A Short History
Of Europe
Since Napoleon

A Short History
of Europe
Since Napoleon

Roger L. Williams

Department of History
University of Wyoming
Laramie, Wyoming

John Wiley & Sons, Inc.

New York   London   Sydney   Toronto

Library of Congress Cataloging in Publication Data

Williams, Roger Lawrence, 1923–
    A Short history of Europe since Napoleon.

    1. Europe–History–1815–1871. 2. Europe–History–1871–1918. 3. Europe–History–20th century.
I. Title.
D359.W5   940   79-39-39034
ISBN 0-471-94749-0
ISBN 0-471-94750-4 (pbk.)

Printed in the United States of America.

10 9 8 7 6 5 4 3 2 1

PREFACE

This short history of Europe since 1815 is about one-third the length of conventional texts in this area, meaning that much detail has necessarily been omitted. This particular format, however, facilitates the use of supplementary readings, and provides the opportunity for diverse approaches to, or interpretations of, the period under survey. The volume is intended for both the beginning college student and the general reader.

This book differs in other respects from the standard surveys of the period. Its organizational focus is upon Europe as a whole, and the reader will not find a compilation of national histories. While the book provides a necessary chronological framework, it particularly features a topical approach to the period since 1815. In some respects, therefore, the book takes on the aspect of an extended essay where a few themes are introduced and developed. Four of the major themes actually appear as section headings in the book: (a) The conflicting claims of cosmopolitanism and nationalism; (b) the gathering centralization of power; (c) the democratization of European society; and (d) the state of the two cultures (the literary and the scientific). But there is also a fifth theme that pervades the history of the nineteenth and twentieth centuries: the crisis of conscience—to believe or not to believe—and the fate of organized religion.

Laramie, Wyoming   *Roger L. Williams*

CONTENTS

PART III

The German Wars 1914-1945   123

PART I
Prologue

The history of Europe in the nineteenth and twentieth centuries, right down to our own day, has an intelligible unity that becomes clear only if we begin by recognizing an aspiration common to thinking Europeans in the eighteenth century: that life on earth should be more humane; indeed, that life on earth could be made more humane. Such a generality is very grand, but if we are to see what the libertarian currents of the eighteenth century, culminating in the enthusiasm for the ideals of the French Revolution, had in common with the scientific and technological progress of that century, we shall have to recognize that these movements and innovations held the promise of a better life for every man, and that the better life was understood to be the freer life. Some even went so far as to propose that every man ought to have the right to the pursuit of happiness!

On one level, critics of European life in the nineteenth and twentieth centuries based their criticisms on these measures of a better life. That is, wherever European states or institutions were seen to be failing to produce liberty and happiness, they were subject to severe social criticism; and the example of the French Revolution would suggest drastic means for producing progress if it could not be had by

1

consent of those in power. On another level, critics of European life in these two centuries raised doubts about the new aspirations of European man and about the possibility of progress itself. Would life in the future be the same old misery carried on behind a glittering facade of growing political liberty, economic development, and the comforts born of technical advancement? What would it mean in the long run to European man to have cast behind him as outmoded his ancient concern for an otherworldly salvation in favor of the more immediate salvation on earth? Answers to such questions have never been clear-cut in the Europe since Napoleon, any more than they ought to be today; but they have provided the intellectual battle lines from that day to our own, until, just recently, it has become possible in Europe to propose that European civilization has become split into two (hostile) cultures.

Whatever may be our judgment of this outcome, we must begin by recognizing that the thinkers and reformers of the eighteenth century not only wished mankind well, but had faith that human reason appropriately applied could bring about that well-being. Most of them, in the spirit of Sir Isaac Newton (1642-1727), saw God's universe as a rational mechanism, and thus, as susceptible to rational analysis. It followed that to apply human reason to the rational solution of earthly problems was to follow God's own method. The notion aroused considerable intellectual optimism, even in those who were thoroughly aware of the magnitude of human dilemmas and of the historical persistence of evil and perversity in human affairs.

THE REVOLUTION IN SCIENCE AND TECHNOLOGY

The contemporary argument about the merits of modern science and technology is simply the latest version of a very old quarrel in European history. Despite widespread assumptions to the contrary, there had been such a thing as medieval science. Whereas modern science, since its origin in the sixteenth and seventeenth centuries, has been humanistic in spirit and increasingly devoted to harnessing nature to serve mankind, medieval science was largely metaphysical in its quests. Thus, the medieval scholar found that the Aristotelian explanation of physical motion also explained why men, by their natures, must seek God. Similarly, the Aristotelian theory of gravity, requiring the earth to be the center of the universe, was consistent with the medieval theological view of the earth as the stage upon which man worked out his salvation. But when we come to men like Francis Bacon (1561-1626) and René Descartes (1596-1650), we find an entirely new world view. "Now the true and lawful goal of the sciences," Bacon wrote, "is none other than this: that human life be endowed with new discoveries and powers." Descartes put it even more pointedly, saying that knowledge ought to be useful to life so that we might "render ourselves the masters and possessors of nature."

What made this new scientific view possible was the increasing secularization of life which came with the waning medieval period. The generations that were witness to that gradual secularization were uneasy in their awareness that changes of profound dimensions were taking place in the European world. Would the search for godly powers ultimately mean that men would cease their search for God? And if so, would mankind overreach itself and come to a tragic end? Not even the great religious reformers of the sixteenth century, however, were able to stem this gradual secularization of life; so that by the eighteenth century, though many men, including the scientists and intellectuals, retained religious faith and a belief in God, the things of this world loomed larger in men's minds. It was left for a philosopher in the nineteenth century, Friedrich Nietzsche (1844-1900), to pronounce the logical conclusion of secularization: "God is dead."

While it is true that a modern scientist, Newton for example, could be too much of a scholar or a philosopher to care whether his ideas were useful, a secularizing society saw in such ideas the possibility of technical progress. Britain was the first of the European countries to demonstrate that conditions of life could be dramatically improved through agricultural, medical, and industrial innovation, so that she became the model for the rest of Europe. As we shall see, her example was the more important in that it became clear to European thinkers that her ability to innovate was related to the political stability and the freer political institutions she had developed by the eighteenth century. On the one hand, innovation is more likely in the community that sets great store in the things of the mind and provides the freer atmosphere for minds to work. While on the other hand, political stability promotes public confidence and lessens the danger for capital investment, meaning that interest rates will be low—and any society wishing technical advancement must find capital for investment.

In the eighteenth century, the British Parliament passed hundreds of enclosure acts to banish gradually the medieval open-field system of agriculture. Enclosure meant individually owned fields, the crops and the livestock to be controlled by the owner alone rather than by the village. Enclosure made investment in scientific agriculture and large-scale food production possible; this was the moral as well as the economic justification for enclosure in the eighteenth century. The statistical results of this scientific, large-scale agriculture are impressive (for example, the average weight of animal carcasses sold at market roughly doubled in the last half of the eighteenth century), meaning that the British population had a far better food supply. But in the process, many of the villagers lost their means to an independent rural existence; some found work as tenants on the big farms, others migrated to towns in search of work. The very technical innovations, in other words, that in the long run improved the conditions of life for every man, also contributed in the short run to the agony and the heartache of some men.

The increase in profits from scientific agriculture was soon so great that the money could not be indefinitely reinvested in agriculture; thus, it served as capital for investment in industry, ultimately providing jobs for the displaced rural folk. Traditionally, manufacturing had been done in homes, a method known variously as the domestic system, cottage industry, or the putting-out system. The availability of capital made the factory system feasible for the first time in the eighteenth century, and the factory system meant the possibility of housing power-driven machinery and thus a larger-scale, more economical production. We know that living and working conditions in the new industrial towns were far from celestial, from which has grown a moral tradition condemning the Industrial Revolution, or more specifically technology, for creating slavelike conditions and smoky skies.

This moral tradition, however, has always omitted considering factors that are equally moral. For one thing, the principal commodities whose production was revolutionized by technology were commodities of general consumption, most notably food and textiles. Imperfect as the distribution system may have been, and unfair and unjust though the conditions of labor still were, it remains to be argued that industrialization, by offering for the first time the possibility of higher standards of living, provided the opportunity to protest against bad conditions. What is more, the moral tradition too easily implied that the evils of material existence arrived with industrialization for the first time. Those who have known rural poverty stripped of its bucolic facade, or who know something of the realities of life in regions untainted by technology, know human life for what it has been for most men throughout history: appalling disease, poverty, and early death. Consequently, whatever the abuses or misuses of technology from the eighteenth century to our own day, the possibility for a better material existence for mankind has depended upon the proper application of modern scientific knowledge.

LIBERTARIAN AND HUMANITARIAN MOVEMENTS

Europeans had known long before the eighteenth century, of course, that happiness and well-being do not depend solely on our material resources. Men aspire not only to be free from arbitrary government, but to be free of ignorance and to enjoy freedom of conscience. Once again in the eighteenth century, the thinkers of Europe saw Britain as one model of greater liberty, if not the only model the eighteenth century had. For one of the paradoxes of the eighteenth century is that two apparently contradictory options were offered in the search for political liberty: One derived from practical English experience in checking royal despotism or absolutism in the seventeenth century; the other was a political derivation from the ideas of the Scientific Revolution. Consequently, anyone criticizing any given regime in the eighteenth century might do so both on the basis of abstract principles grounded in the latest scientific ideas, and on the basis of actual English experience in checking royal power, such as the framers of our Declaration of Independence did.

Twice in the seventeenth century the English Parliament deposed the monarch, and in doing so the second time, in 1689, Parliament seemed to establish the principle that sovereign power lay in Parliament as representative of the nation. The King might not infringe upon time-honored parliamentary prerogatives, nor might he alter the religious establishment without parliamentary consent. This political and religious association was made necessary by the fact that the King, since the Reformation, had been head of both state and church. When Parliament offered the crown to William and Mary in 1689, the offer was accompanied by a Declaration of Rights, which amounted to a contract: the crown had no right to make or suspend laws, nor to levy taxes or maintain a standing army without the consent of Parliament. These principles were not derived from abstract theory, but were issues that had been hotly contended for nearly a century in political life. Yet, by 1690, an active politician, John Locke, had produced a philosophical statement demonstrating that Parliament had not merely had the right, but the obligation, to depose the King.

This English tradition, as codified by Locke, emphasized man's natural, God-given right to enjoy life, liberty, and property, and that reasonable men had originally organized government to protect those natural rights. Consequently, any government that ceased to protect those rights had abdicated its duty and must be removed by society's representatives. To guarantee that government would not become tyrannical, Locke proposed to separate the three branches of government—the executive, legislative, and judicial—so that they would act as checks upon each other, a self-regulating order. Locke's views were widely used to criticize royal despotism in the eighteenth century, notably in America and France. In fact, it could be argued that the defeat of George III's attempt to extend the royal powers in America confirmed, on both sides of the Atlantic, the ideas on sovereignty set down by Locke.

During the eighteenth century, the two-party system and cabinet government developed rapidly to produce the stability and public confidence that would be in marked contrast with the gathering chaos that characterized the absolute monarchy in France. Not only did Britain thus have the edge in economic development, as we have seen, but she prevailed over France in the long duel for overseas empire. It was not lost upon thinking men of that era that the freer society was the more vital one.

Because of our British constitutional heritage, we find it understandable that liberty should be defined as a limitation of government—what government may not do to an individual. Hence, the expression *laissez-faire* which, even though it is often associated with the demand that governments not interfere with trade, really meant that governments ought not interfere with the liberty of the individual, especially his political and religious liberty. It comes as something of a surprise to us, therefore, to discover that the eighteenth century's second model for liberty proposed that the cure for despotism was more despotism. This argument equated liberty with order, and was based on the facts of nature as the eighteenth century knew them.

This rationale would agree with Locke that nature is a state of freedom, meaning that man had been free in the state of nature, but would add what we might call a Newtonian dimension by pointing out that nature is governed by rational, immutable laws. God has given man reason by which he may discover and describe those laws of nature, and God means for us to be free by living according to His laws. In other words, men are most free when their institutions conform to the laws of nature. If one followed *this* formula, then one saw liberty guaranteed more through the well-ordered, rationally administered state than coming from reforms that reduced the authority of the state. This point of view has been called Enlightened Despotism, and one of its enthusiasts (Turgot) perfectly characterized it in his remark, "Give me five years of despotism, and France will be free." As for reforms, rational despotism was specifically identified with the elimination of archaic privilege. The heyday of Enlightened despotism was the last half of the eighteenth century. Frederick II of Prussia, for example, denied his divine right to rule and justified himself as an enlightened, efficient ruler. An even better example was the Emperor Joseph II, who tried to rationalize the organization of the Hapsburg realm, but whose reforms did not survive him. A humane man who wished his people well, Joseph II had no political acumen, and his sad career remains testimony to the folly of bringing pure reason to politics.

Despite the failures of Enlightened Despotism, its benevolent intentions were consistent with a humanitarian movement that gained strength in the late eighteenth century and drew its inspiration from several sources. In Britain, the brutal dislocation of working people brought by enclosure and industrialization focused public attention on misery as never before, though there had been ample misery before. Similarly, whereas children had traditionally been apprenticed at an early age to merchants and craftsmen, the factory system began to attract attention to the evils of child labor. The immediate response was not remedial legislation—that would wait until the nineteenth century and a growing awareness that economic development could be the foundation for destroying economic abuses. For the moment, the call was for the "more fortunate" in society to extend charity to the "lower ranks." Comparable was John Wesley's Methodism, a religion for the poor, which taught that the evils in society would be reformed only through the spiritual transformation of individuals, and counseled thrift, hard work, and abstinence as the virtues that would lead to salvation. Before the end of his life, Wesley sadly recognized that these virtues could also lead to materialism and the erosion of spiritual values.

The intellectual currents of the eighteenth century were a more important source of the humanitarian movement. The rationalist, for example, searched for moral law just as he searched for all other natural laws, because what was natural was both right and good. Rousseau (1712-1778) went beyond the rationalists in his quest for the natural. Believing that we are born disposed to goodness, but that we are altered and corrupted by the artificiality of society, Rousseau taught that we must return to our primitive dispositions. But in calling for a return to the natural, he did not mean a physical return to the realm of nuts and berries as he is so often interpreted, nor did he suppose that man is moral in the state of nature. He meant that man's institutions ought to conform as much as possible to the standards of nature, so as to avoid mutilating man's nature.

A chief characteristic of eighteenth-century intellectuals was their faith that the progress of man on this earth is possible; and in some of them, like the Marquis de Condorcet (1743-1794), the meaning of progress went far beyond mere improvement of our material culture to a faith in the ultimate perfection of humanity. Condorcet argued that, through the use of reason, the human species is "susceptible of an indefinite advancement," and that the day would come when the length of human life would have "no assignable limit." But not all eighteenth-century intellectuals were rationalists. The anti-rationalists, later to be called romanticists, dwelt upon sensibility as the source of our most profound truths; and sensibility also led to compassion for mankind. What rationalists and romanticists had in common, however, was a concern for man's liberty and happiness, qualities then defined in secular terms.

THE ERA OF THE FRENCH REVOLUTION

Of all the movements in the eighteenth century designed to sweep away evils and produce a heavenly city on this earth, none has fascinated posterity more than the French Revolution. At one point or another, it encompassed most of the ideas and passions of the eighteenth century; it brought to the fore an astonishing array of idealists, opportunists, fanatics, and men of real talent; and finally, the peculiarities of its political history made the French Revolution the classic modern revolution, the model against which all subsequent revolutions have been measured. We owe much of the modern revolutionary tradition as well as current political terminology to the French Revolution.

In the coming of the French Revolution, we distinguish—as we ought to in analyzing all revolutions—between the development of both a revolutionary *spirit* and a revolutionary *situation*. The former amounted to the intellectual protest against the premises upon which the established order was based: namely, that the old regime was a wildly inefficient despotism rather than an enlightened despotism; or that the old regime was an absolutism with all power concentrated in the King, rather than a liberal British-style monarchy with the powers separated; or, finally, that society rested upon Christian fundamentals rather than upon the newer fundamentals defined by modern science and expressed as natural, or rational, religion. To put it another way, the old regime was seen as an anachronism and, hence, not likely to be able to cope with the increasing responsibilities of government. Proof of this was seen in the regime's toleration of a privileged, but selfish, nobility, a class that no longer gave the nation the services that had been the original justification for the privileges.

The revolutionary situation amounted to the circumstances which the established order seemed unable to manage. In the first place, the nation suffered from rapid inflation in the eighteenth century, caused in part by the influx of precious metals from the New World, and in part by the increase in population from eighteen to twenty-five million during the century. Production of goods did not keep pace with either the population increase or the increased money supply. Prices rose sharply, wages lagged, and government income declined. In its attempts to reform the economic and financial condition of the country, the monarchy was confronted by a variety of privileges, or inequities, but failed to produce the vigorous leadership necessary to bring order and justice out of the deepening chaos. One major problem was that the tax system varied from region to region, depending upon the circumstances under which a particular province had been annexed to the kingdom, meaning that the tax rate itself was inequitable. Beyond that, the first two estates (or orders) of society were largely exempt from taxation thanks to privileges exchanged for services to the realm, usually dating from the medieval period and no longer appropriate. How much property went untaxed is not precisely known, but there can be no doubt that the state could not tax where much of the money was.

In the national crisis of the eighteenth century, the first two orders (clergy and nobility) refused to sanction any reforms that would reduce their privileges, even in the national interest. Indeed, they pressed their claims to manorial dues from the peasantry as traditional rights despite the fact that most of the peasants by then had become freeholders. Had the King met the crisis by asserting himself in the traditional royal role as defender of the people (the Third Estate) against the privileged orders, a more rational and equitable government might have been devised. But Louis XVI (1774-1792), if he possessed the trappings of absolute authority, was badly cast as a king, and he shrank from the despotic role the fundamental laws provided him. Consequently, we may say that by 1789 France had reached a constitutional crisis, for the wealthiest country in Europe had a hopelessly bankrupt government which was seemingly powerless to reform its own machinery in its own interest. Unable to provide a program, the King called a meeting of the Estates-General, the only legislature the country had—the first meeting in 175 years. Royal absolutism had confessed its failure.

Several factors must be cited to illustrate why the French Revolution, beginning in 1789, came to be regarded as the classic modern revolution. First, when it reached its end, much more than a simple change of government achieved with the aid of violence had occurred. The country had been reconstituted in the several senses of that word: not only was there a new constitution based upon new principles, but a new social order whose principles the new constitution reflected. Many so-called revolutions have been much less thorough-going: Violence may have been used to achieve a change in regime, for which the term *coup d'état* is more accurate than revolution; or violence may have been used by a faction which believes its constitutional rights are being violated (the consequent civil strife becomes dedicated to the legal or proper enforcement of the constitution rather than to its overthrow); or violence may simply come from barbarian assault upon an established order, whether for plunder, whether for violence as a way of life, or out of pure hatred for sophisticated civilization.

Which leads us directly to the second classic feature of the French Revolution: Those who led the assault upon the old regime were true revolutionaries in that they were motivated by real idealism and not opportunism. They were French patriots at the outset, dismayed at the growing national crisis; but in working for the national revival, their intellectual grounding in eighteenth-century rationalism, with its universal truths, led them to believe sincerely that they worked not simply for France but for mankind. Thus, the French Revolution was no mere reform movement, but ultimately a crusade, and its proponents revealed a religious zeal that in some reached fanaticism. They had the Enlightenment in their eyes and the heavenly city on their drawing boards.

Perhaps the most familiar classic feature of the French Revolution was its cycle. That is, it began with the overthrow of the reigning Bourbons and ended with their restoration. During the interim, the country experienced a succession of governments and constitutions, at first increasingly Leftist, then increasingly Rightist, until a military dictatorship was established. The cycle began with the summoning of the Estates-General in 1789, a tricameral body with each estate sitting separately, each estate expressing its will with one vote. Therein lay the first crisis, since the primary motive for calling the Estates-General had been to find a solution for the crown's bankruptcy. A solution depended upon members of the first two estates being deprived of their privileges, especially their tax exemption; but they were in a position to block any reform detrimental to their privileges.

In the absence of any leadership from the King, the Third Estate broke the deadlock on June 17, 1789, by declaring itself to be the National Assembly and inviting the members of the other two estates to join it. Only a few of the more liberal clergy and nobles accepted the invitation. Fearing that the King might use his troops to abolish the assembly, a few radicals directed a mob against the Bastille, a fortress where arms were supposedly stored. The surrender (and massacre) of its tiny garrison led the King to accept the existence of the assembly, and the incident established the precedent that political deadlocks could be broken by violence or threats of violence. What was more, the existence of a National Assembly meant that henceforth all legislation would be made in the name of the nation. Modern nationalism was at its birth.

The National Assembly then set out to construct a constitutional monarchy, a modern national state where the monarch's authority would be limited through the separation of powers, and those powers would be clearly defined in a written constitution. Only then would rational, fiscally sound government be possible; and *that* consideration also dictated the elimination of privileges and made every citizen liable to appropriate taxation. In a special night session, when many members of the assembly were absent, a group of more liberal members voted to abolish many privileges enjoyed by the first two estates and decreed equality of taxation. They abolished tithes also, promising to find new means to provide for the support of the Church.

With inequality abolished, the assembly turned to a formal statement of equality as a basic constitutional principle: the Declaration of the Rights of Man and of the Citizen. The basic assumption in the declaration was derived from Rousseau: "Men are born and remain free and equal in rights; social distinctions may be based only upon general usefulness." The rights listed were to liberty, property, security, and resistance to oppression. Sovereignty was recognized as vested in the nation as a whole, and the law was to be considered an expression of the general will. The assembly also raised an army of its own, the National Guard, to guarantee its independence and to influence the King to sanction the new constitutional legislation whenever he showed himself reluctant.

The French Revolution soon became a matter of international concern. In 1790 the National Assembly completed its constitutional arrangements regulating relations between the state and the French Church, which had the effect of subjugating the Church to the State. The Papacy consequently condemned the French Revolution in 1791, making it impossible for orthodox Catholics, including the King, to accept the revolution. Also, the *emigrés*—those who left France during this political upheaval—were known to be intriguing with foreign governments against the revolution, seeming to put all counterrevolutionaries into jeopardy as potential allies of the foreign enemies of France. When the King made his famous and unsuccessful attempt to flee to the Austrian Netherlands that year, the monarchy was similarly compromised.

Even so, the constitutional monarchy was formally established in the fall of 1791, and elections were held for a new Legislative Assembly. By then, however, the Left-wing minority in the assembly, were emerging as republicans, dedicated not merely to the destruction of the monarchy but to carrying the new liberties in the constitution of 1791 to peoples beyond the frontier. They would, in other words, answer the counterrevolutionary threats from abroad with a counter-crusade against royal governments everywhere. This set the stage for the lengthy wars of the French Revolution, which began in 1792, and for the logical downfall of the monarchy the same year. Louis XVI was brought to trial as a counterrevolutionary (by then meaning a traitor to France) and executed in 1793. A constitutional Convention had meanwhile been summoned to replace the Legislative Assembly for the purpose of framing a republican constitution.

In the process, the republican minority had become dominant through skillful political organization and the calculated use of terror. Once dominant, however, the republicans were revealed to be disunited, so that a curious mixture emerged of political idealism and crass opportunism, as new office-holders supplanted the old. The details of factional differences have a special significance in that these various factions were the forerunners of nineteenth-century French political parties. The two major factions were the Jacobins and the Girondists. The latter seem to have been heavily provincial rather than Parisian in constituency, and their political and economic views were, therefore, decentralist. Once the Jacobins won their showdown with the Girondists in 1793, the victorious Jacobins divided into three warring factions, the followers of Danton, Hébert, and Robespierre.

Close students of the French Revolution will note not only factional differences in principle, but that to a certain extent the success or failure of the factions hinged upon success or failure in the military campaigns against the enemies of France. The Girondists, for example, were hopelessly compromised by military defeat when they were momentarily supreme in government. The subsequent Jacobins could therefore use the military crisis to justify dictatorial executive authority in the emergency, and then use the dictatorial powers to purge political opponents. This is not to say that political idealism was a sham in the bid for power or irrelevant in its seizure. When it came to the warring factions within the Jacobin party, the very loftiness of the Robespierrists' ideology provided them with the unquestioned righteousness that permitted the conscience-free slaughter of the nonbelievers.

With the brief ascendency (1793-1794) of Maximilien Robespierre, a period that has been called the "Republic of Virtue," the French Revolution reached its most democratic moment. Political passions and prejudices aside, the Convention had by then found time to deal successfully with war, insurrection, and a new constitution for the First Republic. Even though this Constitution of 1793 was not implemented because of the military crisis, its universal manhood suffrage served as a model for radicals in later years. With universal rights went universal obligations, notably the so-called *levée-en-masse,* mobilizing the entire nation for the national defense and especially the men for military service. The growing success of French arms owed much to the availability of manpower, but that very success denied dictatorship its justification for existence. Besides, with the right to life now depending upon a reputation for virtue, few members of the Convention could rest easily; and even many Jacobins took part in the plot that brought Robespierre to the guillotine. From that moment in 1794, the Convention and the French Revolution veered to the Right.

The reaction, however, did not bring an abrupt end to the terror nor to the innovations of the revolution. Especially, the Convention proceeded with the development of a public educational system which had earlier been regarded as a correlative to a democratizing society. As for violence, a White Terror began to replace the Red Terror, aimed primarily at known Jacobins; until there was some danger that the reaction would lead straight to a restoration of the monarchy and a cancellation of all the revolutionary reforms. To forestall both that and the "excesses" of democracy, the Convention abolished the Constitution of 1793 and produced a new constitution in 1795 as the basis for a liberal, but not a democratic, republic. This regime became known as the Directory, because the executive power was vested in a five-man board of directors.

With the Directory (1795-1799), the revolution reached its moral nadir. For the most part, those in power were loyal to the revolution only to the extent that it had brought them to power and to wealth; and in society at large, the puritanism of the Republic of Virtue gave way to a gilded licentiousness. Protest against the corruption came from both Left and Right, from those who, respectively, advocated a restoration of the Constitution of 1793 or a restoration of monarchy. The regime met such movements (conspiracies) with force, until there could no longer be any doubt that the Directory was a corrupt dictatorship based on the largest army in Europe. A young upstart general named Bonaparte won prestige for the Directory with the conquest of Italy in 1797, but the popularity and the integrity of the regime continued to deteriorate.

General Bonaparte, meanwhile, who had revealed his independence and ambition during the campaign of 1797, became party to a plot to overthrow the Directory. The conspirators aimed at reestablishing strong executive control in France in the hope of halting the rising tide of both royalism and Jacobinism, both of which, they claimed, would have the effect of destroying the Republic. Their *coup d' etat* took place on November 9, 1799 (or the 18th Brumaire, Year VIII in the revolutionary calendar introduced under the Convention). Parliament was purged of those who doubted that the Republic required such a drastic rescue, and the remaining deputies replaced the Directors with a Consulate of three, with Napoleon Bonaparte as First Consul.

THE NAPOLEONIC AGE

Whatever his title, Bonaparte was the supreme figure in Europe for the next fifteen years. If he is commonly remembered as a military genius, he was no less an administrative genius. The French accepted him overwhelmingly in 1799 after their weariness of ten years of uncertainty and turmoil: he would give them both glory and order. He himself was a product of the French Revolution and had earlier espoused Jacobin principles, but he was also a realist who knew that the revolution had alienated many Frenchmen who adhered either to Christianity or to the old regime. Thus, he set himself to achieving a political settlement that would be a compromise between prerevolutionary ideas and institutions and those of the revolution. Given the fact that the revolution had already radically altered the fundamentals upon which the nation rested, such a compromise might seem to have been impossible. But Bonaparte was greatly assisted in his task by the fact that in some critical respects the Revolution had completed, rather than destroyed, the work of the old regime. The highly centralized power that he enjoyed and developed had been the goal of both the old monarchy and the Jacobins. Also, his pose as the supreme law-giver, who would rationalize the administration of the realm and thus bring liberty through a more perfect order, was a posture advocated in intellectual circles long before 1789. For the moment at least, he could be all things to all people, and no less a figure than Goethe hailed him as the hero of Europe.

The compromise between the old and the new orders became at once apparent in 1799 in the new constitution for the Consulate and in the organic laws of 1800 which reorganized local government and the national judicial system. The constitution, for instance, by providing universal suffrage for males over twenty-one, gave the appearance of democracy; but residence requirements for the vote and a highly indirect system of election effectively diluted the possibility of real democracy and made executive power virtually absolute in practice. The law reorganizing local government virtually brought to an end local responsibility for the administration of national law, but gave a great sense of uniformity. In the new judicial system, except for the justices of the Supreme Court of Cassation (the highest court of appeal), all judges were appointed by the First Consul. Such a system was hardly a separation of powers, but an absolutism that would have been the envy of the Bourbons.

The First Consul also reached a religious compromise within France and with Rome through the Concordat of 1801. Rome saw its authority restored in France with the bishops, if appointed by the

First Consul, being consecrated by the Pope. But the tithe was not restored, the clergy continued to be paid by the State, and the Church had to accept the loss of properties confiscated by the State during the revolution and subsequently sold to French buyers. This confirmation of land titles did much to reassure French property owners that a Napoleonic regime would guarantee the integrity of the French Revolution. Similarly, the new Civil Code of 1800 encouraged belief in the new government—its clauses were not uniformly democratic, but the code was liberal by the standards of that day. Its underlying principle was that all citizens must be equal before the law and must have the right to freedom of conscience and to choice of vocation—a real measure of the degree to which the French Revolution had altered the fundamental structure of the state. Is it any wonder that the French agreed to reward Bonaparte by making him the Emperor Napoleon I in 1804!

Unfortunately, there was another side to the coin, which increasingly rallied much of Europe and many in France against the imperial busybody. Napoleon's ambitions were not limited to France, and he had inherited the crusading universalism of the French Revolution. The rational perfection he was bringing to France in the name of the Rights of Man and the Citizen must also be given to all Europe, by force if necessary. The diplomacy and the wars of the revolutionary governments, therefore, were continued and expanded during the Napoleonic era; until it became clear that unless Napoleon were defeated and dethroned, all Europe would become subject to French military power and to French ideas. That such a cosmopolitan state would be a despotism, enlightened or otherwise, could hardly be doubted, considering the apparent growth of arbitrary rule in France itself after 1804.

Some of Napoleon's proposals on the international scene, it is true, found widespread approval abroad, sometimes winning him enthusiastic foreign support. No German state or ruler, for instance, had ever been able to unite the many German states into a nation. With the sanction of the Diet of the Holy Roman Empire, Napoleon began the rationalization of the German world with a plan in 1803 that obliterated 112 small German states. The second step, however, came in 1806 after the military defeat of Austria, when Napoleon eliminated not only about seventy more German states, but the ancient Holy Roman Empire as well. The surviving German states, all swollen with the territory of the obliterated states, were, with the exception of Austria and Prussia, induced to enter a Confederation of the Rhine which Napoleon sponsored.

The Poles were given hope that their national revival would be guaranteed by Napoleon, when, in 1807, he created the Grand Duchy of Warsaw out of Prussia's share of partitioned Poland; and when, in 1809, he added territory to the Grand Duchy from Austria's portion of partitioned Poland. The Italians, too, saw their national identity emerge for the first time in centuries when Napoleon created the Kingdom of Italy in 1804 in the northern part of the peninsula, taking the royal title himself.

But the great powers, who had seen themselves repeatedly defeated or checked by French power, were gradually forced to emulate the French in order to mobilize the resources necessary to contain and then defeat Napoleon. They not merely copied the newer French military tactics, but recognized that part of French invincibility lay in popular devotion to the national cause. Since that devotion was rooted in the revolutionary reforms which promised a better life for all Frenchmen, it was seen elsewhere that national sentiments had to be mobilized against the French, and that the most effective method would be through liberal reforms. Such programs were promoted in varying degrees in Prussia, Russia, and Austria.

Other factors also contributed to Napoleon's first downfall in 1814. He had lacked sea power, which meant that he was continually frustrated in his ambition to invade England. Thus, he could neither cut off British subsidies to hard-pressed continental allies nor isolate British forces sent to the Iberian Peninsula in support of Spanish guerilla forces. As the French became bogged down in Spain after 1808, it became apparent to the rest of Europe that the French were not invincible. Though in 1812, Napoleon was still powerful and widely feared, he must have known that the tide was running against him. He had detected several of his chief ministers in treasonable relations with enemy powers, and the alliance he had forced upon Russia in 1807 had been shaky from the start. Perhaps only a desperate gamble, which the invasion of Russia was, would reverse his luck. When he failed to crush the main Russian forces and decided to evacuate that country, the resulting winter catastrophe meant that he could not hold down other European areas by force. By 1814 he was on the defensive in France, fighting more brilliantly than ever, but he was hopelessly outgunned. His royalist enemies on the home front, meanwhile, negotiated a peace settlement with the advancing enemy calling for a Bourbon restoration; the Senate deposed him and exiled him to Elba. The revolution had gone full cycle from Bourbon to Bourbon.

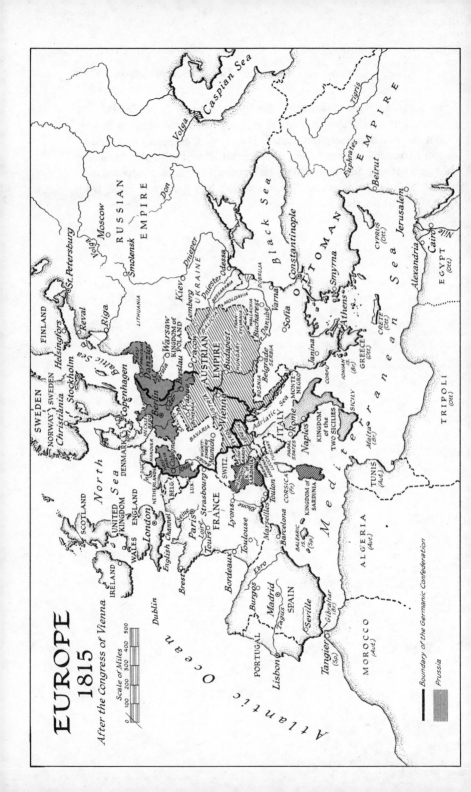

PART II

The Hundred Years

1814–1914

THE CONFLICTING CLAIMS OF COSMOPOLITANISM AND NATIONALISM

1. The Settlement of 1814-1815

The era of the French Revolution and Napoleon gave birth to modern European nationalism in association with liberation, and that combination had immense appeal in the early decades of the nineteenth century. Easy to miss, in the Europe after 1815, is the residue of cosmopolitanism that was an ancient European heritage, and which, as we shall see, ultimately came to be at war with the nationalist ideal.

If we have come to think of Europe as a hodgepodge of nation-states, we may inadvertently obscure those roots common to all European nations which for many centuries gave Europeans a sense of community (despite local differences), and which Europeans have been endeavoring to recover in recent decades. During the medieval era, the dim memory of a powerful Christian empire—the myth of Rome

21

or Byzantium—inspired the creators of Christendom. And the universalism of that Roman and Christian heritage continued to argue against parochialism despite the steady advance of localism and secularization that, together, chipped away at the foundations of the universalist or cosmopolitan dream.

Even the French Revolution, if the breeder of nationalism, came to promote a new universalism—one based not upon transcendent truth, but upon axioms legislated and proselyted by one ecstatic nationality. The very energy of the French nation, in fact, defeated the new cosmopolitanism by revealing the enormous power an emancipated nation could engender. The ultimate defeat of France by a Europe in coalition set the stage for a lengthy conflict between the principles of cosmopolitanism and nationalism.

Many months before the advancing Allies reached Paris in the spring of 1814, they had been formulating their war aims in a series of treaties which were chiefly necessary to hold the wartime alliance together. For the uncomfortable truth of the matter was that the four great powers (Britain, Russia, Prussia, and Austria) had little in common beyond their mutual mistrust of Napoleonic France. Their coalition-warfare against the French had too often been coalition in name only, with their private ambitions and rivalries always working behind the facade of their alliance. Napoleon's very brilliance in the defense of France that spring repeatedly opened the possibility that one or more of the Allies would abandon the campaign and sign a separate peace with the French, providing the opportunity for a French recovery. British diplomacy, backed up by generous subsidies, succeeded in keeping the alliance in the field until the French royalists, led by the realistic Talleyrand, were able to negotiate the restoration of the Bourbon monarchy as a basis for peace. This uneasy experience meant that when it came to constructing the actual peace settlement, the Allied representatives came to the peace table encumbered with prior (and sometimes conflicting) commitments; and that the threat of a French revival loomed large if Allied solidarity should evaporate with the end of the fighting.

This will account for why the peace conference, known to us as the Congress of Vienna, was so lengthy and tortuous, and why the British in particular extended the line of their wartime diplomacy into the peace settlement. In recent times we have come to expect that in the aftermath of great and devastating warfare, all diplomatic energies will be aimed at providing new international institutions designed to maintain the peace and prevent the return of armed conflict. The Congress of Vienna (1814-1815), even if its peace-keeping machinery was far less elaborate or institutionalized than what we have seen in the twentieth century, was the first European peace conference to attempt to define a *mechanism* that would maintain the status quo.

J. B. Isabey's *Congress of Vienna*, November 1814 (Giraudon).

Before sitting down in Vienna to consider the European-wide problems in the wake of the French Revolution and Napoleon, the victorious powers first worked out a settlement for France alone. Talleyrand, the foreign minister who had earlier betrayed Napoleon, had argued for the restoration of the Bourbons in the person of Louis XVIII (1814-1824) on the grounds of his *legitimate* right to the throne. That is, the Bourbons had the hereditary right to the crown, which they had been denied by the now-defeated revolution. Talleyrand's argument not only prevailed, as the victorious statesmen all represented legitimate monarchies, but the principle he advocated came to be a convenient principle of authority when those same statesmen turned to European questions.

It was understood, however, that Louis XVIII would not be allowed to have the absolute power available to the monarchy before 1789. He must grant the French a constitution limiting his powers, as it was recognized that a nation that had gone through the liberalizing period of the revolution would never consent to a return to absolutism. To make the King further acceptable to the French, the Allies blessed him with a peace settlement (the First Treaty of Paris, May 30, 1814) that returned the French to their prewar boundaries, exacted neither indemnity nor territory, and spared them an army of occupation. Such were the first measures taken by the peacemakers in their hope to stifle further revolutionary zeal in the defeated nation, thereby checking the militarism that the revolutionary zeal had earlier produced.

In the autumn of 1814, the representatives of many states gathered in Vienna to discuss the disposition of the great empire that had been won and lost by the French. But the major decisions were made by the chief delegates of the four victorious powers: Chancellor Metternich for Austria, Czar Alexander I for Russia, Viscount Castlereagh for Britain, and Prince von Hardenberg for Prussia; as well as by the wily Talleyrand for France, who exerted critical pressure when disagreements developed among the great powers. He had already advocated legitimacy as the guiding principle in making political and territorial decisions. One alternative would have been to admit the right of each nationality to determine its future. Excepting Britain, where the sovereignty was regarded as vested in the crown *and* in Parliament, the victorious powers regarded sovereignty as the property of the crown alone, and there could be no admission that the people—the nation—shared the sovereignty. The latter notion, in fact, had been held by the revolutionaries in the 1790's, and the peacemakers of 1814 did not mean to embrace revolutionary idealism. Legitimacy it had to be.

Applying the principle, however, proved to be something else. Not only did "legitimate" claims rather generously overlap, but prior commitments necessarily made to ensure wartime cooperation did not always coincide with "legitimate" rights. Moreover, Britain, which had no territorial claims on the continent, preferred to see territory redistributed in a manner that would maintain a balance of power on the continent. Since French military power had not been destroyed in

1814, there remained four military powers on the continent. The British reasoned that on most critical issues these powers would line up two against two, and such a balance would discourage war by making its outcome uncertain. Or, the British could support the weaker pair to restore the balance. In any case, maintaining the balance of power was held to be the key to maintaining the peace.

Conflicting ambitions and goals at the Congress of Vienna finally came to a head in the Polish question—whether to repartition Poland exactly as she had been partitioned in the eighteenth century. The Russians, backed by Prussia, demanded a greater share of Poland than they had previously possessed; but even though the other powers would have been equally compensated elsewhere, this particular transaction would have had the effect of upsetting the balance of power by making Russia the paramount power in Europe. Austria and Britain resisted the demand, finally seeking Talleyrand's support to break the deadlock, thus bringing France into the deliberations of the great powers. If war should be resumed, it meant that France would have two major allies.

This bickering in Vienna, meanwhile, was not lost on Napoleon in exile. Being Emperor of Elba had lost its allure; the Bourbon regime had fallen behind in paying his promised pension; and he knew that many of the French were resentful of this government that had come "in the baggage of the Allies." All seemed to point to a successful return. His landing at Cannes on March 1, 1815, however, shocked the gentlemen in Vienna into quick resolve to mend their differences and deal with the real enemy, whereas Louis XVIII, seeing Napoleon rally many French troops as he moved on Paris, began a discreet retirement northward to await Allied help. Napoleon soon discovered, however, that the most responsible elements of the French population did not favor a renewal of the wars against Europe, which led him to pose as the defender of revolutionary ideals to attract support from the urban masses. He did not wait for the Allies to concentrate against him, but took the offensive northward where he would meet only British and Prussian contingents. Despite initial successes that raised his confidence, he was checked and beaten decisively at Waterloo on June 18. Though he escaped from the battlefield, he abdicated the throne four days later and went to the coast to put himself in British hands, hoping by this voluntary submission to be allowed to live in Britain. Instead, he was caged on the remote island of St. Helena, where he lived until 1821.

His adventure, meanwhile, prompted the Allies to complete the Treaty of Vienna (June 9, 1815), with the Russians obtaining the heart of Poland, and Prussia and Austria obtaining booty elsewhere. The shuffling of frontiers altered the map of Europe dramatically and without much regard for the sentiments of the various nationalities. While the territorial changes can best be understood from a map, it is useful to point out that Prussia, for instance, in annexing the northern half of Saxony, the city of Danzig, and Rhenish territory, was annexing German-speaking people. Whereas Austria, in annexing Lombardy, Venetia, Illyria, Dalmatia, the Tyrol, and the city of Salzburg, gained largely Italians and Slavs, making the Austrian Empire conspicuously cosmopolitan as Prussia became increasingly Germanic. Austria did abandon the Southern Netherlands, which had been an imperial headache during the eighteenth century, so that the two Netherlands could be combined into the Kingdom of the Netherlands to make a more formidable buffer along the northern French frontier.

The Vienna peacemakers necessarily had to eliminate Napoleon's Confederation of the Rhine, but to replace it they could agree neither on the restoration of the Holy Roman Empire nor on the creation of a united German state—a dangerous concession to the principle of national self-determination. The ultimate compromise was a substitute confederation, to be called the Germanic Confederation, comprising thirty-nine sovereign states including Prussia and Austria. A federal Diet was established at Frankfurt under the permanent presidency of Austria: the symbol of national unity without its substance, as the sovereign power was retained by the member states.

In northern Europe, Denmark was punished for her wartime alliance with Napoleon by the loss of Norway, which was given to Sweden. But the Swedes did not get back Finland, which they had earlier lost to Russia. In southern Europe, in Spain and Italy in particular, the "legitimate" governments were restored except in the northern Italian provinces annexed by Austria. The restored regimes looked to Austria for guidance, for she more than any other power came to be regarded as the champion of legitimacy; and the national ambitions of many Italians, which had been excited by the French, went totally ignored.

One further item of business remained after the Treaty of Vienna was signed: a further settlement with France after Napoleon's Hundred Days. The Second Treaty of Paris (November 20, 1815) was understandably harsher than the earlier treaty. France was forced to cede some small, but strategically important, border areas to Prussia, the Netherlands, the Germanic Confederation, and Sardinia-Piedmont; she was now charged a substantial indemnity for an Allied army of occupation in the northeast for a period of five years. Even so, she avoided the partition that Prussia had proposed.

2. Maintaining the Settlement, 1815-1848: The Metternich Era

Because, in 1815, the Allies had been shown the peril that could emerge from their bickering, they signed the Quadruple Alliance, which was designed to maintain their peace settlement, on the very day of their second treaty with France. Article VI of the Alliance recommended that "the high contracting parties . . . renew their meetings at fixed periods . . . for the purpose of consulting upon their common interests, and for the consideration of the measures which at each of those periods shall be considered the most salutary for the repose and prosperity of nations, and for the maintenance of the peace of Europe." Lord Castlereagh was the inspirer of this proposal, which came to be called the Concert of Europe. In fact, the great powers never did meet at "fixed periods," but they did convene periodically when issues arose threatening the general peace. For many statesmen, "maintaining the peace" meant maintaining the status quo as of 1815, a conservatism that regarded liberal ideas as simply the vanguard of revolution. Accordingly, the Concert was soon dominated by the Austrian Chancellor Metternich, for no other power had a greater interest in checking the rise of liberal-national movements than cosmopolitan Austria. In Metternich's hands the Concert of Europe became an instrument of reaction, just as did the Germanic Confederation under Austria's presidency.

The first meeting of the Concert of Europe at Aix-la-Chapelle in 1818 was the most harmonious of the congresses in the nineteenth century. Called at the request of the French, the powers declared that the French indemnity was paid up and withdrew their occupying forces from France. She now joined the family of great powers, but the Allied powers pointedly renewed their Quadruple Alliance. The following year, 1819, Metternich summoned representatives of the nine largest

Germanic states to Carlsbad to deal with liberal-nationalist agitation in the German world. German patriots had looked to Prussian leadership, hoping that the national movement, born during the Napoleonic period, would be crowned in 1815 with constitutional government. But Frederick William III (1797-1840), under Metternich's influence, had abandoned this liberal movement in favor of maintaining the status quo. Out of Carlsbad came proposals for repressive decrees outlawing liberal societies, introducing anti-liberal censorship of the press, and putting universities under police surveillance. These proposals were promptly ratified by the Germanic Diet at Frankfurt.

PRINCE KLEMENS VON METTERNICH (Culver Pictures, Inc.).

The liberal-nationalist sentiments unleashed by the French Revolution, however, were not to be denied. In Spain, the restored Bourbon Ferdinand VII (1814-1833) was preparing his armed forces for the recovery of the Latin American colonies, which had been lost during the Napoleonic occupation of Spain. A revolt led by army officers on the first day of 1820 against the King's vicious and capricious governance made the King a virtual prisoner of the army. He had no choice but to restore the Bonapartist Constitution of 1812. This example encouraged liberals in the Neapolitan army during the summer of 1820 to rise against the despotic Bourbon Ferdinand I (1759-1825), who hastily granted a constitution; and before the summer was over, Portuguese liberals overthrew the regency which had been established in 1807 after the flight of the royal family to Brazil to escape the French.

This led to a crisis in the international establishment, for Austria, Russia, and Prussia, all autocracies, meant to stifle revolution everywhere as inimical to international peace and the Treaty of Vienna. On the other hand, Britain and France, both constitutional monarchies, regarded such intervention into the internal affairs of any nation as a misuse of the international machinery to keep the peace. The upshot, early in 1821, was that Austria acted on behalf of the three despotic powers alone to restore Ferdinand I of Naples to his full powers, following which there was a furious repression in Naples. And the Austrians aided the government of Sardinia-Piedmont in crushing the Italian liberal movement in that country.

Before anything could be done about the Spanish situation, the powers were faced by a Greek national rising in 1821 against the Ottoman Turks. The Greeks, because of their ancient contributions to Western Civilization, were sentimental favorites in Europe; but two issues combined to prevent any immediate European assistance to their cause. The British feared that any weakening of Turkey would simply be the opportunity for Russian expansion in that corner of Europe, with the result of unsettling the balance of power. While Metternich argued that the powers must not support revolution anywhere. Thus, the great powers, at the Congress of Verona in 1822, turned their attention to Spain.

None of the powers had any stomach for a Russian offer to send an army to Spain on behalf of the Concert, but only the British opposed a French offer to restore Ferdinand VII. Louis XVIII's government might argue that their assistance would surround such a restoration with as liberal an atmosphere as possible and perhaps preserve the cause of constitutional government; but the British balked at any encouragement of French militarism. Moreover, the British had developed important trade relations with an independent Latin America. They had no fear that Spain alone could ever recover her authority there, but if the Franco-Spanish Bourbon monarchies were able to revive their eighteenth-century cooperation, it might be another story.

Britain thus separated from the Concert when France was given the mandate to restore Ferdinand VII and warned the French that the British fleet would block the way to Latin America. British hopes that the United States would join in the warning were disappointed, though their proposal did lead our government to issue unilaterally the Monroe Doctrine. In the meantime, the French defeated the Spanish rebels in 1823, but promised the British that they had no intention of intervening elsewhere. The restored Ferdinand VII embarrassed the French by failing to honor his pledge to pardon all revolutionaries, and engaged in a savage extermination of liberals.

The Greek Revolution

Except in Greece, the liberal-national cause seemed crushed by these events, but European enthusiasm for the Greek cause (known as Philhellenism) survived the official indifference of the great powers. As the balance in the struggle began to swing against the Greeks by 1824, the literate classes agitated for intervention. The Greek nationalists, at first led by Alexander Ypsilanti, although inspired by the ideas of the French Revolution, expected Russian aid against the Turks. Not only were the Turks and Russians old enemies, but the Greeks and the Russians were coreligionists with a common desire to see the Moslems driven from Constantinople, their holy city. When Metternich prevailed upon Czar Alexander I (1801-1825) to maintain neutralitiy, the Greek national cause seemed doomed. The Greek uprising in 1822 had caught the Turks off gurad, but in 1824 the Sultan was prepared to invade Greece with new forces from the northeast and had engaged his vassal, Mehemet Ali, the Pasha of Egypt (1811-1848) for a seaborne invasion of the Peloponnesus.

The accession of Nicholas I (1825-1855), a Russian expansionist, brought the question of intervention to a boil, just at a moment when public opinion in both Russia and the West was sufficiently inflamed to permit the Russians to strike at the Turks under the guise of helping the Greeks. It was a difficult moment for the Western governments, forced by public clamor to do something for the Greeks, yet wanting to keep the Turks strong as a barrier to Russian expansion—the old balance of power problem. Initially, three powers (Britain, Russia, and France) tried to force a negotiated settlement that would give the Greeks autonomy under Turkish suzerainty; but the Turks resisted compromise in view of their continuing military success. To underscore their proposal, the three powers then formed an Allied naval squadron which was sent into Greek waters (1827), and these ships inadvertently were engaged by the Egyptian fleet in Navarino harbor, which put an end to the Egyptian fleet. Knowing that the Western governments were embarrassed by this incident, the Sultan still refused to sign an armistice. While Nicholas I, taking advantage of pro-Greek sentiments in the West, soon declared war unilaterally upon the Turks (1828). Britain and France, not wanting Russia to go it alone, then forced the Egyptians to evacuate Greece by threatening military intervention. The Greek cause was finally saved.

The Turks made peace with Russia at Adrianople in 1829, paying a war indemnity and recognizing Greek independence. But the ultimate settlement for Greece, ridden with internal factions, was necessarily worked out by the powers in London. Greek national pride was injured first when the powers chose not a Greek but a Bavarian for the Greek throne, Otto I (1832-1862), and again when the new national frontiers omitted much territory regarded traditionally as Greek by the Greeks: Epirus, Thessaly, and Crete, all of which remained Turkish. Thus, the Greeks had their independence, but cosmopolitan considerations dictated the peace. And a Europe that had officially declared liberal-national movements taboo, had been brought to recognize their possible respectibility.

The Concert of Europe faced a new wave of revolutions in 1830; its firm resolve to squelch revolutions had been badly dented by the events of the previous decade. Conservatives were not surprised, however, when this new wave began in France, which they considered to be the source of most dangerous ideas.

France

Louis XVIII, after 1814, had made an honest attempt to give his people moderate, constitutional government. He faced in Parliament, however, a strong Left wing made up of ex-revolutionaries and ex-Bonapartists, and a strong Right wing made up of ultra-royalists who were absolutist in spirit. The two extremes would often coalesce to make middle-of-the-road government difficult, yet the King felt it necessary to keep the center in power at any price. If either extreme came to power, it could jeopardize the arrangements of 1815 and invite Allied intervention. For a time the stratagem of juggling the electoral laws before parliamentary elections worked to ensure the victory of moderate candidates, but by 1820 it was understood that this dubious practice could not work indefinitely. The government must seek a more permanent alliance with either Left or Right. The very fact that the heir to the throne was the leader of the Ultra faction suggested the practicality of a drift to the Right.

Despite a warning from Metternich that the "established order" in France was the key to the general European peace, Louis XVIII's government introduced reactionary measures in 1821, notably the renewal of censorship and arbitrary arrest, and altered the electoral laws to ensure an Ultra victory that year. The reaction expectedly deepened when the chief Ultra succeeded to the throne as Charles X (1824-1830), with the new King giving clear evidence that he meant to restore a pre-1789 absolutist and Catholic regime. The Constitution of 1814 itself, in other words, was at stake; and moderate royalists began to speak of the necessity of a "French 1688." In July of 1830, the hostility between the crown and Parliament had reached such a point that the King determined to rule by decree and without parliamentary sanction. When he dared to issue four repressive ordinances, which amounted to a *coup d'état,* republicans and liberal royalists aroused Paris against the King. Alarmed too late, the King withdrew the ordinances, then fled from Paris and finally to England. The French Bourbons had fallen for the second and last time.

The constitutional monarchists, rather than the republicans, then got hold of the situation, promoting the candidacy of the Duke of Orleans for the throne. With republican concurrence, he became Louis-Philippe I (1830-1848), King of the French "by the grace of God and the will of the people"—a title which admitted the end of divine right. He promised to uphold the Constitution of 1814, a gesture to reassure Metternich as well as the French; and he took as the national flag the revolutionary tricolor rather than the white banner of the fallen Bourbon. The electorate was immediately broadened by reducing both the voting age and the property qualification for the vote. If not a democracy, the regime announced itself as liberal.

The Concert of Europe was irritated at having to accept the existence of a revolutionary regime; but it made no sense to back Charles X, given his intentions, and refuse to recognize a regime dedicated to upholding the 1815 settlement. What is more, the success of the July Revolution in Paris revitalized revolutionary activity elsewhere for the attention of the great powers.

Belgian Independence

In August of 1830 Belgian nationalists rose against their Dutch king, William I (1815-1844). The union of the Dutch and Belgian peoples, contrived by the Congress of Vienna, had been unhappy from the start; the majority Belgians claimed that they were being governed as a despised minority, subject to religious and economic discrimination. Faced with rebellion, William I offered the Belgians autonomy within the kingdom, but they would have no more of him. Instead, they prepared a constitution for an independent liberal monarchy, and rumor had it that the new French king would be asked to supply one of his sons for the Belgian throne. Meanwhile, the Dutch appealed to the great power to maintain the settlement of 1815.

Louis-Philippe, however, knew perfectly well that the great powers would regard a close Franco-Belgian tie as the beginning of a French resurgence. Knowing that the British in particular were sensitive to a great power moving into the Lowlands, he hastened to reach an understanding with them. The three despotic powers were inclined to intervene on behalf of the Dutch, but the British and French agreed to back Belgian independence. The Concert, therefore, gathered in London to discuss the crisis, and there agreed to recognize Belgian independence. When the Belgians finally selected Leopold of Saxe-Coburg (1831-1865) as their first king, the great powers ratified the choice. The international settlement for the Belgians was known as the Twenty-Four Articles, the sixth article of which recognized Belgium to be "independent and perpetually neutral" under the guarantee of the powers.

Revolutions Elsewhere in 1830-1831

With the Greeks newly freed and revolutions succeeding in France and Belgium, it might appear that the machinery forged to maintain the 1815 settlement had broken down. What the events of 1830 revealed, in fact, was that reactionary government could not be sustained in western Europe: Britain and France, although they were traditional enemies, were being forced together by the liberality of their political institutions. Whereas to the east of them, reactionary regimes could still cooperate to throttle liberal movements. The story of 1830 is full of liberal-nationalist revolutions that were vigorously contained. Uprisings in Hanover, Saxony, Hesse-Cassel, and Brunswick, for instance, forced the respective princes to grant constitutional government. But Metternich, with the backing of Prussia, got the Germanic Diet to vote the Six Acts (1832), leading to the restoration of the absolute authority these German princes had yielded.

Italian secret societies, having failed to achieve national independence in 1820-1821, were inspired to try again by the success in Paris and the foundation of the July Monarchy. Their insurrections began in Parma and Modena, and spread into the Papal States. Metternich, aware of support from Prussia and Russia, repeated his performance of ten years before, and Austrian arms crushed the uprisings. This second failure led the most notable of the Italian nationalists, Mazzini, to believe that Italian unity would never be achieved through the plotting of local secret societies and sporadic uprisings. Fleeing to Marseilles in 1831, he founded the Young Italy movement, designed to organize nationalist agitation on a national rather than a local basis to give unity to what he called the *Risorgimento*—the national regeneration.

The Poles experienced a similar unpleasantness in 1830. Since 1815 the heart of Poland had been within the Russian Empire, and the Czar, as King of Poland, had tried to reconcile the Poles to the arrangement by granting Poland a large measure of autonomy: a constitution, a parliament, and an army. Polish patriots remained dissatisfied with anything short of independence. What is more, they claimed not only territories still held by Austria and Prussia, but provinces to the east taken from Poland in the eighteenth century which were clearly Russian in population. In short, both the nationalist and the "legitimist" claims by the Poles conflicted with those of her three powerful neighbors. When the Poles broke into revolt against Russian rule late in 1830, they recognized the need for outside help and naively expected it from the government of Louis-Philippe. None came, and the poorly organized movement collapsed before a large Russian army. With this failure went the autonomy, and Poland became simply another Russian province subject to a Russification program. Consequently, the Polish refugees who fled (principally to Paris) devoted themselves to keeping Polish culture alive.

The Eastern Question

The Turkish Empire was extraordinarily cosmopolitan. Not only did it include many nationalities, but they were both Asian and European, Moslem and Christian. That Empire had been decaying since the seventeenth century, and various schemes had consequently been advanced for partitioning the Empire in a way that would maintain the balance of power in the east. Yet, the Turks lived on into the nineteenth century, with their territory only nibbled away as by the Greeks in their successful revolt. As Russia had been a major benefactor of Turkish weakness in the previous century. European statesmen in the nineteenth century feared that Russia sought to fill the Turkish vacuum unilaterally as a step toward achieving hegemony on the European continent. The Concert must not merely contain France—but any one power suspected of seeking hegemony.

In the aftermath of the Greek Revolution, the Egyptians inadvertently played into Russian hands. Mehemet Ali had come to the Sultan's aid in that conflict, promised territorial compensation after victory over the Greeks. But the failure of Egyptian arms meant that Mehemet Ali received nothing, and in 1832 the ambitious Pasha occupied Turkish Syria and began an invasion of Anatolia itself. The Sultan Mahmoud II (1808-1839), unable to halt the Egyptian advance, appealed to Britain for support but received none because the British were caught in a domestic political crisis. The desperate Sultan then turned to Russia for help, which was only too eagerly given. The Egyptians discreetly retired from Anatolia as the Turks and Russians concluded a mutual assistance treaty (1833); and western Europe was shocked to realize that Russia had taken a major step toward domination of the eastern Mediterranean.

France responded by encouraging Mehemet Ali in his dream of complete national independence from Turkey and in his hope to build a great Arabo-Egyptian Empire. Turkey, aware of Egyptian ambitions, slowly prepared to counter them, and in 1839 sent an armed force to Syria to expel the Egyptians. The mission miscarried, producing a major European crisis, for it was feared that either Russia or France would exploit the situation. Britain insisted on an international regulation of Turko-Egyptian affairs, and Russia agreed to cooperate, recognizing the opportunity to increase tension between the western liberal powers. The upshot was that the two powers forced Mehemet Ali out of Syria, and the Russians neglected to renew their treaty with Turkey when it came due. The settlement, a diplomatic defeat for the French, gave the Turks a lease on life.

3.   1848:   Year of Revolution and End of the Metternich Era

While the many revolutions in 1848 varied in detail according to nationality, to study them together is to see how many liberal, national, and radical ideas—the heritage of the French and the Industrial Revolutions—came to a head that year. Each group of revolutionaries, whatever the nationality and whether liberal or radical, struggled to found regimes reflecting the ideals of the turn of the century, the very ideals that the statesmen of the Metternich era had tried to eradicate. As these revolutionaries, in general, failed to establish durable regimes, their failures did great damage to the prestige of their ideals. Thus, if the revolutionaries did manage to upset many established regimes in 1848, including that of Metternich himself, the failure to plant successful liberal regimes in their place opened the way for an entirely new species of political leadership. Looking back, 1848 seems not simply to have been a political watershed, heralding an era of tougher, more realistic government, but also a cultural watershed, of which more later.

As in 1830, the wave of revolutions in 1848 began in France. The period of the July Monarchy, which fell between these two dates, saw the beginning of the French industrial revolution; which happened to coincide with a government that was officially liberal, indeed, revolutionary in origin. The liberal of that day, however, as his creed grew out of the eighteenth-century attempt to check royal absolutism, was largely concerned to protect the individual from the tyranny of the state. Let nature rather than the state regulate the system, and freedom would be the result: *"Laissez faire la nature."* The July Monarchy, in short, was too committed to laissez-faire to permit legislative measures to improve the social and economic conditions born of industrialization or urbanization. Not that France became industrialized by 1848—far from it. But what industrial workers there were, along with the artisans in small establishments, soon became alienated from a state that neither set minimum wages nor made any attempt to abolish miserable living and working conditions in the new industrial towns. Understandably, such workers soon felt betrayed by liberalism and began to toy with the various socialist and radical schemes that, in this very period, offered new formulas for the democratization of society. The government responded with repression and censorship, thus gradually losing its claim to be liberal.

Other segments of French society, too, were hostile to the regime: The Legitimists (followers of the House of Bourbon) regarded Louis-Philippe as a usurper; the clergy objected to the government's official anticlericalism; and French nationalists were angered because the government had failed to exploit the Belgian opportunity in 1830 or to back Mehemet Ali successfully in 1840. After that date, a familiar pattern of government reemerged. Guizot, the King's chief policy-maker, answered criticism by manipulating elections to Parliament, buying votes in Parliament, and sharply limiting the electorate through increasing the property qualifications for the vote. Such a regime was doomed in a country that had experienced the liberalization of the French Revolution. When this situation combined with a severe economic depression in 1846-1847, demands for reform proved to be beyond the moral competence of a government based on corruption. Rioting in Paris, led by republican politicians, brought down the monarchy; the King went into exile, and the revolutionaries proclaimed a provisional Second Republic (February of 1848).

This provisional regime was a coalition of liberal and socialist republicans led by Lamartine and Louis Blanc, respectively, meaning that the two groups could agree upon little more than the republican form of government, though they had in common the old Jacobin faith that political democratization would lead to social reforms. When national elections were held in April for a new Assembly, the more moderate or conservative candidates won overwhelmingly against the known radicals, and we know today that many candidates who called themselves republican under the circumstances were in fact recent monarchists with no particular devotion to a republic. By June of 1848, the radicals knew that their dreams of a socialist republic were doomed, and the Parisian mob became convinced that it was again the victim of betrayal by the propertied classes, that the revolution itself had again been betrayed. An insurrection lasting four terrible days in June was crushed by the army, leaving over 5000 dead, after which the Assembly completed work on a constitution for the Second Republic.

In contrast to 1789, this revolution in 1848 never succeeded in establishing a radical regime in France—the reaction set in almost immediately. Moreover, the Left became permanently hostile to political association with moderate liberals. The constitution of 1848, it is true, was a liberal document, providing for universal suffrage and for checks upon executive power. But when new elections were held under this constitution, the electorate revealed itself to be solidly anti-radical and more concerned for order than for liberty. In the presidential election, Prince Louis-Napoleon Bonaparte, nephew of Napoleon I, swamped the moderate and radical republican candidates, beating his combined opposition nearly three to one. Part of his appeal lay in his name, especially attractive after the June Days, when a man of order seemed required. In the parliamentary elections, avowed monarchists won two-thirds of the seats. Though the republic would live on until 1852, it had been given a mortal blow at its birth.

Italy

The Italian national movement, after the failures in 1831, produced three major formulas for achieving national unity. Of the three, that of Mazzini, philosophical child of the eighteenth century and the French Revolution, had the particular characteristic of being at once nationalistic and cosmopolitan. He thought that all nationalities ought to be free and self-governing, that each nationality had unique qualities which could contribute to the enrichment of civilization only when that nationality achieved liberty. As for form of government, Mazzini argued for the French-style anti-clerical republic (to be achieved through revolution) as the best guarantee of individual liberty once national independence had been won. From exile, Mazzini endeavored to coordinate various national movements with his own Young Italy movement, giving the revolutionary movement the aspect of an international conspiracy in the eyes of established monarchical regimes.

Mazzini's hope for a united and anti-clerical Italy with its capital at Rome was unacceptable to those Italian nationalists who remained devoted to Catholicism and to the integrity of the Papacy. The so-called Roman Question included arguments not simply about the proper extent of the Pope's spiritual authority within the various secular states, but about his temporal power within the Papal States. Since that temporal power, dating from the eighth century, had been justi-

GIUSEPPI MAZZINI (Radio Times Hulton Picture Library).

fied as a device to guarantee the spiritual independence of the Papacy, many Catholics feared that to surrender Papal territory to an Italian state would ultimately be to subject Church to State. The experience of the Church during the French Revolution, in other words, seemed to leave the Church no alternative but to be anti-revolutionary and anti-nationalist.

A Piedmontese priest named Gioberti, however, proposed in 1843 a compromise that would give the substance of unity without despoiling the Papacy: a confederation of independent Italian states with the Pope as president of the confederation. That same year, the third formula was proposed by Count Balbo favoring the ruling house of Sardinia-Piedmont. That is, he wanted the house of Savoy to take the lead in Italy, first by banishing Austrian influence from Italy, then by turning Sardinia-Piedmont into a progressive, liberal, constitutional monarchy, to become the nucleus of a united (and monarchical) Italy.

The Gioberti scheme seemed to have the inside track when Pius IX (1846-1878) took the papal throne and gave early evidence of liberal governance in the Papal States. Many Italian patriots became convinced that he would break his predecessor's association with the Metternich system to become an Italian nationalist. Before the end of 1847, the Pope, to his discomfort, found himself a hero of the Italian revolutionaries; for, as the head of a cosmopolitan institution, Pius IX could hardly afford to become recognized as the champion of one nationality against another—especially when the two nationalities concerned were both Roman Catholic. Nevertheless, popular enthusiasm for the Pope forced King Charles Albert of Sardinia-Piedmont (1831-1849) to grant liberal reforms at home in his bid for national popularity.

POPE PIUS IX (Radio Times Hulton Picture Library).

Early in 1848, however, the focal point suddenly shifted southward, where a purely local uprising in Sicily spread to the Neapolitan mainland. Ferdinand II (1830-1859) at once asked for Austrian aid to maintain the status quo, but as Pius IX refused to permit Austrian troops to cross papal territory to get to Naples, Ferdinand was obliged to grant a liberal constitution to his people. In short order, Pius IX, Charles Albert, and the Duke of Tuscany followed suit. Then, with the astonishing news of a liberal uprising in Vienna and the consequent resignation of Metternich, the Milanese rose against Austrian rule in

Lombardy, and the Venetians proclaimed their independence as a republic. Charles Albert of Sardinia-Piedmont, seeing in this his dynasty's great opportunity to take the lead in Italy, announced himself as the champion of the Milanese and declared war on Austria.

This bright beginning for the Italian national cause soon turned sour, beginning with the Pope's refusal to allow his troops to join in an offensive against Austria (though he appealed to the Austrians to withdraw from Italy). In July of 1848, the Austrians overwhelmed Charles Albert, recovered control of Lombardy, and forced an armistice upon the Piedmontese. Meanwhile, Ferdinand II had recovered his own position in Naples by hiring Swiss mercenaries. Through it all, patriotic anger heightened against Pius IX, increasingly seen as the key to the disasters, until the Pope felt obliged to flee to neighboring Naples for protection. Early in 1849, the Mazzinian republicans sought to take advantage of the vacuum in Rome and Charles Albert's defeat by establishing the Roman Republic; but this venture, too, was doomed, and it was a sister republic that brought the Mazzinians down.

The Second French Republic, of course, was republican in name only by 1849. It was a Catholic country with a president whose name and personal ambitions made him an enemy of the 1815 settlement and especially of that country most identified with the maintenance of that settlement—Austria. As the Austrians were recovering from their own revolutionary turmoil, it was assumed they would soon intervene to restore the Pope. Thus, the French decision to go to the Pope's aid really reflected more hostility to Austria than to the Roman Republic, which fell to French arms by midsummer of 1849. Shortly after, the Austrians besieged Venice and destroyed the Venetian Republic—the last of the revolutionary regimes.

Central Europe

The Hapsburg Empire, the very citadel of cosmopolitanism, was itself severely shaken by liberal and national uprisings in 1848. Nationalist sentiments had been on the rise among the various minorities that comprised the Empire in the aftermath of the French Revolution; and even before the news of Louis-Philippe's fall triggered demonstrations and speeches in both Vienna and Budapest, the Hungarian liberal Deák had drafted a plan providing for Hungarian autonomy within the Empire. When the trouble began in 1848, Emperor Ferdinand I (1835-1848) accepted Metternich's resignation, accepted Deák's plan as a constitution for Hungary, and promised the Austrians a constitution of his own manufacture. Rioting continued in Vienna, however, as most Austrian liberals wanted a hand in the drafting of a constitution; and the constitutional movement spread to Prague, with the Czechs insisting on a separate constitution for Bohemia.

Indeed, the Hapsburg Empire seemed to be falling apart at the seams. Other Slavic minorities now aspired to autonomy, and the Czech nationalists launched a pan-Slav movement which proclaimed the solidarity of all Slavic peoples against their German oppressors. When the Croats and Slovenes demanded autonomy from Hungary (which was rejected), the government in Vienna perceived the opportunity to turn the various minorities against each other and thus to recover Austrian hegemony within the Empire. This strategy worked well in Bohemia, where the Austrians exploited quarrels between Germans and Czechs to crush the Czech revolutionary movement. It backfired when the Austrians sought to humble the Hungarians by egging on the Croats. Led by Kossuth, the Hungarian liberals now rejected their newly won autonomy in favor of complete independence, and they invaded Austria to win their point.

Metternich's fall, meanwhile, had particularly shocked Nicholas I of Russia, who felt he must assume the role of policeman of Europe now that Metternich had abandoned it. If the Hungarians were to succeed in making good their claim to independence, their example might inspire the Poles. The new Austrian government, faced with invasion, appealed to Nicholas for help, which he readily granted. Russian forces invaded Hungary from the east in 1849, and the Austrians moved in from the west, smashing the independence movement. After more than a year of turmoil, the Hapsburg domains were reunited by force; the currents of nationalism were at least temporarily confined.

In the German world, the news from Paris in 1848 excited liberal-nationalists into believing that the moment had at last arrived to achieve representative government within a united Germany. The revolutionary movement caught fire, forcing many German rulers to promise liberal reforms. Frederick William IV (1840-1861) of Prussia feared he might have to place himself at the head of this nationalist zeal if he were to maintain his throne. Yet, he had no taste for liberal government and feared retaliation from Austria and Russia if he abandoned them apparently to lead a revolution. At Frankfurt, in the meantime, a self-appointed committee of liberals supervised national elections on a democratic basis, and in May of 1848 the Frankfurt National Assembly convened, suspending the Diet of the Germanic Confederation. In Prussia, meanwhile, the King permitted a constituent assembly to begin preparation of a constitution.

It was all for naught. When news reached Berlin that the new regime in Vienna had successfully dispersed revolutionaries there, Frederick William IV dissolved his own constituent assembly. He then rejected an offer of the throne of a united Germany from the revolutionaries in Frankfurt, making a shambles of their constitutional project. Wanting a united Germany, but on his own terms, Frederick William then toyed with a plan that would have created a Prussian-dominated central European confederation. Neither Austria nor Russia would tolerate this half victory for German nationalism, forcing the Prussian King to cast aside his project in 1850.

4. The Replacement of the Vienna Settlement, 1851-1871: The Ascendency of Napoleon III

After the failure of the liberal-nationalists to achieve their political goals through revolution in 1848, Europe entered a period of reaction similar to that after 1815. More or less autocratic governments justified themselves as the guardians of "order" after the upheavals. Nationalist aspirations, on the other hand, did not fade away; and in the period between 1851 and 1871, a new breed of tough-minded, skillful politicians emerged to advance the claims of nationality. They challenged not merely the liberals' methods for achieving national self-determination, but the liberals' cosmopolitan or European conception of nationalism as a movement that would release unique energies for the benefit of all. The newer view saw nationalities as units of hostility, with each nation-state obliged to strengthen itself for the inevitable competition with other nation-states. By 1871, the liberal-nationalists had been overwhelmed in both the political arena and on the battlefield by the conservative-nationalists, and Europe started her dreadful slide toward total hostility and total war.

The most representative figure of this transitional period was Prince Louis-Napoleon Bonaparte, the man elected to be president of the

Second French Republic in 1848, later Napoleon III (1851-1870). As heir to both the "principles of '89," as he himself put it, and the Napoleonic tradition, he sympathized with all subject nationalities and believed it to be his destiny, once he had achieved power, to work for their emancipation. In the liberal-nationalist tradition, therefore, he represented the view that to liberate subject nationalities would be to remove a major source of conflict and war in Europe. Despite this idealism of an earlier generation, he was also a shrewd, calculating politician, who believed that the national movement could benefit France. He was ready to obtain through diplomacy and war, like the men of his own generation, what the liberals had failed to accomplish in 1848. This uncomfortable mixture of qualities not only baffled his contemporaries, but contributed to the ultimate triumph of other leaders devoted more singularly than he to politics based solely on the realities of power—*Realpolitik.*

EMPEROR NAPOLEON III (Radio Times Hulton Picture Library).

The rise of a new Bonaparte to power was understandably disquieting to the European establishment, based, as it had been since 1815, on containing French militarism. On the other hand, the earlier days of great-power intervention to eradicate regimes thought to be inconsistent with the 1815 settlement were long past, and it would have been folly to have attempted to unseat the elect of such an overwhelming majority of the French. His restoration of the papacy in 1849, however anti-Austrian its real aim may have been, could be seen as the work of a good conservative maintaining the status quo. And when he cunningly outmaneuvered his opponents at home to make possible the supplanting of the Second Republic by the Second Empire after the *coup d'état* of 1851, the great monarchies half hid their irritation over the news by noting with satisfaction the passing of a republic. That the new Emperor's despotism was sanctioned by universal suffrage, a recognition of popular sovereignty, was ominous for the old order; but at least it was despotism. Thus was the Vienna settlement, with its provision against a Bonapartist restoration, peaceably defied.

The Crimean War

The Eastern Question remained quiescent for a decade after the containment of Mehemet Ali in 1841, until the new French Emperor, responding to pressure from Roman Catholic opinion, approached the Turkish government on the matter of the holy places in Palestine, most of which had fallen under the control of Greek Orthodox monks. Napoleon III, in reviving the traditional French right to protect Roman Catholic monks in the Holy Land, thus made his first move to restore French greatness in Europe; and he succeeded in retrieving some of the holy places for the Catholics through Turkish agreement (1852). As the political implications of this success far outweighed the religious, Nicholas I of Russia demanded of Turkey not merely equality with France in the Holy Land, but also the right to protect Greek Orthodox churches in Constantinople and throughout the Turkish Empire.

Even though Britain had been distressed by the appearance of a new Bonaparte in France, and though Britain had previously cooperated with Russia in containing the spread of French influence in the Eastern Mediterranean, the demands made by Nicholas I were so threatening to Ottoman integrity that the British dared not support them—which the Turks soon understood. And their worst fears about Russian intentions were soon confirmed when Nicholas sent troops into Turkey's Danubian Principalities to back up his demands. The remaining great powers now tried to resolve the crisis through diplomacy; but the Turks, increasingly confident of European support, endeavored to exploit this opportunity to give Russian expansionism a sharp slap. Sending Russia an ultimatum to evacuate the Principalities, the Turks declared war upon Russian refusal (1853).

During the Greek Revolution, the British and French had briefly experienced the odd necessity of cooperating to maintain the balance of power. Now the logic of politics forced them together again, and their alliance was popular in the west to the degree that Russia had become odious in the eyes of many western Europeans: a divine-right autocracy was, of course, anathema to liberal opinion; there was much pro-Polish sentiment, especially in France; and the Russian intervention to destroy Hungarian independence in 1849 had awakened horror in the west. Russia, on the other hand, counted on Austrian support, thanks to 1849, to counteract Franco-British pressure. In some respects, therefore, Austria played the decisive role in what became the Crimean War in 1854, even though she never became a belligerent. For the Austrians, whatever their recent debt to Russia, were hardly ready to see Russia dominate the Balkans and the Eastern Mediterranean. After Britain and France went to the aid of Turkey that year, with the public seeing the war as liberalism versus autocracy, the Austrians astonished the Russians by sending them an ultimatum to evacuate the Danubian Principalities. Already at war with three powers, the Russians felt they must comply.

Neither Britain nor France wanted an expensive war, which precluded an invasion of Russia. Their ultimate strategy was to seize the naval base of Sevastopol on the Crimean peninsula and hold it as a pawn, meanwhile applying diplomatic pressure upon Austria to force her active participation against Russia. Vienna was thus the scene of continual negotiations as the fighting developed in the Crimea. Even the Piedmontese joined the western Allies in the hope of a seat at the peace table. The limited nature of the Allied campaign was more than offset by the inefficiency of the Russians in meeting this invasion on the periphery of their Empire, but it took the Allies until the autumn of 1855 to force the Russians to evacuate Sevastopol. Even then, the Russians were reluctant to make peace, as they knew already that the

Allies hoped to solve the Eastern Question by forcing the demilitarization of the Black Sea. It took a second Austrian ultimatum to make the Russians agree to make peace.

Early in 1856 the powers convened for the Congress of Paris to sign the terms which, for the most part, had been worked out in Vienna during the war. Russia and Turkey mutually accepted the neutralization of the Black Sea (a blow to Russia alone); and the Danubian Principalities, the nucleus of the future Romanian state, were put temporarily under the collective jurisdiction of the powers signatory to the Treaty of Paris. The Congress of Paris also proved to be a sounding board, thanks to Napoleon III, for various national groups seeking self-determination and for the revision of the Vienna settlement of 1815. And the general unpopularity of Austria in 1856 for her wartime neutrality—when both sides had sought her belligerency—contributed to a more general willingness to listen to national claims. Between 1857 and 1862, Romaiian nationalists developed the foundations for a nation-state and, in 1866, were granted autonomy within the Ottoman Empire.

The Unification of Italy

The chief spokesman at the Congress of Paris for Italian nationalism was the prime minister of Sardinia-Piedmont, Count Cavour, who represented in particular the Balbo formula for Italian unity: that Sardinia-Piedmont and her ruling dynasty should become the nucleus of an Italian monarchy. Above all else, Cavour was a political realist and he knew, after 1848, that Italy would not be forged by the Italians alone. Recognizing Napoleon III's sympathy and ready to sacrifice Sardinia's two French-speaking territories—Nice and Savoy—to gain the rest of Italy, Cavour bargained privately with the French Emperor. Both men knew that Austria would have to be expelled forcibly from Lombardy and Venetia; while Napoleon III, whose troops had garrisoned Rome after the Pope's restoration in 1849, felt at least temporarily constrained by the need to support Papal independence. Consequently, he favored the Gioberti formula for Italian unity; the formation of a confederation of independent Italian states.

In 1859, Cavour provoked Austria into an attack upon Sardinia-Piedmont, making it easier for Napoleon III to come to the side of Sardinia. After two military victories by the French over the Austrians, however, Napoleon's luck in Italy began to run out. Prussia suddenly mobilized on the French frontier and volunteered to come to the aid of Austria, clearly a bid to seize the leadership of the German world from the Austrians. Since neither Austria nor France welcomed Prussian intervention, they hastened into armistice and arranged terms far short of what Napoleon had originally promised Cavour. Austria ceded only Lombardy to France (which gave the province to Sardinia), but retained Venetia. Napoleon's hopes for an Italian confederation were soon dashed, partly because of the Pope's continuing refusal to become its president, and partly because Cavour's agents, some of them Mazzinian, stirred up Italian opinion in favor of a unitary state. Following nationalist uprisings (1859 and 1860) in Tuscany, Parma, Modena, and Romagna (part of the Papal States), plebiscites were held in those territories, and the inhabitants voted overwhelmingly to be annexed by Sardinia-Piedmont (1860). Plebiscites were also held in Nice and Savoy, where the vote was to join France.

Meanwhile, in the south, Garibaldi (a former Mazzinian who now rallied to the Sardinian monarchy) successfully invaded the territories of the Neapolitan Bourbons. Fearing that he might move next against Rome, where he had commanded briefly in 1849, the Sardinians quickly sent a force to occupy Naples to avoid an embarrassing clash with French arms. Pius IX tried to prevent the Sardinians from crossing Papal territory to reach Naples, but lost his tiny army in the process. The upshot was that two more bits of Papal property, Umbria and the Marches, as well as Naples, were given the option of voting to join Sardinia. So that by the end of 1860, only Venetia and Rome itself remained outside the realm. Early in 1861, Sardinia renamed herself the Kingdom of Italy. Napoleon III, in short, had done much for Italy, if not exactly in the manner he had anticipated. In the process, French Catholic opinion had been offended and the Pope outraged, hardly grateful for the French troops who still protected him.

The Waning of French Prestige

If Napoleon III was instrumental in producing a modern Italy and a Romania, in the process of which he apparently returned France to the continental paramountcy lost in 1815, his luck with other nationalities turned sour in the 1860's, paving the way for the rise of the modern Germany. Some of the reverses were due to French miscalculations, and others to foreign misreading of French intentions abroad.

An example of the former was the French intervention in Mexico, beginning in 1861. No doubt the Mexican Republic invited trouble by suspending payments on debts to European investors, but the real motives for Napoleon III's conquest of Mexico were those of a visionary. He had long been interested in the construction of a Central American canal as the focal point for Latin American economic development, a cosmopolitan scheme worthy of a Napoleon. When he became convinced that the Mexican Republic was depriving the majority of Mexicans of their preferred Catholic monarchy, he intervened on behalf of Mexican monarchists, enabling them to install the Austrian Archduke Maximilian as Emperor in 1864. When the truth dawned in Paris that Napoleon III had been misled about the state of popular opinion in Mexico, a French evacuation was inevitable; and it came toward the end of 1866 when alarming developments in the German world made it necessary to bring the troops home.

A costly and apparently senseless expedition such as this only increased European mistrust of French ambitions. And a foreign policy that sought European-wide benefits, rather than benefits for France alone, was an anachronism in a day of the new nationalism and, thus, easily misperceived. The British, in particular, still haunted by the image of the first Napoleon across the Channel, concluded that his successor ought to be isolated. When in 1863, the Poles rose a second time against Russian domination, the great powers were given an opportunity to behave toward a revolution as they had in the 1820's and to contain the supposed militarism of the French as they had in that era.

The Polish Revolt of 1863 was a highly complicated movement, as the revolutionaries were deeply divided into factions. In the aftermath of the Crimean War, which had revealed gross inefficiencies in Russian government, Alexander II (1855-1881) had begun major social and administrative reforms within his empire, which eliminated many of the abuses and hardships endured by the Poles after their rebellion in 1831. Though the Czar hoped to reconcile the Poles to integration with the Russians, the relaxation in fact aroused hopes for independence. As earlier, Polish patriots dreamt of reestablishing their prepartition boundaries of 1772, meaning territory that was not strictly Polish in population, and that by 1863 was claimed by Prussia and Austria as well as by Russia. Polish demands, in other words, soon exceeded what Alexander II either would or could concede.

When fighting broke out, the hopelessness of the Polish cause was underscored by a Prussian offer to give Russia any aid that might be necessary to quell the revolt. Polish appeals to France for aid put Napoleon III in a quandary: On the one hand, the Polish cause was popular in the West and consistent with well-known Napoleonic principles. On the other hand, he had striven to be conciliatory to Russia ever since the Crimean War, his aim being the reconciliation of all the Crimean opponents as the basis for a durable peace. He tried to save both causes by avoiding unilateral action in Poland, calling upon the great powers to do something for Poland in concert. The three eastern powers, with their common interest in the subjection of the Poles, were unenthusiastic, and Britain found in the crisis the opportunity to promote French isolation. Consequently, Polish independence went down the drain, and Napoleon III's attempt to reconstruct a new European authority suffered a fatal defeat. The future belonged to those whose ambitions were parochial rather than cosmopolitan.

The Unification of Germany

The gradual isolation of France provided a favorable climate for the aggrandizement of Prussia under William I (1858-1888), just as the Franco-Sardinian success against Austria encouraged Prussia to play a Sardinian role in the German world. Vigorous attempts to reform and enlarge the Prussian military establishment were for a time stalled in the Landtag by the Liberal majority, which wanted control of the budget and saw the army as the bulwark of the autocracy. Indeed, when the monarchy had granted constitutional and representative government during the crisis of 1848, the royal intention had been to preserve royal authority behind the mere facade of representative government; and the crown took a dim view of this liberal attempt to check royal power. In 1862, after several years of parliamentary squabbling, William I appointed as his minister-president a tough conservative known for his hatred of parliamentary institutions: Otto von Bismarck.

Bismarck was not so much a German nationalist as he was a Prussian patriot, but his policies soon won him the support of nationalist opinion and ultimately the acclaim of many liberals. This despite the fact that he ordered the collection of taxes without parliamentary consent and thus destroyed the liberals' position. His quick successes in foreign affairs were the key to his popular support; and German nationalists, in abandoning their earlier alliance with liberalism, effectively promoted the Prussification of Germany in the name of unification. Both Napoleon III and Bismarck were consummate politicians, but unlike Napoleon III, Bismarck was not harnessed to a set of political ideals. His genius lay, therefore, not in promoting a preconceived program, but in exploiting international crises for the benefit of Prussia.

PRINCE OTTO VON BISMARCK (Radio Times Hulton Picture Library).

Since the eighteenth century, the rise of Prussia in the German world had been at the expense of Austrian power, and certainly in the nineteenth century Austria had used her power to bind the Prussian government to anti-nationalist policies. Thus, the wedding of Prussia to German nationalism in the 1860's was seen as a great peril in Vienna. As an Empire whose vulnerability had been exposed in 1848 and again in 1859, the Austrians would have done well to cede Venetia to Italy after 1863 in exchange for a firm understanding with Italy and France, freeing Austria to face the north. Napoleon III, in fact, proposed a characteristically elaborate scheme by which the Austrians would annex Turkey's Danubian Principalities (then preparing for autonomy) as compensation for the loss of Venetia; and Italy would pay the Turks an indemnity for the ceded Principalities (which they seemed likely to lose ultimately anyway) as the price for Venetia.

As the Austrians rejected any such transaction, they became the victim of an Italo-Prussian alliance (1866) which had the blessing of Napoleon III. For he not only was anxious to see Italy obtain the Venetia he had been unable to deliver in 1859, but he was logically sympathetic to German as well as Italian nationalism and had long expected that Prussia must one day be enlarged into a Germany. What is more, Bismarck hinted at territorial compensation along the Rhine, presumably those areas lost by France in 1815, in exchange for French neutrality. It remained for Bismarck to provoke a war with Austria, which he accomplished by suddenly proposing that the Germanic Confederation be abandoned in favor of a new federal system which would eliminate Austria. Most of the small states in the Germanic Confederation sided with Austria to avoid being swallowed up by Prussia; and the Austrians, fearful of French intervention, at once ceded Venetia to France to guarantee French neutrality.

The shortness of the ensuing Seven Weeks War (1866) astonished European military opinion, which had expected a lengthy, indecisive conflict. Even though the Italians were defeated by Austria, the Prussians won a great victory for the Alliance by routing the Austrians at Sadowa. Bismarck at once offered the Austrians an easy peace, based on the exclusion of Austria from further participation in the German world, and the Germanic Confederation was scrapped. In its place he formed the North German Confederation under Prussian presidency, to include the states north of the Main river. Napoleon III, of course, handed Venetia to the Italians; but when the French approached Bismarck for the expected bits of territory that would have wiped out the vestiges of the 1815 settlement, they had their first experience with his deviousness. During 1866 and 1867, he methodically scuttled the very projects for territorial adjustment which he himself initiated. In retrospect it is easy to see that, having pushed Austria from the German scene, Bismarck used the occasion to enrage French opinion as the basis for future conflict. That conflict, when it came in 1870, was a major tragedy that ought to have been avoided, since Napoleon III had long since accepted the legitimacy of Prussian aggrandizement in Germany. Instead, Bismarck believed that Prussian aggrandizement required a national war against a common enemy as the context for unification, and the French defeat in 1870 did much to destroy what remained of a sense of a European community.

This is not to say that Bismarck plotted the Hohenzollern candidacy for the Spanish crown, which proved to be the incident leading to the Franco-Prussian War. Instead, when a Hohenzollern prince seemed to be the Spanish choice to fill the throne that had been vacant since 1868, Bismarck secretly abetted the cause, certain that the French in general would see this Hohenzollern "encirclement" as intolerable. The House of Hohenzollern itself was far from anxious to become the cause for another war, and Bismarck very nearly saw his plans go awry as the Hohenzollern candidacy was withdrawn in the face of French pressure. The French, however, too anxious to avenge their humiliations of the recent past, pressed the Prussians to promise that there would never be a renewal of the candidacy in such a way as to force them to admit they had been guilty of wrong-doing in the first place. William I rightly rejected the demand, and Bismarck altered the report of the King's last interview with the French Ambassador to make it appear that the French had made insulting demands upon the King, and that the King had dismissed the Ambassador in an insulting manner—which had not been the case. The French fell into the trap, and, in declaring war, appeared to be the aggressors.

To general surprise, the army which had won in the Crimea, in Mexico, and in Italy did poorly from the start, notably out-generaled by the Prussians under Moltke. After the capture of Napoleon III and a portion of the army at Sedan, the Parisians overthrew the Second Empire and established a Government of National Defense which was republican in form. Energetic attempts to mobilize the entire nation for defense in the manner of the 1790's stood some chance of success had it not been for the untimely surrender of a second French army at Metz. Paris itself endured a dreadful siege during the winter of 1870-1871, until the responsible elements in the provisional government knew they must seek an armistice. For a time, they had hoped for European intervention to prevent Prussia from becoming too overwhelming on the continent. The other powers, however, could not be roused to act in concert. Britain rejoiced to see Napoleon III in captivity; the Russians announced that they would remilitarize the Black Sea; and when the Italians were certain of the French defeat, they seized the city of Rome as their national capital.

As for Prussia, she crowned her victory by swallowing up all of Germany. The other German states no longer dared to defend their sovereignty, and the King of Bavaria was induced to invite the King of Prussia to take the imperial title. Early in 1871, the German Empire was proclaimed at Prussian military headquarters, the Palace of Versailles. Peace terms were then given to the French: the loss of Alsace and Lorraine, an indemnity of five billion francs (which was believed to be beyond the power of the French to pay), and an army of occupation in the northeast until that indemnity could be paid. The intent of such terms was obvious, and the treaty marked the beginning of a new era of harshness and bitterness in international relations.

5.   The Road to Total War, 1871-1914:
The Hegemony of the German Empire

Having been the architect of Prussian aggrandizement, Bismarck became the first chancellor of the German Empire; and having achieved his aims, he emerged after 1871 as the devoted champion of the European status quo. His diplomacy had to cope with three major factors that would remain constant right down to 1914: First was the need to keep defeated France isolated, for her unanticipated financial recovery by 1873 raised the specter of a war of revenge if she could find an ally against her larger neighbor. The foundation of the Third Republic in 1870, however, seemed to suggest indefinite isolation amidst the monarchies of Europe. Since Britain had been following an isolationist policy herself after the Crimean War, Bismarck felt that an understanding with the Russian and Hapsburg Empires would suffice to contain France.

Second, the Hapsburg Empire had been much altered by the reverses beginning in 1859. After their defeat in 1866, the Austrians felt obliged to make concessions to Hungarian nationalism, and in 1867 the Austrian Empire was formally converted into the Dual Monarchy of Austria-Hungary. Bringing the Hungarians into foreign policy-making amounted to a diplomatic revolution. They were able to deflect Hapsburg energies away from the traditional involvement in German and Italian affairs, forcing the monarchy to devote its attention to the Slavic minorities within the Empire, a stance which in time came to be a policy of hostility to Slavic peoples. The new orientation may have facilitated Bismarck's desire for reconciliation with the Hapsburgs, but it jeopardized his plan to develop close ties between Germany, Austria-Hungary, and Russia. Not only did the Russians remember with bitterness what they called Austria's "betrayal" during the Crimean War, but the Hungarians nurtured a passionate hatred of Russia for suppressing their national movement in 1849.

One can see the extent of Bismarck's diplomatic task when one adds to this picture the traditional rivalry of these two eastern empires to replace the declining Turkish Empire in the southeast. Toward that goal, the Russians increasingly picked up the banner of pan-Slavism, first flown by the Czechs in 1848, as the device to increase Russian influence among the peoples of southeastern Europe. The Dual Monarchy tried for a time to counter this by opposing Slavic nationalism and favoring maintaining the status quo in the Turkish Empire.

Finally, the third factor in the diplomatic picture was the rise of little Serbia under the leadership of Prince Michael Obrenović (1860-1868), an ardent Serbian nationalist. During his brief reign, he reached an understanding with the Prince of Montenegro and with the Bulgarian Revolutionary Committee (within the Turkish Empire) for an eventual union with Serbia, clear evidence of Serbian expansionism in the Balkans. This Slavic nationalism was as distressing to the Hungarians as it was to the Turks.

With these factors present, Bismarck achieved his first postwar diplomatic success in 1873 when he brought the three eastern empires into the Three Emperors' League *(Dreikaiserbund)*. This arrangement, not a formal alliance, simply provided for mutual consultation in case the peace should be threatened. The fragility of this arrangement was soon revealed in 1875 and 1876 when insurrections in the Turkish provinces of Bosnia and Bulgaria provided opportunities both for Slavic nationalists and for international intervention into Turkish affairs. In the summer of 1876, the little Slavic states of Serbia and Montenegro invoked the pan-Slavic ideal and declared war against Turkey, entrusting the command of their armies to a Russian general well-known for his pan-Slavic views. Though the representatives of the *Dreikaiserbund* tried to regulate the crisis by agreeing not to allow the formation of a large Balkan state, the quick defeat of the Serbs by the Turks put Serbian independence in jeopardy and offered Russia a fine opportunity for intervention.

To meet this general Balkan crisis, the great powers convened in Constantinople. The Turks, however, confident of British backing in resisting Russian pressure, rejected the international attempts to meddle in Ottoman affairs—all while negotiating a status quo-antebellum peace with Serbia. In secret, meanwhile, Russia and Austria worked out an agreement, which revealed that neither power was seriously concerned for the welfare of Serbia. Both reaffirmed that the formation of a large Balkan state would be blocked, and agreed that Russia might unilaterally declare war on Turkey for refusing to improve the administration of her Christian subjects. After the expected Russian victory, she would annex Bessarabian territory along the Danubian frontier, while the Austrians would be free to occupy Turkish Bosnia and Herzegovina at any time. Accordingly, Russia declared war on the Turks in 1877 and was promptly joined by Romania, who hoped to transform her autonomy within Turkey into complete independence.

Once the Turks were overwhelmed and agreed to Russian peace terms (1878), Bismarck learned how difficult it was to keep Austria and Russia on good terms. The Russians had dictated peace terms to Turkey that were entirely inconsistent with the prior understanding with Austria. They provided for the creation of a large, independent Bulgaria (which Russia hoped to dominate), and for an autonomous Bosnia and Herzegovina. To avoid a possible war between Austria and Russia, Bismarck invited the great powers to resume their Balkan deliberations in Berlin. This Congress of Berlin (1878) forced the Russians to invalidate their previous peace terms and to accept the Treaty of Berlin, which greatly whittled down Bulgaria and left her merely autonomous within the Turkish Empire. Romania, however, did win her complete independence. As for Bosnia and Herzegovina, the treaty put a brake on the Austrians, too, by permitting them a *temporary* occupation of the two provinces if order there should need to be restored. The events of 1878, in sum, revealed that both Russia and Austria had expansionist ambitions in the Balkans: Russia by trying to create a large Bulgaria, Austria-Hungary by her increasing interest in Bosnia-Herzegovina.

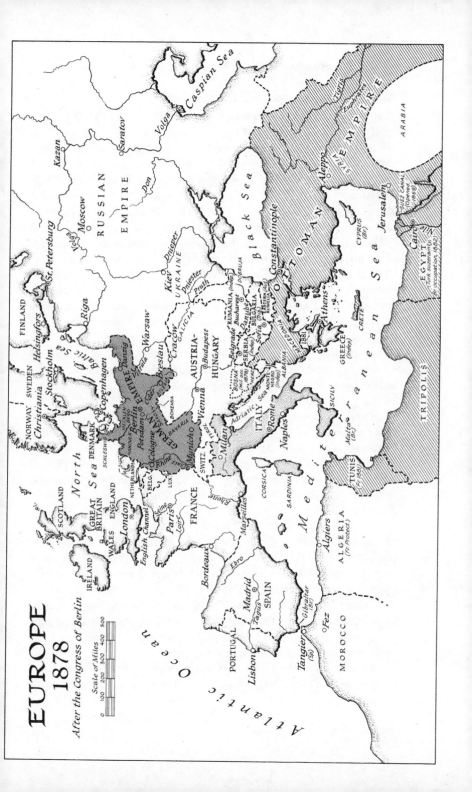

The Dual and Triple Alliances, 1879 and 1882.

The events of 1878 also revealed the ineffectuality of the *Dreikaiserbund,* and as the angered Russians hinted that they might seek an alliance with France, Bismarck felt he must draw closer to Austria-Hungary. He found the Austro-Hungarians willing to sign an alliance with Germany, providing it was directed against Russia alone. Thus, the Alliance of 1879 pledged the two countries to assist each other in case of an attack by Russia; but they were under no obligation in case of an attack from another country (France or Italy, for instance) unless that country was aided by Russia. This agreement was the first of the arrangements that would become effective in 1914.

Both partners in the alliance, meanwhile, had been aware of potential trouble from France and Italy: the former were anxious to recover territories lost in 1870, the latter were claiming the Trentino (the Italian-speaking part of the province of Tyrol). Consequently, both Germany and Austria urged France and Italy, respectively, to seek their territorial goals in North Africa rather than in Europe; and for reasons we must consider in greater detail elsewhere, both powers settled upon Tunisia as their proper area of expansion. The French suddenly occupied Tunis in 1881, to the dismay of the Italians, and established a protectorate. Bismarck, though personally disdainful of Italy, preferred under the circumstances to accept Italy as an ally. Otherwise, the frantic Italians might feel themselves forced to reach an understanding with France for the partition of North Africa, in which case France would cease to be isolated. The upshot was that Germany and Austria formed the Triple Alliance with Italy (1882), the terms of which were specifically anti-French rather than anti-Russian.

Bismarck had not, in fact, abandoned his hope of reestablishing the *Dreikaiserbund,* and had cajoled the Russians into renewing the ties ruptured at the Congress of Berlin. Toward that end the three emperors agreed in 1881 to consult on matters relating to the Eastern Question. And to rebuild this accord, Bismarck, who had presided at the Congress of Berlin as a self-styled "honest broker," now secretly agreed to the undermining of the Berlin settlement. Austria withdrew her objection to a large Bulgaria and received in exchange the right to annex Bosnia and Herzegovina at any time.

The years after the Congress of Berlin were increasingly worrisome for the small Balkan states, caught as they were in the crossfire of

Russian and Austro-Hungarian ambitions. Moreover, each Balkan state had its own expansionist dreams, the revival of some ancient or medieval greatness before the arrival of the Turks; and without exception each national ambition was incompatible with that of every neighboring nationality. Add to this hints from some Italian nationalists that Italy might well lay claim to territories within the Roman Empire, and one had in the Balkans the ultimate madness that the new nationalism could create. Under the circumstances, these small states sought the protection or sponsorship of a great power; but in becoming clients, they risked becoming mere pawns of the great powers. The domestic politics of these small states, therefore, reflected these gross ambitions and elaborate fears, which gave to Balkan politics the atmosphere of comic opera based upon nightmares.

The potentiality for disaster in this mixture of great-power and small-power rivalries was illustrated in 1885. Bulgaria, hoping to convert her autonomy into complete independence, had taken advantage of Russian sponsorship to prepare to seize Eastern Rumelia (a Bulgar-speaking territory in Turkey immediately south of Bulgaria, which she had been denied in 1878), meanwhile quietly mobilizing Bulgarian national opinion to resist becoming a Russian puppet. When the Bulgarians suddenly moved into Eastern Rumelia in 1885, the jealous and anxious Serbs declared war on Bulgaria. Austria, for the moment regarding Serbia as her client, failed to intervene until the Serbians were quickly defeated by Bulgaria. Then, without informing her *Dreikaiserbund* partners of her intention to intervene, Austria forced an end to the conflict and prevented the unification of Bulgaria. Had not the Russians already been irritated by their inability to manipulate Bulgaria, a general war could have developed that year, for Russia was infuriated by Austrian high-handedness.

The *Dreikaiserbund* failed to survive this second major clash of Austrian and Russian interests, and in 1887 Bismarck endeavored to keep his foreign policy intact by seeking a treaty with Russia that would be compatible with his treaty with Austria. This meant that he could not guarantee German neutrality in case of an Austro-Russian war. The result was the three-year Reinsurance Treaty, more a testament of good will than a document guaranteeing mutual aid. Germany's real alliances, indeed, were those with Austria and Italy.

The Accession of Kaiser William II (1888-1918) and the Franco-Russian Alliance of 1894

Bismarck's system, if already in difficulty, did not long survive the accession of a new Emperor in 1888. Much influenced by the military and political views of the German General Staff, William II believed that an Austro-Russian war for domination of the Balkans and the Straits was unavoidable. As the national interests of Germany were more reconcilable with those of Austria than with those of Russia, the German General Staff favored an Austro-German "preventive war" against Russia while she was relatively weak. Bismarck had opposed that view, arguing that such a war would be the opportunity for France to try to recover Alsace-Lorraine. But Bismarck's long-term policy had been to maintain the European status quo, whereas William II was nurturing ideas of German expansionism. Clearly, the two divergent views could not long remain in the same house, and when, in 1890, Bismarck offered his resignation, the Emperor accepted it. An immediate result was a German failure to renew the Reinsurance Treaty, apparent proof that Germany was abandoning Bismarck's policy of being friendly simultaneously with Russia and Austria.

In retrospect, German foreign policy between 1890 and 1914 seems to have been as erratic as the restless, ambitious Emperor himself. Its first result was to drive the Russians into an alliance with France, no matter how repugnant such a marriage was for the autocratic Alexander III (1881-1896). Though it was known in Europe that the two powers were seeking an agreement, the actual terms of the military convention signed in 1894 were kept secret (Russia wished to avoid irritating Germany). Completely defensive in nature, the alliance was to remain in force only as long as the Triple Alliance existed. Even so, it marked the end of French isolation.

Aware of the negotiations, William II tried to tie Britain to the Triple Alliance. The British, arguing that their cabinet system of government precluded binding future governments with long-term obligations, would enter no alliance system. The Germans believed the British argument was disingenuous, and it made them suspicious of British intentions. William II consequently had second thoughts about his rejection of Russia, and his uneasiness was underscored when the questionable effectiveness of Italy as an ally was revealed to all by a monumental defeat inflicted on the Italians when they tried to establish a protectorate over Ethiopia in 1896.

In the 1890's, therefore, a new German policy gradually evolved which was based not upon securing the isolation of France, but upon securing the isolation of Great Britain. The effect would have been to merge the Triple Alliance with the Franco-Russian Alliance, to destroy the balance of power on the continent, to give Germany practical hegemony on the continent, and to leave Britain alone facing a situation uncomfortably reminiscent of the Napoleonic Empire. William II found the key to this new orientation in East Asia, where Britain had commercial interests and where Russia had become the competitor of Japan—both powers were endeavoring to expand at the expense of the declining Chinese Empire. Encouraging Russian expansion in the Manchurian-Korean region, if a German bid for Russian friendship, had the added advantage of turning Russian energies away from the Balkans and a possible clash with Austria. The strategy seemed the more workable since it coincided with Anglo-French squabbling in North Africa.

This rivalry had begun to fester in 1875, when the British government, taking advantage of the Egyptian ruler's indebtedness, purchased his shares in the Suez Canal Company, and became the majority stockholder in what had been a French enterprise. In the ensuing years, the French saw their traditional influence in Egypt replaced by that of Britain, with the British gradually drawn southward up the Nile valley to defend Egypt's claim on the Sudan and to protect the water supply for the canal region. In the 1890's, French nationalists counterattacked with a scheme designed to give France control of the headwaters of the Nile; and the two Western powers seemed near war in 1898 when the French established a small base at Fashoda in the Sudan.

By then, however, the British were too alarmed by German policies and tactics to allow relations with France to degenerate into war. In 1896, for example, on the twenty-fifth anniversary of the German Empire, William II proclaimed an aggressive "pan-German" program: "The German Empire has become a world empire. Everywhere at the most distant points on the globe dwell thousands of our fellow countrymen. German merchandise, German science, German energy sail the oceans. The value of our sea trade amounts to thousands of millions. It is your duty to aid me in creating firm links between this greater Germany and our fatherland." Already possessing a formidable army, the Germans announced in 1897 the development of a large navy to implement the new global policy. The British read the challenge correctly and knew that their security depended upon naval supremacy. A belated attempt to reach an understanding with Berlin was rebuffed, as the Germans were increasingly confident in the ultimate success of their continental system. This gave the British no option but to seek a reconciliation with France. Thus was born the series of commitments that would serve to block William II's world policy.

Britain Renounced Her Isolation, 1899-1907

In backing away from her long-term isolation, Britain entered into a number of agreements with foreign powers, but never concluded an alliance in Europe such as all the continental powers had arranged by 1900. Her international position, therefore, remained ambiguous, especially in German eyes; as she was suspected of having made, by 1914, firm European military commitments in secret—which, in fact, she never did. Though, like the other powers, she had signed the Treaty of London (1831) which guaranteed the independence and neutrality of Belgium. In 1899, she reached an African settlement with France, by which the French agreed to evacuate the Nile watershed; west of this the British gave the French a free hand. This immediately alarmed Italy as a possible barrier to her still frustrated African ambitions, leading her to undertake secret talks with the French. In 1900 they mutually recognized Italy's "interest" in Tripoli and France's in Morocco, actually a first step in undermining Italy's loyalty to the Triple Alliance.

Britain's second move was an attempt to restrict Russia's German-backed penetration of East Asia by signing a five-year alliance with Japan in 1902. The two island empires recognized Japan's economic interests in Korea, but guaranteed the independence of both Korea ?nd China. This treaty had the effect of making Russia promise to vacuate Manchuria, but her failure to live up to the promise gave the Japanese pretext for war. Early in 1904, the Japanese launched a surprise attack, which gained them early advantages from which the Russians never recovered. What is more, the Russian government met these disasters so ineptly as to provoke a political crisis at home and to provide opportunity for a radical uprising against the autocracy in 1905. The political crisis forced the Russians to make peace at the very moment when their forces in East Asia were finally reaching the strength to make a Japanese defeat probable. The pro-Japanese

Theodore Roosevelt mediated the conflict, and the Japanese were left with a foothold in Korea and the southern half of Sakhalin. Like the Crimean War, the Russo-Japanese War revealed the inefficiency of the Russian autocracy and forced both military and political reforms upon Czar Nicholas II (1896-1917). But the outcome of the war also obscured Russia's true military strength, just as the Japanese victory excited Asian and African nationalists.

Meanwhile, the French developed their African settlement with Italy by securing Italy's promise to remain neutral in case the French found themselves "directly provoked" to declare war. This gave the Italians the latitude to decide who would be the "real" aggressor in a future Franco-German conflict and, thus, the opportunity to shirk the obligation to aid Germany. However advantageous to Italy, no power could any longer predict how she would behave in a crisis, and she was mistrusted after 1902. The French also hoped to develop their African settlement with Britain, and toward that end Anglo-French diplomats systematically reviewed and compromised a backlog of disputes that had divided the two nations. Their efforts were summed up in the *Entente Cordiale* of 1904, which removed the major grievances and made close cooperation henceforth possible. William II's hope of uniting the continent against Britain was slowly being checked.

We can certainly see by the turn of the twentieth century that Europe as a cosmopolitan entity had almost disappeared. Even those proposals that seemed to embody an international idealism were too often expressions of mere national interest. The First Hague Conference (1899), for instance, came following a proposal of Nicholas II that the powers ought to seek agreement on the limitation of arms. No power felt it was politic to ignore the proposal. Yet, Russia's motive, when she was conducting an aggressive policy in East Asia and falling behind Germany's military expenditures, was widely (and rightly) suspect. With Russian sincerity questionable at The Hague, the Germans vetoed a Russian suggestion that all armies be kept at current levels for five years. The British then proposed that the powers establish a permanent court for compulsory international arbitration, which the French warmly supported. Such a court was established at The Hague, but the Germans rejected the idea of compulsory arbitration and put themselves in a bad light. In the aftermath, the French and Russians tightened their alliance by prolonging their military convention indefinitely. Moreover, as part of the search for their *Entente Cordiale,* the Anglo-French agreed to refer all their future disputes to the International Court.

The strengthening of the ties between Britain and France, and between France and Russia, made the French logically eager to see Britain and Russia be reconciled after a century of hostility. The destruction of Russian naval power in the war with Japan did a good deal to relieve traditional British worry over Russian expansionism, while the post-1905 reforms in Russia brought to power men more sympathetic to the British than to the German form of government. Consequently, Anglo-Russian diplomats reviewed and compromised the entire gamut of Anglo-Russian frictions, especially those along the inner frontiers of Asia. And in 1907, they signed an entente—an understanding—rather than an alliance. The last of the prewar alignments had been achieved.

The Descent into War, 1908-1914

Beginning in 1908, Europe experienced a series of crises in the very regions that had long been the focal points of international tension; but the great powers now responded to such crises in the light of the recent British commitments (some real and some imagined) to her continental friends. The Austrians, for example, presumed that the British, in reaching an understanding with Russia, had abandoned their traditional support of Ottoman integrity and had agreed to aid the Russians in getting the Straits opened to Russian warships. (The Straits had been closed to all warships since the Crimean War.) For her part, Germany, learning that the French and British had been engaged in secret military and naval discussions, presumed that the Entente of 1904 masked a firm military alliance. Both these assumptions were incorrect, but the misunderstandings affected international relations.

Thus, in 1908, when a group of young Turkish nationalists dedicated to stemming the long decline of Ottoman Turkey seized power in Constantinople, the Russian and Austrian foreign ministers met at Buchlau to discuss their mutual ambitions in the Balkans, as the sudden revolution seemed to be the opportunity to annex Turkish territory. Their "Buchlau bargain" permitted Austria to annex (rather than merely occupy) Bosnia-Herzegovina, with the Russians getting Austrian support for opening the Straits to Russian warships. Evidently, the Russians assumed that such major changes could not be undertaken without obtaining the sanction of all the powers signatory to the Treaty of Berlin—and set out to secure their permission—and were thus caught short when the Austrians suddenly announced the annexation of Bosnia-Herzegovina. To their chagrin, the Russians then discovered that Britain and France would only support the opening of the Straits for *all* warships, not merely those of Russia. And nationalistic Serbia, her own eyes on Bosnia-Herzegovina, was furious at Austria's action; as was Germany, for her ally had taken this major step without prior consultation. War between Austria and Serbia-Russia was a real threat when the Russians insisted that they had not approved the Austrian annexation; but that lie was so evident that the German government felt itself obliged to support Austria in the crisis, giving the unfortunate impression that Germany would support any Austrian move to maintain the Triple Alliance. The Turks put the final fires out by accepting an indemnity from Austria for the lost provinces.

A second war crisis blew up in 1911 over Morocco. A turbulent country in the nineteenth century thanks to continual uprisings and conflict among four major ethnic groups, Morocco had become as early as 1880 the subject of international intervention designed to produce order. The consequent rise of anti-foreignism in Morocco not only threatened to undermine such international efforts, but gave the French, whose interest in Morocco was evident by 1900, an opportunity for establishing the same special status for themselves in Morocco that they had won in Tunisia in 1881. The initial French move in 1905 was blocked largely by German initiative, but in 1911 anti-foreign riots in Morocco led the French to occupy Fez. Again the Germans reacted in a manner that suggested that they themselves were conniving for naval bases on the Moroccan Atlantic coast. The British naturally backed the French in the crisis, and the issue was successfully mediated when the French gave the Germans bits of the French Congo and some adjacent territory.

With France getting a free hand in Morocco, the Italians concluded that it was high time to utilize their earlier agreements by grabbing Tripoli from the Turks, who were now the butt of everyone's nationalist ambitions. If all the great powers had earlier encouraged Italian penetration of North Africa for reasons of their own, by 1911 no great power wanted to see at that moment any further assault upon the

Ottoman Empire for fear it would light new fires in the Balkans. The Italians proceeded, nevertheless, but found the Turks unexpectedly well-entrenched in Tripoli. A second Italian fiasco in Africa was in the making when, in 1912, the Turks felt forced to make peace in order to confront a far greater danger in the Balkans.

After their humiliation in 1908, the Russians had been secretly urging the little Balkan states to form an alliance against further Austrian expansion. Until 1912 Balkan rivalries had precluded such cooperation; but with Turkey vulnerable during the Italian attack, Serbia and Bulgaria concluded an alliance that was ostensibly anti-Austrian (as the Russians wished), but secretly anti-Turkish (which the Russians knew). The Russians, on the other hand, expected to be able to use this alliance solely as an anti-Austrian tool. With the adherence of Greece to the alliance, however, the Russians recognized that the situation was not under their control, and they joined the other powers in warning the alliance not to disturb the peace. The warning came on the very day that Montenegro declared war on Turkey, the fight being immediately joined by Greece, Bulgaria, and Serbia.

While the Turks were easily defeated in this First Balkan War, the vectors immediately squabbled over the spoils as their various national ambitions all collided. Before the year was out (1913), Greece and Serbia declared war on Bulgaria, and Turkey and Romania joined the war against Bulgaria, who was quickly defeated in this Second Balkan War. The most significant result of the two wars was the enlargement of Serbia to nearly double her former size and the consequent whetting of her nationalistic appetite. Bulgaria was the chief, and the embittered, loser.

Turkey herself proved to be the scene of the last serious crisis before 1914. If in the nineteenth century Britain was the chief power to bolster declining Turkey, she began before the end of the century to recognize the hopelessness of preaching reform to the sultans to forestall the end. The waning of British interest in Turkey happened to coincide with an upswing in German interest in Turkey, which at first seemed little more than a German search for a place to invest capital—thanks to the phenomenal growth of German technology and industry after 1871. Though German activity in Turkish business enterprise and railroad construction exceeded that of any other power by 1900, the commercial value of this economic penetration was small. It led, however, to the Germans furnishing military missions to train the Turkish army; while the railway concessions, by tying Berlin to the Persian Gulf via Constantinople and Baghdad, were suddenly perceived in Europe (notably in Russia) as a major military advantage to the Dual Alliance powers and as a development entirely consistent with William II's world policy. Especially after 1907, the German presence seemed designed to cut Russia off from her Western friends in case of war. Thus, in 1913, when a German general was appointed by the Turks to the actual command of Turkish troops around Constantinople, the Entente powers blew up in protest. The German government admitted the legitimacy of the opposition and worked out a compromise with the Turks, so that the officer remained in the Turkish service but not in command of troops.

The Assassination at Sarajevo, June 28, 1914

The murder of the heir to the Austro-Hungarian throne, Archduke Franz Ferdinand, by Serbian nationalists in the Bosnian capital proved to be the final straw in 1914. Even today the events surrounding that fatal incident remain somewhat mysterious. Especially after the Austrians annexed Bosnia-Herzegovina in 1908, they were seen by Serbian nationalists as the chief barrier to the creation of a large Serbia; and even though the principal Serbian nationalist organizations were unofficial, major Serbian officials joined such organizations, making it difficult to distinguish between official and unofficial Serbian actions and attitudes. As for Franz Ferdinand, though an autocrat at heart, he was widely believed to have accepted the necessity for reforming the Dual Monarchy to accommodate the minority nationalities; meaning that he was as much feared by conservatives within the Empire as by ambitious nationalists in Serbia and Romania.

The announcement that the Archduke would visit routine army maneuvers during the summer in Bosnia was made several months before the event, giving the assassins ample time to organize their attempt upon his life. Meanwhile, the Serbian government, aware of the plot but finding it impolitic to warn the Austrian government directly, sought to pass on the information through indirect channels. Whether this method proved to be ineffective (thus giving the Austrians grounds to claim that they had not been properly warned), or whether the Austrians chose to ignore the warning in their search for a show-down with Serbian nationalism remains unclear. The fatal shots were fired by Gavrilo Princip, a Bosnian Serb belonging to a group that advocated the unification of the southern Slavs.

The Austrians took the official line that unless they dealt promptly with Serbia, the Hapsburg dynasty, its territories, and thus the Triple Alliance would be in mortal danger. William II informed the Austrians that he would back their settlement with Serbia, thus giving the Austrians what has been called a "blank check"—perhaps anticipating that under the circumstances of the murder the Russians would not come to the aid of Serbia, and the conflict would remain local. Austria's ultimatum to Serbia was deliberately constructed to make it unaccept-able to a sovereign government, and the terms were not revealed to the Germans until they had been sent off to Belgrade. In other words, the war was deliberately provoked—the Austrians declared it on July 28. Any hope that the conflict could be localized was dashed in a few days, and Europe entered the era of total war.

THE GATHERING CENTRALIZATION OF POWER

1.   The Heritage of the French Revolution and Napoleon

One of the oldest traditions of the continental monarchies was their tendency to increase their power and efficiency by centralizing their authority and making their governance as uniform as possible through-out their various realms. To accomplish such a goal, monarchs had necessarily struggled against the aristocracies of Europe, whose titles reflected local powers and interests. If in those struggles over the centuries most kings gradually reduced the power of their nobles, the process of centralization was far from complete in most states by the eighteenth century—and government was still notoriously inefficient. Even the much-vaunted centralization achieved by Louis XIV before his death in 1715 left France a country without uniform or equitable tax rates, with internal tariffs detrimental to the national economy, with no national standard for weights and measures, and with a nobility so exempt from taxation as to contribute to the central government's bankruptcy before the end of the century.

In Part I, we noted that many intellectuals, especially on the continent in the eighteenth century, responded to such imperfect government by advocating what we have come to call "enlightened" despotism. That is, government based upon the same rational principles that presumably also govern the universe. Such government could only be ordained by a philosopher-king who would both understand the principles of nature and possess the authority to reform man's institutions to conform with those principles. The argument ran that such a system would not only produce a highly centralized and rational order, but liberty as well, for the equation held that inefficient government led to disorder and tyranny; whereas liberty could only derive from rational order. The whole notion depended upon the assumption that nature is a state of rational order and a state of perfect freedom. Thus, the old prescription that man ought to return to a state of nature in order to find freedom was not meant to be an invitation to return to the woods, but a plea to discover all natural laws and to regulate society according to them.

Many royal governments experimented with what they thought was enlightened despotism in the later eighteenth century as the newest formula for enhancing centralization. And while the French Revolution certainly did not derive from a single cause, it is very much to the point that the French monarchy failed to produce anything like enlightened despotism, led the nation into bankruptcy and constitutional paralysis, and had to be overturned before the century was out. What is more, the republican and Napoleonic heirs of the old monarchy labored successfully to perfect the centralization of government. By 1814, the revolution had transformed France into a highly centralized nation with local authority utterly subservient to Paris—the perfect political instrument for any would-be dictator—and all in the name of order and liberty.

The paradox gradually dawned on Europe as a whole. Even though most of the libertarian ideas and slogans of the French Revolution remained in the nineteenth century to inspire Europeans seeking national or individual liberty, many European liberals in fact turned to the English experience as a more practical guide to freedom. The British record by 1815 was impressive: During the long duel with France, which had begun in the time of Louis XIV and ended with the final surrender of Napoleon, British political institutions had been steadily liberalized. That is, royal power had been checked without destroying the monarchy; the unitary state retained its paramouncy without destroying the integrity of local government; and public confidence in the system—if occasionally strained—provided the credit the regime required to sustain the unequal contest with France. No doubt much remained to be done if Britain were to become a heavenly city. But by European standards of that day, she stood alone and beyond as the model for the future, though she functioned through institutions out of the past. It was not lost upon European liberals that this freer society had prevailed over the more autocratic one.

Nineteenth-century liberals, because their creed had been born of the long fight to contain royal absolutism, were seriously concerned to define what the state must *not* do. Though they might still thrill to the emancipatory currents undammed by the French Revolution, they were also inevitably distressed that the French Revolution had shown the way to a more effective centralization that could become a new absolutism. The liberals' desire to free nations and individuals, which they knew often required centralization, when combined with a reluctance to organize and use power, put nineteenth-century liberalism on the horns of a dilemma from which it never entirely escaped. They were often centralizers when in power, decentralizers when out of power. Just as the European liberals gradually lost direction of the various national movements because of their relative political ineffectuality, so did their reluctance to use the power of the state often make them ineffective social reformers. The particular seriousness of this impotence lay in the fact that the Industrial Revolution, already well underway in Britain, began to creep across the continent.

We know today that the Industrial Revolution did not necessarily worsen the economic conditions of life for those caught up in the transition from country to town. But whatever the momentary economic conditions of life, the long-range implication of industrialization was a higher standard of material existence for all. By raising popular expectations, industrialization contributed to the development of a revolutionary situation; not because hardships were created, but because the poor, with their eyes on immediate amelioration, were easily disenchanted. Rapid urbanization, moreover, was another form of centralization whose implications went far beyond the political or the

economic. Highly self-sufficient rural folk found themselves in special-
ized routine factory jobs, living and working in a crowd—conditions
that can affect negatively everything from morale to fertility. A
sixteen-hour work day was not unusual for a factory laborer, and his
wages were usually too small to support his family unless his wife
and children were also employed.

The average liberal of the post-1815 period, hoping for nature
rather than the State to regulate men's lives, no longer had any
reason to believe that the outcome of nature's regulation would be
happiness for the majority of mankind. Writing an essay on population
growth in 1798, an English clergyman named Malthus had calculated
that an unchecked population increases geometrically (doubling roughly
every twenty-five years), while food production merely increases
arithmetically. Workers, in particular, he believed, tend to multiply
until checked by starvation and misery. He argued that nature limits
our population growth through wars, poverty, and vice; and that if
social reformers tried to remove those evils, the population would
swiftly outstrip the food supply. This pessimism was shared by David
Ricardo, another laissez-faire liberal, who believed that economic life
is governed by unalterable natural laws. Among them he included the
natural antagonism between the three classes: landowners, capitalists,
and laborers. Believing that there is a fixed amount of goods and a
fixed amount of wages to be divided among workers (and knowing
Malthus' work on population growth), Ricardo calculated that the
lot of workers must inevitably decline. The supply of workers, in
other words, would increase faster than the demand for them. Social
reforms designed to keep them alive were actually an unkindness to
them. If you paid them higher wages to keep them alive, the capitalists'
earnings would necessarily be smaller, meaning smaller investments
and fewer jobs in the future. This fixed system he aptly called *The Iron
Law of Wages* (1817). The pursuit of happiness, deemed feasible by
some liberals in the eighteenth century, was banished by these dismal
scientists of the nineteenth.

2. The Liberal Regimes and the Rise of Radicalism

Doctrinaire liberalism enjoyed its heyday in western Europe between
1830 and 1848, during which time various radical and socialist theories

also found their adherents in western Europe. In the face of a greater awareness of social problems, the fact that liberals were political, rather than social, reformers largely accounts for the rise of radicalism. In fact, following the decline of liberalism after 1848, no recovery would be possible for liberalism until liberals could find a way to accommodate their traditional concern for individual freedom with a concern for general welfare.

The first of the regimes to be officially liberal was the July Monarchy of Louis-Philippe (1830-1848). In 1831, silk workers in Lyons succeeded in negotiating better wage rates with their employers; but the government, viewing this collective activity as a violation of laissez-faire, did not regard the new wage agreement as legal. Troops were used on several occasions to maintain order, which was distressing to liberals who shrank from the idea of a government based on force; while the workers felt themselves betrayed by the state and learned that the benefits of liberalism were for the few. A similar ambiguity could be seen in the liberal Education Law of 1833. Liberals were genuinely concerned for the intellectual and moral improvement of individuals and were heir to the French Revolutionary notion that public educational facilities must be established to make that improvement possible. The law of 1833 made all French municipalities responsible for providing primary education for boys; but, attendance was not to be compulsory to safeguard the individual's liberty. In a day when many children were employed in factories and mines, such a law gave the appearance of giving the employers' needs higher priority than the children's. On the other hand, the latest "science" sanctioned such an outlook, so that sincere humanitarian intentions were often overborne by a faith in laissez-faire.

In Britain, where political reform (as opposed to revolution) had often been successful in meeting abuses, both major political parties—the Whigs and the Tories—had become increasingly conservative during the long years Britain had fought the French Revolution and Napoleon. Reforms projected in the later eighteenth century had consequently been shelved. Thus, after 1815, when the nation began to suffer from the dislocations produced by the change from a wartime to a peacetime economy, the prior failure to reform left the political system peculiarly unresponsive to the economic crisis. The parliamentary system in particular revealed two major constitutional flaws: First, constituencies had not been revised to reflect the dramatic shift in population from rural to urban areas which came with the Industrial Revolution, leaving some rural constituencies as grossly overrepresented as the new towns were underrepresented. Second, since land alone had been traditionally regarded as real property, the property qualification for the right to vote and to hold public office had the effect of disenfranchising many of those who owned the commercial or industrial property that was becoming the economic backbone of the nation.

Though the Whigs had historically been more liberal than the Tories, both parties necessarily represented the landed interests. After 1815, a new breed of radical (or democratic) politicians emerged who saw that the new conditions of life in the nineteenth century would require the democratization of British institutions. A journalist with great credit among British workers, William Cobbett, argued that if parliamentary constituencies should be revised so that representation in the House of Commons would once again reflect the nation rather than the few, the necessary social and economic reforms would follow. Jeremy Bentham formulated a political philosophy called "unitarianism," which advocated political democracy as the most practical political form. Wanting a system that would provide men with what they *need* and *desired*—which would bring "the greatest good for the greatest number"—Bentham also wanted to secure the greatest happiness for the greatest number. Political democracy seemed to satisfy these requirements: If each individual best knows his own interest, then it follows that the general interest can best be judged by the majority. The system reconciled individual egotism with the general welfare. Another radical, James Mill, saw popular education as a necessary concomitant of democracy and a free press as necessary to check arbitrary government.

In the 1820's, a bizarre reformist alliance appeared. The aristocratic Whigs, desperate for office after nearly a half century of Tory rule, were finally ready for the reform of Parliament even at the expense of the landed interests, making possible an alliance with the unrepresented manufacturers and with the Radicals. Their opportunity came when the Whigs won the elections of 1830. The subsequent Reform Bill of 1832 reformed the constituencies, redistributing the seats in Commons to reflect the shift in population from country to town, while the property qualifications for the vote were modernized. In fact, the bill did not greatly enlarge the electorate, since the property qualifications remained high; but the bill gave the middle class a greater participation in politics and reinforced the liberal, if not the democratic, climate.

What followed was reformist legislation by a liberal regime which, like its contemporary in France, practiced laissez-faire to the distress of those Radicals who had expected social and economic reforms. In the matter of slavery, the Whigs and Radicals did see eye to eye and cooperated to end slavery throughout the Empire in 1833. But when Parliament then took up the reform of poor relief, by then an archaic dole system by which public funds were given to parishes to make up the difference between a worker's wage and a minimum living wage, the Liberals and Radicals parted company. If the old system was both morally and economically outrageous, the new Poor Law of 1834 held no charm for workers. No relief could now be given to the able-bodied unless they resided in a poorhouse, where conditions were kept deliberately wretched to encourage a man to accept any work at any wage to stay out of them. The reform provided a large supply of laborers eager for work, while taxes for poor relief diminished. It also revealed that the liberal principle of laissez-faire could be a guarantee of inhumanity. Europe was ready for new doctrines that would reduce the exploitation of human beings.

Count Henri de Saint-Simon was the first well-known socialist writer of the nineteenth century. Rather than exploit each other, he argued, men should work together to exploit nature for the common good. He envisioned the future State as a giant cooperative, a highly centralized and authoritarian State, which would supervise both production and distribution of goods. As for the sharing of goods, he would have each person receive "according to his capacity and according to his services." Toward the end of his life, Saint-Simon tried to extend the social and economic aspects of his system into a secularized morality that he called the "New Christianity," with himself the messiah for the new cult. His disciples developed his ideas into a formal religion where salvation lay in organizing the means of production so as to improve the lot of the poor as quickly as possible. The French government outlawed the cult in 1832 for advocating the abolition of private property.

Obviously, men had exploited the resources of nature long before Saint-Simon; and Christian sects had sometimes conveniently adjusted their doctrines to sanction human rapacity, especially in frontier communities. On the other hand, traditional Christianity had taught that nature, including human nature, must not be violated, just as the eighteenth-century rationalists had seen nature as our proper model rather than as our victim. The Saint-Simonian invitation to exploit nature as a moral duty was especially enticing in a day when the Industrial Revolution promised a burgeoning production, and the utilitarian ethic he substituted for a spiritual or metaphysical ethic made man's material welfare the new measure of the good and the true.

Charles Fourier was another early socialist who, like Saint-Simon, opposed an economy based upon competition as likely to lead to human exploitation. Rather than antagonism, let us have harmony, he said, which he thought could best be achieved through the founding of small cooperative communities, not through a centralized administration. This idyllic communalism was rooted in the eighteenth-century faith in the inherent goodness of human nature. Where competition and antagonism were removed to make the environment sweeter, human instincts would naturally work for peace and happiness. Each person who entered such a community was to be given property to give him a stake in the community, and each person was to be free to choose his own vocation. The first of such communities was established southwest of Paris in 1832, but the movement's heyday was in the 1840's in the United States, where sixteen communities were founded.

The contemporary Owenite movement was also decentralist and similar in spirit to the Fourierite movement. Robert Owen (1771-1858), a Scottish cotton mill owner, was an environmentalist who was determined to turn his typically wretched factory town into a model community with no unemployment. He raised workers' wages while reducing the work day from seventeen to ten hours; constructed decent housing and improved factory conditions; and required the workers' children to be in school between the ages of five and ten. He hoped this model would lead other manufacturers and the state to found similar communities, never to exceed 3000 people, but he was not emulated. His ideas, however, did contribute to the founding of many cooperative stores in Britain where workers could purchase goods at little more than cost, and to the founding of a number of Owenite communities in the United States.

During the 1830's, when the labor movement in France was being driven underground by the July Monarchy, and when British workers became increasingly dismayed by the failure of the reformed Parliament to enact social legislation, the labor movement itself became more radical. Two British artisans, William Lovett and Francis Place, drew up the "People's Charter," a petition to Parliament that asked for universal male suffrage, the removal of the property qualification for the vote, and annual elections to Parliament—terms that implied popular sovereignty and democracy. Nearly a million and a quarter signatures were attached to the petition before it was submitted to Parliament in 1839. But the Whigs and Tories, holding that sovereignty was vested jointly in the Parliament and the crown, rejected the petition. The energies of the movement were soon channeled into the drive for free trade (which would have the effect of reducing food prices for the British public). This was achieved under the leadership of Richard Cobden in 1846 after the failure of the Irish potato crop and poor harvests in England. In France, Louis Blanc published a book called *The Organization of Labor* (1839), which presented statistical evidence of the miserable conditions of employment in the industrial cities, attributing them to free enterprise. He extended the revolutionary doctrine of the Rights of Man by arguing that every man has not merely the right to live, but also the right to live by the fruits of his own labor. To provide full employment at decent wages, Blanc insisted that it was the obligation of the centralized state to provide interest-free loans to cooperatives, a device he believed would ultimately ruin private operators and pave the way for a complete socialization of capital.

This growing awareness that industrialism was producing an entirely new complex of social problems led directly to a new field of academic study: sociology. Its father, Auguste Comte (1789-1857), ought to be specially noted as epitomizing the main currents of mid-nineteenth century thought. Originally a Saint-Simonian, Comte's studies led him to sum up mankind's thought as an evolutionary progress through three principal phases: The theological phase, a period when man's knowledge was so limited that he necessarily ascribed all phenomena to supernatural powers; the metaphysical phase, the period in which man sought to discover the causes of phenomena by observing nature and by using his reason; and finally, the *positive* phase in which man has progressed to a point where he no longer asks *why* things happen but is wisely content with the "scientific" facts which tell us *how* things happen or *what* is happening. This school of thought, known as positivism, advocated the gathering of information about man and his society so that our political, religious, and ethical systems could be given a scientific foundation. This emphasis on giving man a better life was soon transformed into a worship of mankind; and like Saint-Simonianism before it, positivism became a secularized religious cult.

Karl Marx, the father of scientific socialism, also based his sociology upon his particular views of the history of mankind; and he, too, found an evolutionary mechanism which he claimed not only explained the past but predicted the future. In his *Communist Manifesto* (1848), he introduced his fundamental premise that "the history of all hitherto existing society is the history of class struggles." This meant that he saw all historical change resulting from the conflict between the propertied and the propertyless—that the course of history had been determined by economic factors. This conflict or dialectic became known as dialectical materialism. According to his theory, the class owning the means of production inevitably becomes politically ascendant. Thus, when machines and factories became the principal means of production, the middle class replaced the feudal aristocracy. In the future, the proletariat—the operators of the machines—would replace the bourgeoisie.

In predicting the inevitable triumph of the proletariat as the outcome of the nineteenth-century conflict between the owners of capital and labor, Marx made no claim that capitalism would fail because it seemed ethically defective, but advanced on economic explanation known as the theory of surplus value. Much influenced by Ricardo's inflexible views on wages and profits, Marx argued that capitalism would fail because the low wages paid to laborers would make it impossible for them to buy the products of their own labor. Prices would not be lowered, because this would be inconsistent with the capitalists' necessary profits. Since he believed that bourgeois governments would never act to limit bourgeois profits, the rich would get richer, the poor poorer. Much of the middle class would erode into the proletariat, which would end by seizing the state and the means of production. The immediate result would be a dictatorship of the proletariat, a totally centralized State where capitalism would be abolished in favor

KARL MARX (Radio Times Hulton Picture Library).

of a cooperative commonwealth: the first classless society in history, where workers would presumably for the first time receive full value for their labor. But since the disappearance of classes meant, according to the original premise, the disappearance of conflict in society, Marx's long-range forecast was that the dictatorship would cease to be necessary, that the State would wither away—a heavenly vision, but necessarily an earth-bound Eden.

Marx's French contemporary, Proudhon, also wanted the State to wither away, but he called himself an anarchist. Recognizing that when men had originally emerged from the state of nature, they had necessarily organized government to create order, Proudhon went on to argue that as men become increasingly sophisticated in society they become increasingly resentful of government authority. The rational response to this is to seek greater liberty and equality through decentralization of political authority, until such a point that authority is entirely self-imposed rather than imposed by the State. Proudhon's influence during the 1850's and 1860's in France, the most centralized of European countries, was much greater than Marx's; but Proudhon's ideas, thanks to his particular prose, were especially open to misconstruction. He did not, for instance, advocate the abolition of private property, but merely denounced those who used their property to exploit others. And as for anarchy or self-government, he meant self-discipline, not self-indulgence, his goal being perfect justice for all.

3.   The Aftermath of 1848

The general failure of liberals and radicals in the revolutions of 1848 left conservative governments in the saddle; these justified themselves as the guardians of "order" in the wake of the uprisings. Just as they seized control of the various national movements after 1848, so did the conservative regimes press forward with the traditional tendency to centralize power. In multinational Austria-Hungary, for example, the provincial Diets (legislatures) enjoyed by the various national groups were now abolished, the revolts in 1848 being sufficient excuse. Local government became entirely administered from Vienna, one of the long-range goals being the Germanization of the Hapsburg Empire. In Prussia, though Frederick William IV granted his subjects a constitution of his own manufacture after the defeat of the German liberals in 1848, the constitution preserved the King's ultimate authority. Centralization was promoted by denying towns and rural districts further participation in the choice of local officials. All office-holders came to be appointed by the crown.

In France, where administrative centralization had been perfected before 1815, executive power made itself once again absolute after 1848. As we have seen, popular reaction to radical violence undermined the democratic institutions of the Second French Republic. The National Assembly played into the hands of President Louis-Napoleon Bonaparte by being more reactionary than he, allowing him to pose as the heir to his uncle's alleged dual role—the guarantor of order *and* the hope of democracy—a latter-day crowned Jacobin, for the crown was his goal. And like his uncle, he staged a *coup d'état* against his parliamentary opponents (1851) to secure dictatorial powers. The following year, the Second Republic was easily converted into the

Second Empire, with the President becoming Emperor Napoleon III. These changes were overwhelmingly sanctioned in national plebiscites. A Caesarian democracy, in other words, a dictatorship established by popular vote.

Unlike Prussia (later Germany) and Austria-Hungary, where highly centralized, autocratic institutions remained intact until 1914, France experienced a gradual liberalization of her political institutions, but no decentralization. Beginning in 1860, when the still-popular Napoleon III enjoyed the prestige of his victories over Russia in 1856 and Austria in 1859, he began to dismantle the dictatorship. Parliament, which had lost its right to initiate or amend legislation, was periodically granted new legislative powers, labor won a limited right to organize in 1864; and four years later, the regime all but abandoned its censorial power. This led, in 1870, to a new constitution establishing the so-called Liberal Empire, a limited monarchy whose development was cut short by the untimely onset of the Franco-Prussian War. The Emperor's initiative seems to have been motivated by his realization that France (unlike Austria or Prussia), with her liberal and radical traditions dating from 1789, would not indefinitely tolerate absolutism. If his dynasty were to endure, he must move in the direction of the British model—though he hoped to be his own prime minister.

The liberal tendencies Pius IX (1846-1878) evinced upon taking the papal throne vanished after his unhappy experiences in 1848-1849. Thereafter, his reaction took several allied forms: He worked to centralize the administration of the Roman Catholic Church to increase papal administrative authority at the expense of the various national hierarchies (a tendency known historically as ultramontanism); and his doctrinal innovations were conservative and directed toward papal absolutism. Earlier in the nineteenth century, men who called themselves Liberal Catholics had championed ultramontanism, thinking that by strengthening papal control, they could reverse the modern tendency of the secular states to dominate the national churches. For them, ultramontanism was a device to secure separation of Church and State, a goal of all nineteenth-century liberals. Consequently, these Liberal Catholics were dismayed as they saw the ultramontanism of Pius IX lead not to greater separation, but to closer relations with illiberal governments and to doctrinal attacks upon liberalism.

In 1864 he issued the Encyclical *Quanta Cura,* to which was attached a *Syllabus of the Principal Errors of Our Time.* Its tenor was summed up in the eightieth "principal error," namely, that "the Roman Pontiff can, and ought to, reconcile himself, and come to terms with progress, liberalism and modern civilization." This papal extremism reflected the Pope's view that modern civilization had become highly secularized; and that if religion, which he held to be the true foundation of justice and legitimacy, were finally to be excluded from society, we would enter an era of materialism and brute force. Pius IX capped his challenge to secularism by summoning a Vatican Council (1869), which he induced to proclaim the dogma of Papal Infallibility in 1870. This meant that when a pope speaks *ex cathedra* on matters of faith and morals, he is infallible. The centralization of spiritual authority, at least, seemed complete.

Meanwhile in Russia, which had not experienced an uprising in 1848, the Crimean War exposed the shocking inefficiency of the central government. Moreover, since it has become apparent that much of this inefficiency was grounded in the archaism of the fundamental institutions of Russian life, Czar Alexander II (1855-1881) reluctantly recognized the necessity of thorough-going reform. Moreover, the initial reform—the long-overdue decree abolishing serfdom—dictated the nature of the subsequent reforms. It is estimated that the emancipation decree (1861) freed forty million people, after which the state took the responsibility for providing the ex-serfs with land, compensating the original landowners. Such lands were not given outright to the peasants, but were administered by the villages where the peasants lived; and the peasants repaid the government for the land in installments over a period of forty-nine years. The system was a financial expedient, it being easier to collect taxes and installment payments from the villages than from each peasant.

The emancipation of the serfs had profound political and legal implications by instantly removing traditional feudal relationships, and Alexander II knew that he would have to provide new institutions of local government and law. He did so in 1864, first by creating local and provincial assemblies and giving them the right to levy taxes for local needs. And second, by decreeing equality before the law regardless of class, and by establishing a bar. If the Czar stopped short of a national assembly so that Russia remained an autocracy, his reforms did make the central government more efficient and rational; and they stimulated demands for a more thorough-going democratization of Russian society and government. Because there was little consensus among would-be reformers as to the methods to achieve their goals, the autocracy proved to be invulnerable until it would once again inefficiently conduct war after the turn of the century.

4.   The Commune of Paris, 1871

As we have already seen, the capture of Napoleon III in the Franco-Prussian War allowed his Parisian republican opponents to seize power. But their efforts, through a Government of National Defense, to reverse the unfavorable war proved to be in vain, and early in 1871 this provisional regime signed an armistice with Bismarck. This national disaster only exacerbated the internal questions that had divided the nation ever since 1789. During the final months before the armistice, the liberal Republicans in power had been continually criticized and intimidated by more radical Republicans in Paris. The latter not only succeeded in convincing large numbers of Parisians that they were invincible, but that the liberals sought an armistice simply to avoid having to inaugurate social and economic reforms. Thus, when the national elections which followed the armistice produced a National Assembly that was overwhelmingly conservative, while the Parisian delegation was largely radical, the defeated nation found itself seriously divided—with Paris against the country.

The humiliation of defeat and a deep sense of betrayal were compounded when the harsh peace terms from Germany became known; and the radicals in Paris ended by defying the rest of the nation by establishing an independent government in city hall known as the Commune of Paris. While the regular government based in Versailles prepared to reduce Paris by force, the Commune struggled to define its program, a nearly hopeless task since its membership included a wide variety of radicals whose principles could not be made to coincide. Consequently, the rhetoric was far more radical than the deeds. The popular support for the regime in the city quickly fell off, but those who fought against the assaulting troops did so desperately and were massacred. In the final week, between seventeen and twenty thousand Parisians lost their lives.

Above all else, the Commune did represent the decentralist principle, whereas the ultimate victory of the central government amounted to one more example of the contemporary European drive toward the unitary state. This vicious civil war proved to be the last of the uprisings within the revolutionary tradition that had begun in 1789; and though a highly centralized republic finally emerged from that revolutionary tradition, the great majority of the French, remembering the violence, voted for a republic that was resolutely conservative. Marx's pamphlet, *The Civil War in France* (1871), saw the revolt as an attempt to establish a dictatorship of the proletariat, tailoring the facts to fit the Marxian theory of class conflict. Since both radicals and anti-radicals tended to see the Commune in this Marxian light, the misinterpretation affected French politics for several decades and served as a major contribution to Marxian mythology.

THE TWO CULTURES OF THE NINETEENTH CENTURY

1.　The Democratization of European Society

European civilization, deriving as it did from two major sources—the Roman and the Christian—had always borne within itself contrary tendencies and impulses that reflected its parentage. One has only to recall the various polarities encountered in the study of European history to illustrate the point: the spiritual and the temporal, the common law and the canon law, scholasticism and humanism, the classical and the romantic, the universal and the particular. Such tensions were challenges that contributed to the vitality of European civilization. Consequently, to find contrary tendencies within the civilization of nineteenth-century Europe is in itself hardly novel. Rather, what strikes one as new about the various polarities found in the nineteenth century was the deepening suspicion in that era that such tensions either could not, or ought not, be reconciled to give civilization stability and balance. One no longer rendered appropriately unto both Caesar and God. The whole was no longer the sum of its parts, the parts often being seen as the whole.

The contemporary novelist-physicist C. P. Snow (1905-) has noted that our intellectual and practical lives have become polarized into literary and scientific groups, between which there is incomprehension, distrust, and open hostility. The roots of this dangerous schism are deep in the nineteenth century: the emergence of two divergent cultures. No single explanation suffices to account for this civilizational fragmentation, though a study of nineteenth-century history reveals that many of the ingredients contributing to the crisis were related.

We know, to begin with, that European society was becoming democratized in the nineteenth century, and at the same time it was becoming secularized and industrialized. Also, the pace of life—or the pace of change—had begun to accelerate in a manner previously unknown to Europeans; the acceleration was due principally to the practical applications of modern science. Men were called upon to adjust to novelties at a rate that often became uncongenial and seemed inhumane, and the continual need to choose between the "old way" and the "new way" introduced new tensions in every man's life and between the generations. If we can understand that the tempo of life for most Europeans in 1850 was more comparable to that of the thirteenth century than that of the twentieth century, we may get some sense of the distressing adjustments that life was beginning to require. An agonizing paradox was not lost upon the intelligentsia in particular: As men were becoming freer politically, socially, and economically, the very dynamism of science, which contributed to that freedom, also contributed to the cultural crisis. The upshot was that not only would every "advance" increasingly be questioned, but that the notion of progress itself would become a matter of doubt.

Take, for instance, the gradual democratization of European society in the nineteenth century. This movement, grounded in the revolutionary idea of the sovereignty of the people and a secularized expression of belief in the importance of every man, differed greatly in both form and substance depending upon the particular nation or empire, the movement in general being most advanced in western Europe. If in theory a democratic constitution was supposed to guarantee the rights of all citizens regardless of class, in fact democratic constitutions were employed in the nineteenth century in both liberal and autocratic regimes. We have seen already how universal suffrage was granted by the Second French Republic in 1848 as the foundation of modern, liberal government; and that the same universal suffrage was used as the foundation of Napoleon III's autocracy in 1852, and used again by him as he liberalized the Empire after 1860.

The new German Empire in 1871, through which Prussia really swallowed the other German states, was the outstanding example of democracy in an autocracy. The imperial constitution created the facade of a federal empire and representative government with a bicameral system. Sovereignty was vested in the upper house, the *Bundesrat,* which represented the governments of the member states. But since state delegations had to vote as a unit and their size was fixed by the constitution, the system was rigged to preserve Prussian dominance. These state delegations were appointed by the states they represented—not popularly elected. The *Reichstag,* the lower house, presumably shared the legislative duties with the *Bundesrat,* and here the delegates were elected by universal suffrage. By giving the *Bundesrat* the power, however, to dissolve the *Reichstag,* the imperial government possessed an easy means of checking the lower house and universal suffrage. The constitution did not even pretend to provide responsible government. Federal affairs were directed through the chancery, the chancellor being appointed by the Emperor and responsible to him alone. The whole apparatus enabled autocratic Prussia to give Germany a Prussian regime.

The ambiguities in this anachronistic empire were revealed by Chancellor Bismarck's attitude toward socialism. In 1875, various socialist factions fused to form the German Social Democratic party, which was dedicated to achieving social advances through the democratically elected *Reichstag.* Bismarck, suspecting that all socialists were at heart really anarchists, was horrified by their parliamentary gains; and in 1878 he pushed through an Anti-Socialist Law banning socialist and communist organizations and publications. Yet, even Bismarck saw the need for social legislation in an industrializing country, and in the 1880's he sponsored social security laws for the protection of workers—legislation that was liberal in spirit but in violation of laissez-faire: an accident insurance law (1885) which forced employers to insure their employees against accidents while on the job; a sickness insurance law (1885) which forced every employee making less than $500 a year to insure himself against sickness; and an old-age insurance law (1889) requiring employees

PEOPLES OF CENTRAL EUROPE 1914

Teutons
Latins
Slavs
Other Indo-Europeans
Ural-Altaics

LAPPS

KARELIANS

FINNS

GREAT
RUSSIANS

NORWEGIANS

SWEDES

ESTONIANS

LETTS

LITHUANIANS

WHITE
RUSSIANS

CELTS

DANES

ENGLISH

DUTCH

FLEMINGS

WALLOONS

GERMANS

POLES

LITTLE
RUSSIANS
(RUTHENIANS)

CZECHS

SLOVAKS

FRENCH

AUSTRIANS

MAGYARS

SLOVENES

CROATS

RUMANIANS

SERBS

SERBS

BULGARS

GREEKS

SPANIARDS

ITALIANS

CORSICANS
(FR.)

ALBANIANS

TURKS

(SP.)

SARDINIANS
(IT.)

GREEKS

SICILIANS

Scale of Miles
0   100   200   300   400

making less than $500 a year to contribute, along with their employers, to a pension fund. Bismarck's leadership in "state socialism" inspired most western government to adopt similar laws.

Democratization within the Austro-Hungarian Empire was a problem much complicated by the cosmopolitan nature of that Empire. After the *Ausgleich* of 1867, when the Hungarians obtained full autonomy in their half of the Empire, the Austrians and Hungarians viewed democratization differently. Whereas the former tackled the problem of getting the minority nationalities to tolerate each other in their common loyalty to the Hapsburg dynasty, the Hungarians directed their energies toward keeping their minorities in check. Thus, Hungarian franchise laws reflected not democratization but attempts to Magyarize the minorities. In Austria, meanwhile, especially during the prime ministry of Count Taaffe (1879-1893), the minorities were urged to participate in elections for seats in the imperial *Reichsrat;* and the franchise was broadened, by a law of 1882. Since a concession to any given nationality was seen as an affront by the remaining nationalities, the Austrian government saw this greater participation in central government as the only possible alternative to granting local concessions. Similarly, the Austrians sought to play down the nationality issue by turning to social reforms in the manner of Bismarck.

The Austrian policies were from the start jeopardized by the strong appeal that nationalism had in the nineteenth century, as well as by the autocratic nature of the monarchy. While it is true that prime ministers usually gave up or lost office when unable to command a majority in the *Reichsrat,* in fact they were legally responsible only to the Emperor. When universal male suffrage was at last granted in 1907 and seats in the *Reichsrat* were redistributed to national groups according to their population, the reforms had the effect of multiplying political factions along national lines. Instead of strengthening the monarchy, political parliamentary life became more chaotic.

Even the democracy of the French Third Republic had its equivocal aspects. The constitution of 1875 provided for a bicameral National Assembly and for universal suffrage. But while the lower house, the Chamber of Deputies, was elected by direct vote of the people, the Senate was elected by a highly indirect and undemocratic procedure. The president was not popularly elected, but was chosen by the

National Assembly for a seven-year term; and his cabinet ministers were all responsible to the National Assembly. This deliberate attempt to shackle executive power revealed French awareness that their highly centralized state was a ready-made vehicle for any would-be dictator; and that a dictator might just as easily be voted into office by the people as through a military *coup d'etat.*

The turbulence of the political life of the Third Republic owed much to a continual attempt of the democrats to eliminate the anti-democratic features from the constitution, while the anti-democrats strove in the opposite direction. Thus, every crisis or every scandal to come along would be blown up out of proportion to its real significance in order to make it serve the fundamental constitutional dispute. Consequently, every crisis seemed to threaten the existence of the Republic itself. The rise of a popular minister of war in the 1880's, General Boulanger, initially an ally of the democratic elements in society, was first seen as a maneuver to strengthen the democratic Republic. When the Left came to perceive his political incapacity and withdrew support, he obtained the support of the Right, stimulating fear that he would overthrow the Republic. In the 1890's, the more celebrated Dreyfus Affair, growing out of an espionage case, may have begun as an attempt to obtain justice for a man probably falsely accused. But the affair quickly enlarged into a contest between the Republic and its opponents. That Dreyfus ultimately obtained justice was almost incidental in the fight to save the democratic Republic. We know today that the Republic was less threatened by such crises than it appeared to be at the time—that the great majority of the French wanted to preserve the reforms that had come from the French Revolution and would support a Republic as long as it did not become radical.

In Britain, meanwhile, both major political parties had come to realize that the Reform Bill of 1832 had fixed a property qualification for the vote that was altogether too high. Many artisans were intellectually qualified to vote, yet did not possess sufficient property or pay sufficient rent to qualify. Proposals for a second reform of Parliament were introduced as early as 1851, but all of them fell victim to intra-party strife in both parties. The impact of the American Civil War upon British public opinion forced the reform issue to a head. Whereas the gentry had seen its way of life at stake in the

Southern cause, and the textile manufacturers had been injured by the Northern blockade of Southern raw cotton, the British urban workers had favored the North as representing the more democratic society. Consequently, the Northern victory seemed to presage the advance of democracy everywhere. Also, the trade union movement had then reached a point where it could agitate effectively for democratization. The Second Reform Bill of 1867 again reapportioned parliamentary seats to reflect population shifts; but more important, the qualifications for the vote were lowered so as to give virtual universal suffrage to the urban workers. The bill had little effect upon rural workers.

This gradual democratization of the European peoples, however, was not the only important feature in the population profile. What we today call the population explosion had actually begun in the eighteenth century, and the European population more than doubled itself in the nineteenth century—from about 187 million in 1800 to 401 million in 1900—and this despite a substantial emigration from Europe during the century. On the other hand, the birth rate in most European countries peaked and began to decline before the end of the century, evident first in France, Norway, and Sweden before 1850, and ultimately in Italy in the 1880's. Therefore, the greatest factor accounting for the growth was the decline in the death rate, a decline which was more notable after 1870 when the germ theory of disease became accepted and antisepsis was practiced. Since Europe was simultaneously undergoing industrialization, the surplus population migrated to the industrial cities, accelerating the urbanization of Europe; and something over twenty million people left Europe entirely in the last three decades of the century. While it is true that European technical and economic development was astounding in that period, such an emigration reveals that economic development lagged behind the population explosion.

2.   The Prestige of Science and Technology

Since in the contemporary world, the sciences and the humanities are often believed to be working at cross-purposes, it is useful to point out that in its origin modern science was one of the humanities. That is, modern science was one of the intellectual disciplines which grew out of the rejection of medieval scholasticism by the humanist scholars during the Renaissance. Whereas the medieval scholastic hoped that his science would help mankind achieve an otherworldly salvation, the goal of the humanist's science was more immediate. Or, as Francis Bacon put it, "that human life be endowed with new discoveries and powers." Also, if science is currently unpopular among many educated people, the opposite was true during much of modern history. For science was seen as the key to our understanding the universe, on the basis of which we might reform human institutions; and applied science (or technology) could improve every man's standard of living. The growing enthusiasm for science and technology, often indistinguishable in the popular mind, reached its peak in the thirty years following 1870, what a distinguished historian called "a generation of materialism." By this time many in the "literary group" were highly alarmed about the future of European civilization. They saw the democratization of a rapidly increasing population as the forecast of a mass culture where creature comforts would be man's highest goal. Theirs was a vision of a new barbarism based upon technology—the vulgarization of culture—a society in which individual greatness would become impossible.

Great scientific discoveries in the nineteenth century, like those in the preceding centuries, may have led to practical results but their immediate significance was to contribute information to philosophical speculation about the nature of our universe. The climate of scientific opinion had been predominantly Newtonian in the eighteenth century, a faith that the universe is an immutable mechanism governed by unchanging laws discoverable through the proper use of human reason. But some natural scientists in that same century, by calling attention to biological evidence which suggested that species are not permanently fixed or unchanging as a result of their creation, cast doubt about the validity of the mechanistic outlook. In 1830, Charles Lyell published his *Principles of Geology*. By showing that the earth gets its appearance from the continual action of geological processes, like erosion, volcanic action, and earthquakes, Lyell contributed evidence to those who had begun to argue for an evolutionary rather than a mechanical view of the universe.

On the other hand, Lyell's contemporary, Michael Faraday, made a celebrated report to the Royal Society in 1831 which seemed to confirm the Newtonian view. Convinced from the outset that those phenomena which he called "the forces of matter" are mutually dependent and have a common origin (in other words, that magnetism, electricity, gravitation, cohesion, heat, and light are different manifestations of the same basic power), Faraday designed his experiments to find the relation of these "forces." He was, in fact, the synthesizer of a number of contributions made by his predecessors during the 1820's in the attempt to understand electromagnetism, beginning particularly after the Danish scientist, Oersted, published his observation that a magnetic needle was deflected when a current of electricity flowed through it. Faraday found that a steel needle could be magnetized by subjecting it to an electric current, not only confirming the relationship of these "forces," but opening the way for practical electrical machinery, which depends upon the principles of the induction of currents.

Theories of evolution had been in the air for a hundred years, not only in natural science, where they had been offered by Buffon and Lamarck, among others; but in philosophy, history, and sociology as well, as we have seen in the cases of Comte and Marx. And Charles Darwin, in the course of his studies which led to the publication of his *Origin of Species* in 1859, knew of the evolutionary implications in Lyell's *Principles of Geology*. We ought not to say, therefore, that Darwin was the first to conceive of evolution, but that he achieved a refined and novel view of evolution and successfully popularized the idea. And if the idea of evolution became acceptable after 1859, it is not merely that Darwin's views were plausible, but that many factors had paved the way for their acceptance.

In asserting that species are not permanently fixed, but are in a process of continual change, Darwin initially offered three mechanisms to explain how such differentiation and changes occur: natural selection, sexual selection, and the inheritance of acquired characteristics. He thought that the primary mechanism is natural selection. Meaning that in the struggle for life, those individuals within a given species with special variations favorable to survival tend to survive and reproduce. Repeated variations and improvement through many generations result finally in a new species. It is not the least of Darwin's significance that his ideas seemed to reconcile the mechanical and evolutionary views of the universe, in that he proposed that evolution is really a mechanism. Therein lay the real grounds for intellectual dispute.

CHARLES DARWIN (Courtesy American Museum of Natural History).

Contrary to popular notion, Darwin neither denied the existence of God nor professed to know how life was originally created. But in limiting himself to describing the mechanism which presumably governs life itself, a mechanism evidently involving neither choice nor act of individual will, he suggested that there is no purpose to life. Earlier, Lamarck (1744-1829) had explained differentiation and change through the inheritance of acquired characteristics, a deliberate response by an individual to special environmental conditions. Lamarck's view had been congenial to the romantics of the earlier nineteenth century, who not only rejected a mechanical view of life but insisted on the ability of the individual to act and triumph in unique ways. The decline of romanticism after 1848 (of which more later) helped to provide a climate of opinion that was more congenial to Darwin's views.

Even though Darwin had emphasized natural selection, he recognized that it could only account for why a given mutation survived or failed to survive. Thus, he had reluctantly added Lamarck's assumption that acquired characteristics are inheritable to account for variation in the first place. The German zoologist Weismann refined Darwinian theory by making a distinction between the ordinary bodily (somatic) cells and the reproductive (germ) cells. Since hereditary characteristics are transferred by the germ cells alone, it meant that acquired characteristics, being variations in somatic cells, could not be inherited. His findings left Darwinism a theory which explained the survival of variations, but not the reasons for variation.

Another major contribution to inheritance theory was made by the Augustinian monk Gregor Mendel. By carefully controlling plant fertilization, Mendel found that he could breed for certain characteristics, and that these characteristics would appear in subsequent generations in proportions that he could predict mathematically. He reasoned that this could only happen if the germ cells of each parent contained conflicting or opposite characteristics, one being dominant and the other recessive. In the union of male and female germ cells, the dominant characteristics will appear more frequently than the recessive, and always in a set mathematical proportion. Mendelian genetics could, therefore, account for the systematic perpetuation of variation in species, but shed no more light on the purpose or meaning of evolution than Darwin had. Mendel's contribution, though published in 1870, was not discovered and publicized until 1900.

Because of the title of Darwin's 1859 book, it was too easily inferred that his subject was the origin of life rather than the variation and survival of species; and the misunderstanding fed the well-known controversy between the Darwinians and the religious fundamentalists. Many materialists and anti-religionists of that period also misunderstood

Darwin's findings, believing erroneously that he had given them a mechanical solution to the origin of life which, in particular, refuted the Bible. Scientific opinion in the mid-nineteenth century was predominantly materialistic in outlook and prepared to accept mechanistic theories about life, including the notion that life is generated spontaneously and does not require some act of creation.

Pasteur, whose prejudices were formed by his continuing Christian faith, rejected the very idea of spontaneous generation. The experiments he began in 1860, which led to the process we call pasteurization, were based upon his assumption that if one could first destroy the microbes in putrescible liquids and then isolate such liquids from microbes in the air, the liquid would remain pure indefinitely, because there would not be any spontaneous generation in the liquid. Similarly, in 1865, Pasteur was able to solve the silkworm epidemic in France only because he was prepared to treat the disease as an infectious matter rather than as a phenomenon of spontaneous generation. Having thus demonstrated the validity of the germ theory of disease, Pasteur worked for the next several decades to produce vaccines to give immunity to both animal and human diseases by learning how to attenuate the virulence of disease germs, so that a benign infection of a given disease could be used to provide immunity from that disease. Pasteur's research enabled Lister to develop procedures for antiseptic surgery in hospitals, greatly reducing the septic diseases that had always made surgery so risky and had given hospitals an evil reputation.

For the first half of the nineteenth century, the world of chemistry had been a battleground. In 1808, John Dalton had published an atomic theory. Each element, he proposed, has its distinctive kind of atom, and the different atoms have different weights. It was then known, for example, that water is a compound of oxygen and hydrogen. Dalton assumed that a molecule of water contained one atom of each combining gas; but when he subjected these atoms to gravimetric analysis, he found that seven parts *by weight* of oxygen combined with only one part *by weight* of hydrogen to form a molecule of water. This meant to him that an atom of oxygen is seven times heavier than an atom of hydrogen. In 1811, however, Avogadro argued that the relationship of atoms should be established by volume rather than by weight, saying that equal volumes contain an equal number of atoms, whatever the gas.

Confusion reigned until 1860, when, at an international convention of chemists, Cannizzaro proposed a way to harmonize the data on atomic weights with that on the volume of gases: Atomic proportions should be established by relative weight, oxygen being assigned a weight of sixteen; but molecular proportions should be established by gas volume. A molecule of water, therefore, since it actually contains two atoms of hydrogen and one atom of oxygen, should be written H_2O, a formula that does not reflect the relative weights of the combining atoms. During the 1860's, many chemists contributed information about atomic weights to produce the periodic table—an arrangement of the elements according to their atomic weights. And in 1870, Mendeleyev capped the work with his periodic law: When arranged by atomic weights, the periodic sequence of the elements reveals a mechanically perfect progression, and the gaps in the chart simply mean undiscovered elements. It was a stunning statement for the rational perfection of the universe.

The organization of impressive bodies of facts into systems, such as the chemists of the 1860's and Darwin did, served the prestige of science enormously; and the field of physics had a great synthesis in that perod, too, with the statement of the laws of thermodynamics. The nature of heat, and particularly the motive power of heat, had been of increasing interest beginning with the use of the steam engine. Here the key contribution was James Joule's discovery that water could be warmed by agitating it with a paddle, from which he derived a formula relating the rise in water temperature to the amount of work spent on the paddle—the mechanical equivalent of heat. This led directly to Helmholtz's statement of the first law of thermodynamics in 1847, also known as the law of conservation of energy: When heat is transformed into any other kind of energy, or vice versa, the total quantity of energy remains invariable; that is to say, the quantity of heat which disappears is equivalent to the quantity of the other kind of energy produced and vice versa. The second law of thermodynamics—the law of dissipation of energy—was described by Lord Kelvin in 1851. Admitting that the total energy of the universe is constant, he added that the useful energy was being diminished by its conversion into dissipated heat. The law implied the ultimate death of the universe with the gradual cooling of the sun.

The prestige of science, however, did not depend upon its discoveries or their philosophical implications, but was enhanced by the increased practical use of scientific knowledge as the pace of industrialization quickened. This activity was especially brought to public attention after mid-century in an organized manner through what we would call a world's fair—the first was the London Exhibition of 1851, which was then followed by the Paris Exposition Universelle of 1855. Visitors saw the latest application of building materials, new farm machinery, and household items designed to raise the living standards of the poor. Science, philosophy, and the arts all were engaged in the pursuit of truth; but science alone produced engines, medicine, and domestic comforts.

The phrase "generation of materialism," to characterize the last thirty years of the nineteenth century, referred both to the mechanization of thought—that is, the vogue of Darwinism with its mechanical implications—and to the enormous expansion of European industry with its promise for better material living for the average man. Even though that generation had its important skeptics, it was popularly supposed that science and technology would soon solve all human dilemmas. That the proof of such an assumption lay in the appearance of the first telephone (1876), the incandescent lamp (1878), electric cars and trams (1881), the electric sewing machine (1889), and wireless telegraphy (1896) suggests the shallowness of the popular appraisal.

The discoveries in science, however, continued to be impressive. In 1895, Roentgen found x rays while investigating cathode rays, and the practical application of x rays in diagnostic medicine was almost immediate. What is more, the x rays proved to be the key to other discoveries that brought physics from the Newtonian to its modern (or quantum) stage. Studying some of Roentgen's observations led Becquerel to the discovery of radioactivity a few months later; and in 1899 Marie Curie concluded that radioactive atoms are unstable atoms in the process of disintegration, thus releasing energy. In the same decade, Thomson, trying to relate electrical and atomic properties, found particles within atoms which carried negative charges of electricity. These were later called electrons, and the phenomenon revealed that atoms are composite, not simple, entities.

Soon after the turn of the century, two more revolutionary ideas further undermined traditional physics to lead us into the atomic age. Classical physics had held time to be an absolute, so that the past, present, and future were perfectly clear and unmistakable terms. Space, too, was seen as an absolute, within which all phenomena were seen in three dimensions. The system was applicable to this world alone; but in 1905, Einstein began his description of new laws of mechanics that would be absolutely applicable in all coordinate systems—not merely to earth. Since the only constant factor to be related to motion is the velocity of light, he proposed that motion is always relative to the motion and position of the observer. This made it possible for Einstein to suggest that the interval between the past and the future has a finite extension in time which depends on the distance in space between an event and its observer. In this view, space and time attain an absolute character only when they are fused (space-time) and become part of a four-dimensional continuum. Einstein's proposal was called the theory of relativity for evident reason, but was in fact a new absolutism.

ALBERT EINSTEIN (Philippe Halsman/Magnum).

Because the Newtonians had regarded the universe as a precise mechanism whose motions could be predicted with exactness, it was disturbing to discover at the end of the nineteenth century that the classical electromagnetic theory could not account for the emission and absorption of radiation. Max Planck suggested a new physical mechanism to account for the phenomenon—the quantum theory. It had been held that the energy of an oscillator depends solely on its frequency and amplitude, but Planck suggested that an oscillator may possess only discrete amounts of energy—even though he was distressed philosophically by the idea that natural processes could be discontinuous.

MAX PLANCK (Photo World).

3.   The Protest Against Mechanism and Materialism

The literary, philosophical, and artistic protest against materialism—and particularly the protest against the popular view that technology is the road to human salvation—was rooted in what we have called the "romantic spirit." One can, in fact, trace the origins of the romantic movement back to the eighteenth century, to those who already rejected the mechanistic, rigid view of the universe characteristic of rationalism and classicism. Instead of the eternal and the universal, the romanticist emphasized the changing and the particular—a more subjective, individualized, complicated view of reality. Nature was no longer the elegantly perfect mechanism to be comprehended rationally, but a thing of beauty revealed through our senses. The set values of the classical or rational outlook were giving way to relative values, truth defined as something individually perceived. This willingness to emphasize both the particular and those things which change contributed to the European climate which fostered empiricism and made it easier to accept evolutionary theories in a variety of fields. Therefore, one must be careful to note that the romanticist was not opposed to science itself, merely to those scientific theories which saw man and his universe as mechanisms.

Perhaps the most distinctive philosopher of the romantic period was Hegel (1770-1831), because of his idea that *being* is a process of *becoming*, which epitomized the changing, or evolutionary, view of life. In this view, to exist is to change, to grow, to evolve toward a goal. Moreover, he believed that the *striving* for a goal gives life its significance and meaning, and that the goal which the human spirit seeks is freedom. He meant us to understand that freedom emerges not from passivity, but from conflict; and he used an argument, or dialectic, to illustrate how we progress toward higher truths in our striving. It is the conflict between a thesis and its necessary antithesis, which ultimately produces a synthesis—which is at once a higher statement of truth and a new thesis. The process continues endlessly, like evolution itself, meaning that the goal is never really achieved. Thus, the meaning in our lives derives not from attaining the goal, but in our awareness of the goal and our struggle to reach it.

When one has reviewed the various traits of romanticism—individual expression, subjectivity, the rejection of classical rigidity, the reliance on intuition and the senses—one must note that not all romantics shared these qualities to an equal degree. In particular, some were equivocal in their rejection of rationalism, seeking to harmonize the universal with the individual to achieve a balanced view of reality and the human condition. Goethe (1749-1832), for instance, feared that the subjectivity in romanticism could lead to self-indulgence or

GEORG WILLIAM FRIEDRICH HEGEL (Culver Pictures, Inc.).

despair, yet he insisted in the best romantic fashion on the striving for a rich personal life, struggling for the noble goal regardless of its attainability. We are thus introduced to a tragic vision, as in his *Faust,* of man's existence: that we must struggle for fuller knowledge in the full realization that we will fall short of fulfillment. And there can be no surrender, even though we recognize our goal to be forever elusive. "This is wisdom's final word," he wrote, "Worthy alone is he of life and freedom, Who conquers them anew each day." This tragic view of human reality, characteristic of the romantic spirit, was a far cry from the enthusiasm engendered by the technological progress of the nineteenth century.

Another aspect of the rejection of rationalism emerged from the apparent failure of "enlightened" laws to bring peace and order in the time of the French Revolution and Napoleon. Traditions and standards may have been destroyed by the revolution, but the perfect society had not replaced them. The general disenchantment characteristic of so much of the European intelligentsia by the beginning of the nineteenth century led some of them to seek a spiritual awakening as the key to man's dilemma. Chateaubriand (1767-1848) was the outstanding example of a former rationalist who became reconciled with traditional Christianity, claiming it to be the only salvation for mankind. Mysticism and pietism enjoyed a revival, especially in the German world—intensely private religion directed toward individual rather than universal salvation. Yet, under the influence of German mysticism, Czar Alexander I proposed his Holy Alliance in 1815, which was not so much a treaty as it was a statement of principles as a basis for international cooperation. He hoped that the European monarchs would regard each other as "brothers" and their subjects as "families" in the Christian sense.

As Goethe had recognized, romanticism could reach extremes of despair, a condition he had flatly called disease. The black melancholy of Kierkegaard (1813-1855), for example, while it clearly derived from a dreadful childhood and physical deformities, left him incapable of concern for society or mankind. In that century when most intellectuals continued to reject Christianity, Kierkegaard was a believer; but he was entirely indifferent to the misery of others in his concern for his private despair. "The thing is to find a truth which is a truth for me," he wrote in 1835, "to find the idea for which I can live and die." His Christianity was intensely private and existentialist.

Schopenhauer (1788-1860) was another philosopher of despair. Like Kant in the previous century, Schopenhauer believed that the contradictions represented by theses and antitheses are generally beyond solution by human reason, and he had no patience with Hegel's confidence in inevitable progress. For Schopenhauer, the world is inherently evil, and its only reality is what we perceive through our senses. This loathesome reality is to be avoided at all cost, all the more difficult in his view as our basic drive is our will to live in this

SOREN KIERKEGAARD (Radio Times Hulton Picture Library).

world of misery. One can only avoid this real world by giving himself to contemplation, and to the contemplation of art in particular.

On the whole it is fruitless to try to associate romantic philosophers and artists as a group with a particular political party or faction. Indeed, if one seeks generalizations about their public attitudes, one might first note that the romantics' penchant for individual perception of truth and beauty, their willingness to break with convention, inclined them to radical postures, whether on the left or the right. Lacking practical political experience—and often despising those who did—their views were as brilliant and humane and imaginative as they were often impractical or naive. This in itself might not distinguish them from their counterparts in other centuries. What was characteristic of artists and writers in particular in the romantic century was their refusal to come to terms with a society caught up in swift commercial and industrial expansion, seeing themselves as the sword and shield of a civilization endangered by the dragon of crass materialism. For them, mankind was not to be saved by advancing technology nor by a religious revival, but somehow to be redeemed by art. Science was fine so long as it remained speculative and unapplied, and especially when it used its heaviest guns to blast at religious positions. But the redeemer's role was reserved for art. As the century deepened, the democratization of society—the rise of the masses—was seen as another dimension of barbaric materialism, at which point artistic protest often became elitist rather than liberal.

Lord Byron (1788-1824) and Shelley (1792-1822), who scandalized their nation with advanced opinions and erratic behavior, were characteristic of the earlier romantic generations. They were rebels against all authority and convention, seeing their own homeland as the worst possible example of obtuseness and repression. Both left England for the continent after 1815. In Paris, Victor Hugo sought to have his romantic drama *Hernani* produced in 1830. Aware that neoclassicists were out to destroy the play with hisses, Hugo mustered a throng of romanticists to defend his right to have the play staged, including Balzac, Stendhal, Gautier, Berlioz, and Delacroix. Which should remind us that neoclassicism lived on into the nineteenth century with distinguished representatives like the painter Ingres (1780-1867), even though romanticism had become the dominant creed. The neoclassical calm and impersonality, as well as the superb drawing, in Ingres' canvases, was a far cry from the boldness of design, the bright colors, and the fascination with action and struggle characteristic of Géricault (1791-1824) and Delacroix (1799-1863). Berlioz was the composer who was most revolutionary in abandoning traditional symphonic form, in the liberties he took in orchestration, and in the lavishness of his individualism. His *Symphonie Fantastique,* first performed in 1830, still sounds astonishingly modern, yet came on the scene only three years after Beethoven's death.

In its rejection of universal truths and rigid form, romanticism emphasized not simply individualism, but often the individual nationality within European civilization. The subject matter of the arts was increasingly historical or patriotic; and Weber (1786-1826), endeavoring to develop a German opera distinct from the Italian, drew upon folklore and folk melodies. Most of Sir Walter Scott's (1771-1832) well-known novels, appearing after 1814, were set in either historical England or Scotland; just as the elder Dumas's (1803-1870) were set in historical France. Aside from appealing to the national past, such works were nonpolitical.

Yet, the romantic novelist could give his work a contemporary setting—the greatest of them did—and it is much to the point that many such novels were either acid commentaries on the conventions of bourgeois society or protests against the conditions of life in the industrializing towns. Such romanticists were but a step from the literary realism that became predominant in Europe after 1848, and they exuded the pessimism common to all those who had become disenchanted with classical idealism. In 1831, Stendhal published *The Red and the Black,* the story of a young upstart who chose clerical black rather than military red in his scheme to rise in a corrupt society. His calculated love affairs and his blatant opportunism were Stendhal's way of commenting on the public and private morality of his day, a morality that Stendhal both despised and feared he shared. In *The Charterhouse of Parma* (1839), Stendhal revealed the pettiness of the reactionary regimes restored after the greatness of the Napoleonic era. The protest movement took a feminist twist in the novels of George Sand, whose heroines were restless romantics. She drew in particular upon her own emotional experiences for *Indiana* (1831) and *Lelia* (1833).

In 1842, Balzac began a detailed survey of French life through a series of novels under the overall title *The Human Comedy,* establishing the tradition of "documentary" novels which Zola would perfect later in the century. Balzac's hatred of the society of industrializing, commercial France is continually evident in his novels. He had the romanticist's contempt for the unexciting, stingy standards set by King Louis-Philippe himself, a world in which bankruptcy was the greatest of all possible tragedies. His subjects were taken from real life, though he used his imagination freely in their rendering.

Even the Russian czar admitted that Gogol's exposure of corruption and hypocrisy in high places in his play *The Government Inspector* (1836) was fair, and Gogol went on to include a sharp denunciation of serfdom in his novel *Dead Souls* (1842). Gogol's crisp characterizations remind us of his English contemporary, Charles Dickens, the most popular of early Victorian novelists. At once realistic and melodramatic, some of Dickens' works were also propagandistic. His *Oliver Twist* (1838), for example, commented on the harshness of the Poor Law of 1834; and in *Nicholas Nickleby* (1839), he revealed the need for school reform. On the whole, Dickens' novels portrayed lower-class life. For criticism of upper-class life, one may turn to Thackery's *Vanity Fair* (1847) or to his *Henry Esmond* (1852). The lithographer-journalist Daumier (1808-1879) was spiritually akin to such novelists. His subject matter, with few exceptions, was the unpleasant, the ugly, the grotesque, the inhumanity to be found on all sides, and the shallow pompousness of the middle class. One finds here no visions of beauty or progress, but contempt for that which degrades humanity—the conviction that the human comedy is really the human tragedy.

The failure of the political romantics in 1848 and the consequent emergence of the "blood and iron" politicians had its artistic counterpart in realism. In true realism, the artists not only rejected the ideal or the rational, but abandoned the personal and the individual, deliberately choosing subjects from the everyday world, striving to be impersonal in recording what they saw. And generally they saw life as brutish and mankind as weak. Realism continued, therefore, the tradition of social criticism; and the writers became zealous fact collectors to provide the raw material for their novels. What was new in this school, most notably represented by Flaubert (1821-1880) and later by Zola (1840-1902), who called himself a naturalist, was a conscious desire to close the widening gap between those in the literary culture and those in the sciences. Theirs was, in fact, a faith in science, Flaubert arguing that the only hope for the human race was to make "science prevail." Zola went even further by trying to turn literature into a scientific enterprise, insisting on "scientific" objectivity in the portrayal of reality. Beginning in 1870, this Darwinian of the arts sketched out a series of twenty novels through which he meant to describe all aspects of life under the fallen imperial regime: *The Natural and Social History of a Family Under the Second Empire.* This great endeavor was completed in 1893, a vast canvas of social evils. But for all its documentation, the focus on the sordid and the appalling did not provide a balanced view of life under the Second Empire. What was great in Zola was his art, not his science.

GUSTAVE FLAUBERT (Radio Times Hulton Picture Library).

The main thrust of cultural opinion after 1848, however, was hostility to materialism and commercialism, the very things which science, through technology, was aiding if not intentionally abetting. This passion took the form (as it had with the earlier romanticists) of contempt for everything bourgeois. Though they identified the bourgeois with all that was gross, they meant by *bourgeois* a spirit, an attitude, rather than a class, just as Matthew Arnold (1822-1888), condemning the barbarism of mid-century life, used the term *Philistine* to describe the "exuberant self-satisfaction" of those Englishmen who saw material progress as the guarantee of human happiness. Both Arnold and John Ruskin (1819-1900) warned against the development of an ethics founded on acquisitiveness. If the right to acquire should become the standard measure, Ruskin predicted that national destruction would follow.

They referred to acquisitiveness for its own sake, and to all those—regardless of class—who never subordinate self-interest to exterior claims. To be *bourgeois* was to prefer security to grandeur, to seek wealth rather than truth or beauty. Cultural vitality, therefore, was still equated to the old romantic passion for individual greatness. The poet Baudelaire (1821-1867), in despair for the future, thought that the time was soon at hand when the young man would leave home, "not in search of heroic adventures, not to deliver a beautiful prisoner from a tower, not to immortalize a garret with his sublime thoughts: but to start a business, to grow rich, to enter into competition with his vile papa." Indeed, since the economic realities of the nineteenth century pointed to the increasing availability of the things of this world, and to their worship, the cultural protest against materialism took on the guise of a crusade against the Philistines.

Such cultural zealots, seeing themselves as the few pitted against the masses, often saw themselves as a new aristocracy. Their elitism, however, took a variety of forms: In some, we see the search for new energy, for boldness; in others we find extreme individualism and extravagent preciousness. In the 1860's, the word "impressionism" was used to describe the work of a new school of young painters, notably Manet, Degas, Monet, and Renoir, who were opposed in theory to both neoclassicism and romanticism. They painted "what they saw," especially the outdoor world, seeking to create the visual impression of the moment, but as the human eye sees, not the camera. Hence, they blurred, often distorted canvases to suggest how we really see things at a glance. In the following decade men like Van Gogh and Gauguin, calling themselves expressionists, went beyond impressionism by insisting that the painting should reveal the artist's emotion when he is recording his impression on canvas. The result was great individuality and vivid color.

Elitism did not necessarily bring its practitioners spiritual relief. Gauguin's well-known abandonment of his family for a life of art on Tahiti may have symbolized the artist's challenge to bourgeois conventionality, but his heroic gesture ended in wretchedness. The playwright Ibsen (1828-1906), abhoring the social conventions of his native Norway, went into Italian exile; yet, haunted by his past, he set his plays in the dark, cold country of his birth, thus achieving even a grimmer view of reality. Because the majority in any society are necessarily wedded to social conventions, the libertarian Ibsen equated democracy to mediocrity and conventionality. Similarly, Flaubert, in the 1870's, toyed with the idea of leaving France as a place likely to become uninhabitable for people of taste. The Goncourt brothers predicted that man's rash ventures into science would bring mankind to its end. Having heard a famous scientist estimate in 1869 that in a hundred years our knowledge of organic law would enable us to create life in competition with God, they recorded that at such a moment, God in His white beard would descend to earth, swinging a bunch of keys, and say to mankind as the attendant at the museum says at five o'clock: "Closing time, gentlemen."

That the great Russian novelists after mid-century seem so different from their Western counterparts reflects the backwardness of Russia and a different set of problems. Dostoevski's exile was imposed by the state in 1849—four terrible years in Siberia among the Empire's most vicious criminals—for having been a member of a revolutionary society. His later novels, especially *Crime and Punishment* (1866), were admired for their psychological insights, another characteristic of realism. Hating the social evils and the autocracy of Russia, Dostoevski still had the capacity to perceive the evil in all men. Tolstoy (1828-1910), whether in his novels or in his religious essays, was consumed by moral and philosophical problems, relating them to the way people ought to live. The ancient Russian preoccupation with the mystical flowered anew in Tolstoy. Though he struggled to believe that, in this evil world, mankind's salvation lies solely in ultimate redemption and rectification, the lack of serenity in his personal life suggests that he shared the spiritual doubts of the generation of materialism. "I have been thinking about the Divinity of God for a long time," he wrote in 1877, "Don't say that we must not think about it. Not only we must, but we ought. In all ages the best people, the true people, have thought about it."

Such concerns were a far cry from those elitists whose sense of civilizational doom led them into what we might call aestheticism. Here the manifestations ranged from dandyism to a high-minded hedonism; that is, the belief that the richest life is the one spent in pursuit of pleasure through beauty. Theirs was not an art of social criticism, but, in the phrase of Walter Pater (1839-1894), the "love of art for art's sake." In this view, art should give us nothing but the highest quality to the moments as they pass. Aestheticism seems to have been a logical protest on the part of those who rejected the

COUNT LEO TOLSTOY (Radio Times Hulton Picture Library).

implications of material progress, who associated such progress with the democratization of society, and who had come to the conclusion that the rare, creative imagination of artists was being prostituted by the vulgar fact collectors of the realist school: the mechanistic bondage of the creative soul. These aesthetes, in other words, lumped the realists with the very bourgeois society the realists had condemned.

Though the aesthetes were highly individualistic by definition, they all equated beauty with art—with artificiality. The poet Baudelaire, with a poisonous hatred of nature and for most of society, transmuted the most appalling aspects of the industrializing, urban reality about him into poetic beauty, the *Flowers of Evil* (1857). His lines may have enabled others to see beauty where it had not been seen before; but for Baudelaire, the lines amounted to a perverted glorification of all that he hated, which included his own defects. Thus, if Baudelaire was among the first to enlarge the scope of artistic subject matter to include the vulgar, he was also among the first to protest against vulgarity.

Elitism, in its variety of forms, now seems to have been the attempt to create a cultural aristocracy to replace the fading blooded aristocracy: an aristocracy of talent made possible only by the democratization of society in the nineteenth century, yet in revolt against that democratization and contemptuous of innovations that were making the lives of ordinary people increasingly bearable. The people were seen as a stupid, destructive beast, which must be contained by the authoritarian state. The earlier hope that the arts could redeem mankind through the revelation of the most fundamental truths had given way to the notion that art is superior to life. A true religion, in other words, had been corrupted into an idolatry of the arts. The precious artificiality of the idolators was well-epitomized by Stefan George, the German poet (1868-1933): "My garden requires no air and no sun."

4.   Reflections on Violence

After the gigantic calamity that was the First World War, historians necessarily sought its causes, looking in particular through the diplomatic records to find out which power, or powers, had been most responsible for bringing on the war. This endeavor, while intellectually respectable, often concealed the fact that the European climate of opinion after 1848 had been subtly drifting toward violence. One must hastily add that, of course, violence has always been present in history. What changes historically is our attitude toward violence: That is, the degree or the pervasion of violence can be affected by a society's view of its desirability or its inevitability. The conservative order that held sway in Europe after 1815, for instance, was determined to use both diplomacy and force to maintain the general peace settlement, holding the localized use of force to be preferable to the generalized European conflict of the previous twenty-five years. Throughout the century, Britain used her monopoly of sea power toward the same end: to limit rather than to eliminate violence.

After 1848, however, we become aware that the moral abhorence of violence had weakened, and that the future belonged to those who hitched violence to progress. The benevolent, cosmopolitan nationalism of the early century brought freedom to no nationality. That required blood and iron—notably in the cases of Italy and Germany. The history of radicalism seemed to parallel that of nationalism: A benevolent utopianism gave way to a belief in violence after mid-century. This is seen not simply in the Marxian summons to revolution, but in the anarchism of Bakunin (1814-1876), who advocated the immediate destruction of the state. His ideas, his insistence that men should obey nothing but the laws of nature, might remind us of Proudhon; but Bakunin went far beyond him in demanding the *violent* destruction of existing society. Bakunin's anarchism, in fact, illustrates another form of political extremism: the rejection of contemporary morality or religion upon which all social, economic, and political institutions are based; hence the justification for their destruction. The later nineteenth century called that prescription *nihilism.*

It takes nothing away from the elegance of Darwin's work if we recognize that his theories reached an audience well-prepared to think of life as a struggle for survival. Any intellectual worthy of that name had to have an opinion on evolution after 1859, and not simply to keep apace with the nonintellectuals. Darwin himself saw "grandeur" in his view of life—that from a simple beginning "endless forms most beautiful and most wonderful have been, and are being evolved." Some of the Darwinians, furthermore, saw in the principle of evolution the guarantee of progress—that progress is not an accident but a necessity. Consequently, Herbert Spencer (1820-1903) could happily look forward to a day when evil and immorality must disappear and man must become perfect.

Racial theories and racism had been known in Europe since antiquity, and the word "racial" had long been used loosely to mean national. So that after Darwin, when it became fashionable to discuss species and, in particular, those fittest to survive, it was but a step to compare the European "races" as to their "fitness." Thus, German political and military preeminence after 1860 was said to prove that the Germanic "race" was the fittest; hence, it was a superior "race." This seemed to square with Gobineau's *Essay on the Inequality of Races,* published in 1854. An aristocrat, Gobineau had actually not meant to ascribe racial superiority to any one nation. On the contrary, he tried to prove the superiority of the French aristocracy over the masses of the French people on the grounds that the aristocracy represented pure Germanic or Frankish stock, while the people were an impure mixture of many "races." Indeed, he thought that the German masses were just as "racially" mixed as the French masses. But because he described aristocratic superiority in Frankish or Germanic terms, he was widely understood by the 1880's to have demonstrated the superiority of all Germans. Thus, Richard Wagner, working to construct a national German art, could conclude that a purely Germanic art (his own) must necessarily be superior to that of other "races."

Such racial theories were more easily swallowed in that day, not merely because Darwinian biology was claimed to sanction them; but because in an era of increasing national antagonisms, patriots grasped at any facts which seemed to justify those antagonisms. To think of nationalities or races as superior or inferior was a long step away from regarding them as unique and possessing different (and valuable) qualities. Racial theories, indeed, have historically always been advanced for deliberate political goals. After 1871, especially, "racial" prejudices were cultivated to help justify discriminatory legislation against minorities in various nation-states in the interest of centralization and national unity. National as well as religious minorities felt the lash of discrimination: "One law, one language, and one religion," as one Russian statesman put it. A feature of such nationalist programs was an upswing in antisemitism, in response to which a Hungarian Jew, Theodor Herzl, in 1896 launched the Zionist movement: the search for a Jewish national state, preferably in Palestine.

For some like Herbert Spencer, the theory of evolution may have been an optimistic guarantee of human progress, but for others the theory seemed to underscore our brutish qualities, permitting only pessimism. Nietzsche (1844-1900), Spencer's contemporary, prepared for a pessimistic outlook by Schopenhauer, saw that the distinction between man and animal had been abolished by Darwin. This was the ultimate in secularization, if one may so state it, and led Nietzsche logically to conclude that "God is dead." Moreover, he turned the tables on those who argued for inevitable progress by pointing to the immense time it takes for evolutionary changes to be effected. It made no more sense to wait passively for mankind to evolve than to believe that our animal ancestry permits us instincts for the good, the beautiful, and the true.

FRIEDRICH NIETZSCHE (Radio Times Hulton Picture Library).

Our true nature, Nietzsche said, is to strive for power, to strive for greatness, so that an aristocracy of supermen shall emerge. His was a reassertion of the romantic spirit, an elitist protest against the substitution of mass culture for vital individualism, an attack upon all aspects of the vulgarization of life. The violence of Nietzsche's words were later taken to mean that he was the champion of brute force, that he thought of the superman as a superior physical animal who would smash culture as a decadent and odious phenomenon. While it is true that he hated the climate of democratization in the late nineteenth century, his supreme value was culture and its creation. His superman's strength was the vitality and refinement of the truly civilized man. He had no sympathy for racism and its associated nationalism, predicting that they would destroy the German spirit, which he defined as the concern for eternal, universal questions. Since he saw the great dilemmas of mankind as unchanging, he could not avoid being contemptuous of notions of human progress; he was clearly a man of the "literary culture."

In 1907, Henri Bergson published his *Creative Evolution*. He proposed, as evolutionists like Hegel and Darwin had before him, that the world is in a state of flux, that change is the fundamental truth about reality. Bergson's particular twist, however, was his statement that, beginning with the original creation of matter and mind by God, evolution has been the continuing creation of new forms in the universe. The world may be mechanical, obeying strict laws, he argued, but man's *intuition*, his consciousness, enables him to overcome such rigidities and to be free of mechanical determinisms in his search for truth and freedom. "To exist is to change, to change is to mature, to mature is to go on creating oneself endlessly." This may not give evolution a precise meaning, but it gave evolution vitality, what he called creative vitality: *élan vital.* Bergson would admit that man may be an animal—but an intelligent animal. Our intuition, in other words, is not animal instinct, but one form of human intelligence.

The immediate popularity of his ideas suggests how eager Europeans were to find explanations for life that both coped with the latest scientific discoveries and gave man a role which transcended the mere mechanical. By the beginning of the twentieth century, in fact, one sees signs of a growing awareness that, though man may have originated in the state of nature, his emergence into the state of society put him into a realm where nature's laws do not necessarily apply. Man may still have to contend with his ancestry and with the fact that he shares the planet with the other creatures of nature; but in society man has become so various, able to manifest himself in so great a variety of forms, as to raise doubts about our ability to know about *the* nature of man. If this is so, the proper study of man cannot be limited to biology. As Wilhelm Dilthey (1833-1911) believed, "What man is, only his history tells."

Such an outlook implied that we have to settle for something less than certainty, to accommodate ourselves to the mysterious. It pointed the way not merely to religion but, as in Bergson's case,

HENRI BERGSON (Photo World).

to mysticism: the private, romantic search for unique knowledge. Organized religion, too, showed signs of accommodating itself to the modern world by the end of the century. Many Europeans had come to assume that the Church was losing its fight for survival in the modern world, not simply because Pius IX had announced in 1864 that he would not come to terms with modern civilization; but because the spiritual truths the Church represented lacked believers in the generation of materialism, and the peace of God was nonsense to those who saw violence as the key to progress.

During the pontificate of Leo XIII (1878-1903), however, the papacy abandoned its traditional alliances with conservative governments, repeatedly warning that the Church was not married to any form of secular government. Through a series of encyclicals, the Pope showed that Christianity had constructive alternatives to the evils of materialism, and that Christianity could become progressive and scientific in spirit. If Leo XIII attacked socialism for denying men their "natural right" to possess property, he also rejected the laissez-faire view that labor should be regarded as a commodity in a free market. He denied that class warfare is the natural state of man, but added that "it is shameful and inhuman to treat men like chattels to make money by, or to look upon them merely as so much muscle or physical power." Roman Catholicism, in other words, while still professing its faith in an otherworldly salvation, served notice of its intention to fight all dogmas that held men to be mere brutes and all institutions that reduced men to brutish existence.

Whereas Dilthey studied history as the key to mankind's "nature," Sigmund Freud focused on the private history of each individual. Freud is known to us as the inventor of psychoanalysis, which he defined as the "discovery of the unconscious in mental life," and which has made us more aware of the nonrational impulses which underlie human nature. He taught a new technique of observation—that we must try to see others as full individuals: both the rational and the nonrational, the conscious and the unconscious, the obvious and the mysterious. Psychoanalysis was based on the theory of repression—that is, that society necessarily represses the individual, and the individual represses himself. Thus, the individual really disowns some of his ideas and desires, forcing them into his unconscious, where the conscious will no longer be aware of them. But banishment does not render them impotent. Dreams, neurotic symptoms, and slips of the tongue reveal both the presence and the nature of our unconscious ideas and desires.

Freud concluded that we are all neurotic, for the reason that civilization itself, as the initial represser, is the source of neuroses. His view of man, therefore, was entirely pessimistic. Though Freudian therapy was designed to force the unconscious into the consciousness so that we might understand the wellsprings of the conflicts within us, Freud saw that human life is fraught with pain, disappointment, and insuperable tasks. We may have the right to the pursuit of happiness, but we find only suffering.

The intellectual and cultural life of Europe in those years immediately before the outbreak of general war, in sum, was immensely vigorous, if often pessimistic. But on the whole the thinkers did not anticipate the great war, perhaps because as a group they were so nonpolitical. The intellectual and artistic elitists remained essentially

SIGMUND FREUD (Brown Brothers).

indifferent to international affairs in particular. If they predicted catastrophe, it was their reaction to the technological revolution and to the decline in moral values. Yet the forces of nationalism and socialism, increasingly militant in the decades before 1914, were on the verge of destroying the old order of nineteenth-century Europe.

The case of Georges Sorel (1847-1922) illustrates the point. A retired railroad engineer, he was an advocate of violence without ever suspecting the actual form of the violence that was to come. Hating the politicians of the Third Republic and seeing its democracy as the road to mediocrity and moral degeneration, he published, in 1908, his *Reflections on Violence* as a formula for national regeneration. His ideas were a curious mash of Marxian dialectical materialism, the

Nietzschen will to power, and Bergsonian *élan vital.* The energy and the regeneration of the future he thought could come only from the proletariat; and he saw the labor union (or syndicate) as the logical organization to promote the proletarian revolution. The general strike, moreover, would be the ultimate weapon in class warfare. This formula came to be called syndicalism. It called not for reason, but for violence—for direct action. Sorel may not have predicted World War I, but his ideas proved to be congenial to those men who would lead the postwar dictatorial states: men who, whether Leftist or Rightist, accepted violence as *the* solution to social and international problems. As Ortega y Gasset would later write, Sorel's system amounted to the Magna Charta of barbarism.

SUGGESTED READINGS

Albertini, Luigi. *The Origins of the War of 1914.* 3 vols. Oxford: Oxford University Press 1952-1957.

Artz, Fredrick B. *Reaction and Revolution 1814-1832.* New York: Harper, 1934.*

Barzun, Jacques. *Romanticism and the Modern Ego.* Boston: Little, Brown, 1943.*

Barzun, Jacques. *Darwin, Marx, Wagner.* New York: Doubleday Anchor, 1958.*

Binkley, Robert C. *Realism and Nationalism* 1852-1871. New York: Harper, 1935.*

Bonnin, Georges. *Bismarck and the Hohenzollern Candidature for the Spanish Throne.* London: Chatto and Windus, 1957.

Broglie, Louis de. *The Revolution in Physics.* New York: Noonday, 1953.*

Bruun, Geoffrey. *Revolution and Reaction 1848-1852, A Mid-Century Watershed.* Princeton, N.J.: Anvil, 1958.*

Cameron, Rondo. *France and the Economic Development of Europe 1800-1914.* Chicago: Rand McNally, 1965.*

Chapman, Guy. *The Dreyfus Case, A Reassessment.* New York: Reynal, 1955.

Durell, Clement V. *Readable Relativity.* New York: Harper, 1960.*

Duveau, Georges. *1848: The Making of a Revolution.* New York: Vintage, 1967.*

Eiseley, Loren. *Darwin's Century, Evolution and the Men Who Discovered It.* New York: Doubleday Anchor, 1961.*

Feis, Herbert. *Europe, The World's Banker, 1870-1914.* New Haven, Conn.: Yale University Press, 1950.

Goldberg, Harvey. *The Life of Jean Jaures.* Madison: University of Wisconsin Press, 1962.

Graña, César. *Bohemian Versus Bourgeois, French Society and the French Man of Letters in the Nineteenth Century.* New York: Basic Books, 1964.

Halévy, Elie. *The Growth of Philosophical Radicalism.* Boston: Beacon, 1955.*

Hayes, Carlton J. H. *A Generation of Materialism 1871-1900.* New York: Harper, 1941.*

Himmelfarb, Gertrude. *Lord Action, A Study in Conscience and Politics.* Chicago: University of Chicago Press, 1952.*

*An asterisk indicates that a paperback edition is available.

Howard, Michael. *The Franco-Prussian War: The German Invasion of France, 1870-71.* New York: Macmillan, 1961.*

Jackson, J. Hampden. *Clemenceau and the Third Republic.* New York: Collier, 1962.*

Jelavich, Barbara. *The Hapsburg Empire in European Affairs 1814-1918.* Chicago: Rand McNally, 1969.

Kedward, Roderick. *The Dreyfus Affair..* London: Longmans, Green, 1965.*

Kissinger, Henry A. *A World Restored: Metternich, Castlereagh, and the Problems of Peace.* Boston: Houghton Mifflin, 1957.*

Kohn, Hans. *Pan-Slavism: Its History and Ideology.* New York: Vintage, 1960.*

Langer, William L. *Political and Social Upheaval, 1832-1852.* New York: Harper, 1970.*

Lukacs, Georg. *Studies in European Realism.* New York: Grosset & Dunlap, 1964.*

Malia, Martin. *Alexander Herzen and the Birth of Russian Socialism.* New York: Grosset & Dunlap, 1961.*

Manuel, Frank E. *The Prophets of Paris.* New York: Harper, 1962.*

May, Arthur J. *The Hapsburg Monarchy 1867-1914.* Cambridge, Mass.: Harvard University Press, 1951.

McConnell, Allen. *Tsar Alexander I, Paternalistic Reformer.* New York: Thomas Y. Crowell, 1970.*

Moraze, Charles. *The Triumph of the Middle Classes.* New York: Doubleday Anchor, 1968.

Mosse, George L. *The Crisis of German Ideology, Intellectual Origins of the Third Reich.* New York: Grosset & Dunlap, 1964.*

Mosse, George L. *The Culture of Western Europe: The Nineteenth and the Twentieth Centuries.* Chicago: Rand McNally, 1961.

Mosse, W. E. *Alexander II and the Modernization of Russia.* New York: Macmillan, 1959.

Namier, Lewis B. *1848: The Revolution of the Intellectuals.* New York: Doubleday Anchor, 1946.*

Nochlin, Linda, ed. *Realism and Tradition in Art: 1848-1900.* Englewood Cliffs, N.J.: Prentice-Hall, 1966.

Remak, Joachim. *The Origins of World War I.* New York: Holt, Rinehart & Winston, 1967.

Rich, Norman. *The Age of Nationalism and Reform, 1850-1890.* New York: Norton, 1970.*

Robertson, Priscilla. *Revolutions of 1848: A Social History.* Princeton, N.J.: Princeton University Press, 1952.*

Rudé, George. *The Crowd in History, 1730-1848.* New York: John Wiley, 1964.*

Schenk, H. G. *The Mind of the European Romantics.* New York: Doubleday Anchor, 1969.*

Sedgwick, Alexander. *The Third French Republic 1870-1914.* New York: Thomas Y. Crowell, 1968.*

Stavrianos, L. S. *The Balkans 1815-1914.* New York: Holt, Rinehart & Winston, 1963.*

Stewart, John H. *The Restoration Era in France 1814-1830.* Princeton, N. J.: Anvil, 1968.*

Walker, Mack. *Plombières: Secret Diplomacy and the Rebirth of Italy.* Oxford: Oxford University Press, 1968.*

Willey, Basil. *Nineteenth-Century Studies, Coleridge to Matthew Arnold.* Baltimore: Penguin, 1941.*

Willey, Basil. *Darwin and Butler, Two Versions of Evolution.* London: Chatto and Windus, 1960.

Williams, Roger L. *The World of Napoleon III.* New York: Free Press, 1965.*

Williams, Roger L. *The Commune of Paris, 1871.* New York: John Wiley, 1969.*

Williams, Roger L. *The French Revolution of 1870-1871.* New York: Norton, 1969.*

Woodham-Smith, Cecil. *The Reason Why.* New York: Everyman, 1960.*

PART III

The German Wars

1914–1945

THE OPENING ROUNDS

1. World War I

Since the responsibility, or guilt, for inaugurating the era of violence has never been historically settled, it is useful to ponder the variety of causes that have been thrown into the debate. Some historians have stressed the long diplomatic prelude to the war, the series of international crises after 1871, to suggest an almost inexorable drift toward a violent showdown. Others, in contrast, by stressing that diplomacy had successfully contained those crises, pointed to the immediate events in 1914 where international diplomacy evidently collapsed. Another group has argued that what really made a general war probable was the growing climate of violence during the later nineteenth century, a kind of fatalism which assumed that reason must ultimately fail in the affairs of men, with violence to determine what should survive. To this, the response has been that there seems to have been no general expectation that a war was coming.

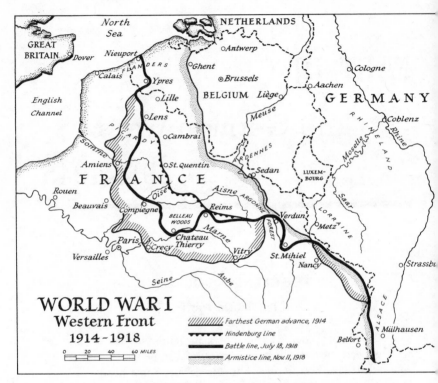

World War I, Western Front, 1914-1918

Other historians labored to pin the guilt on one particular nation or alliance, an industry which included the peacemakers at Versailles, who wrote into Article 231 that "Germany accepts the responsibility of herself and her allies for causing all the loss and damage to which the Allied and Associated Powers and their nationals have been subjected as a consequence of the war imposed upon them by the aggression of Germany and her allies." In the historical literature after 1918, one can find learned arguments designed to demonstrate the primary guilt of all the major participants. An alternative was to see this evidence as proof that no nation was uniquely guilty, but that the responsibility belonged to *all* the participants to a greater or lesser degree. If this is so, then Article 231 was patently unjust.

The argument for corporate guilt was ultimately buttressed by showing that no power in the crisis of 1914 wanted a *general* European war, and that the diplomatists all worked either to avoid war entirely or to localize it. The political consequences of a general war were too uncertain, the losses in life and property were likely to be too high, for any power to have wanted general war. But if one went behind the immediate crisis of 1914 and its frantic diplomacy, then German responsibility loomed larger. For after 1890, German foreign policy, apparently aiming at hegemony in Europe and in the world, was the principal factor that threatened the continental balance of power which had succeeded in localizing conflicts since 1815. It is argued that, in those twenty-five years before 1914, the Germans merely sought in the world what others had earlier achieved. Be that as it may, her expansionism, often poorly planned and clumsily defined, gave Germany an aggressive posture. It took a second World War, however, when German designs were more transparent, to reveal the aggressive continuity of German foreign policy in the twentieth century. In which light, Article 231, if perhaps unwise and too exclusive, was not far off its mark.

Thus, while the well-known German invasion of Belgium in 1914 (in violation of the Treaty of 1839) served to bring Britain into the war, there can be little doubt that she would have of necessity entered the war in any case. A continental victory for William II's aggressive policy in 1914 was as intolerable for British security as a similar victory for Hitler's ambitions would prove to be for the United States in 1940. Such observations must immediately be tempered: First, by recognizing that the Germans did not plot the war in 1914, which depended upon the quarrel between Austria and Serbia. And second, by noting that the United States entered the war in 1941 only when attacked, and not because the general public yet understood the consequences of a German victory in Europe.

By 1914, most European military strategists had been taught by the swift Prussian victories of 1866 and 1870, rather than by the lessons of the American Civil War. Instead of a war of deadlock and attrition, they saw victory quickly achieved through vigorous offensives. The improvement in communications after 1870 confirmed their faith in the technical feasibility of swift movement. Every power had its contingency plans, the most critical of which proved to be the Schlieffen Plan, named for the man who headed the German general staff from 1892 to 1905. His plan of attack (1905) assumed from the Franco-Russian alliance that the Central Powers, in case of general war, would face a two-front war. To await an attack from two sides would have been madness, especially in view of Italy's doubtful loyalty to the Triple Alliance; and given the likelihood of a slow Russian mobilization, the opportunity to avoid a two-front war lay in the swift defeat of France.

Schlieffen expected (correctly) that the best French troops would be concentrated for an invasion of Alsace-Lorraine. If, therefore, the Germans moved swiftly and in great strength through Belgium into a region less well-defended by the French, moving upon Paris from the northwest, the French would have to abandon their own offensive plans and rush to the defense of Paris. The invasion of Belgium, which the Germans admitted to be a violation of international law, was a military requirement designed to force French capitulation within six weeks. Meanwhile, the Russians would have to be held in check by inferior forces in the east, giving some ground if necessary; for the Germans were not confident that the Austrians alone could contain Russia.

The critical factor was time, and that went against the Germans in 1914 from the start. The Belgians fought hard, delaying the German advance two weeks and giving the British an opportunity to join the French. Still the Germans came on, forcing an Allied retreat eastward. So confident was General von Moltke of victory, that he detached several corps for service on the eastern front. In fact, his gigantic operation became exposed on its right flank to counterattack by French reserves; and though he saw the danger, communications with his fast-moving forces were inadequate to make adjustments in time. French counterattacks thus forced Moltke to halt his advance and to retreat into defensive positions. By the spring of 1915, a stalemate was achieved with the battle lines extending from Switzerland to the North Sea; and the Germans found themselves condemned to a two-front war.

Had the Russians been ready for war, therefore, the Central Powers would have been in serious difficulty from the very outset of the campaigns. But Russian military reforms, projected after the defeat by Japan in 1905, were not scheduled for completion until 1917. Disorganized and unready for battle, they moved prematurely into East Prussia to try to divert German pressure from the French and were beaten back. On the other hand, the Russian advance against the Austrians in 1914 was a spectacular success and came at a time when the Austrian attempt to knock Serbia out of the war had failed. Russian shortages in arms and equipment, however, forced a halt to the offensives in the late fall, and the real opportunity to eliminate Austria-Hungary from the war was lost. Thus, the eastern front became stabilized by the end of the year, much like the western front.

Campaigns after 1914 followed a familiar pattern: attacks launched at great human cost without any appreciable decision being attained. The long defensive lines on both fronts presented no vulnerable flanks to be turned, and defensive firepower proved to be superior to offensive tactics. Machine guns, especially, were murderous against advancing infantry, masses of barbed wire were employed to prevent surprise assaults, while elaborate systems of dugouts protected troops on the defense from artillery fire. The entry of new powers into the war, Turkey late in 1914 and Italy in 1915, offered new threats to break the deadlock, but the results were the same: broken offensives after appalling casualties.

In the West, both sides saw their sea power as another means to break the deadlock. Britain's initial blockade of the Central Powers was concentrated on the Channel and the North Sea. But since the United States insisted on the right of Americans to trade with neutrals, American goods reached Dutch and Scandinavian ports. Since the British and French knew that a great part of such imports ultimately reached Germany, they came to increasingly rigid definitions as to what constituted contraband; and late in 1914 they declared the North Sea to be a military zone. Faced with a shrinking flow of supplies, the Germans risked a naval raid against the British early in 1915. Its failure led the Germans to their last naval ace: their submarines. They declared a counterblockade of Britain and the Channel, warning that enemy ships in that war zone would be destroyed without warning—for the effectiveness of submarines depended upon surprise attack. The Germans warned neutrals to stay out of that war zone, since mistakes could easily be made, especially after the British advised their merchantmen to fly either neutral flags or no flags at all in British waters as a protection against submarines.

Although there is no legal difference between the seizure of neutral merchandise as contraband and the sinking of neutral ships, world opinion reacted quite differently to the two procedures—for the sneak attacks cost many lives. Before the end of the year, American opinion, especially, had been so outraged as to make the Germans doubt the wisdom of their submarine campaign; and William II gave assurances that there would be no more surprise attacks upon passenger ships or neutral vessels. This decision led to new massive efforts on all sides to break the military deadlock with giant offensives in 1916. The one that came closest to success was the Russian drive against the Austrians, as the Austrians were found to be seriously demoralized. But the drive halted when the Russians again became starved for ammunition.

New weapons were introduced to overcome the stalemate. In 1915, the Germans experimented with poisonous gas against British infantry, a frightful tactic, but of limited offensive value. By 1916, furthermore, when the Germans used gas again at Verdun in a desperate bid to break French resistance, the defenders were ready with gas masks. Meanwhile in Britain, Churchill had sponsored the development of a vehicle that could smash through barbed wire, protect its occupants from enemy fire, and bridge enemy trenches. The "tank" was the answer, so called because its development was hidden from the Germans with the pretense that the British Navy was constructing new water storage tanks. First used experimentally against the Germans in 1916, the thirty-six sent into action were inadequate for any military success; but the British saw their future and ordered a thousand more.

As 1917 approached, the Germans, well aware that time was not on their side, once again turned to naval tactics; for food supplies were running short, and the home-front morale was cracking. German surface ships were sent on raids in the North Sea in the hope of destroying isolated units of the British fleet without engaging the entire British fleet. On one such sortie, a British advance guard was lured into action off Jutland with the main German fleet and might have been destroyed had not Jellicoe's grand fleet suddenly appeared out of the mist. The Germans had to flee and might have been destroyed had not Jellicoe been overcautious out of respect for their gunnery. (Though outnumbered, the Germans had some ship-for-ship advantage, as their navy was of more recent construction.) Though the victorious Jellicoe was supreme on the North Sea, his caution allowed the Germans to slip into the Baltic where the British dared not follow, meaning that Britain lost the opportunity to close in on the Baltic submarine bases, not to speak of the opportunity to open a supply route to Russia.

The only remaining naval alternative for the Germans, however, was a return to unrestricted submarine warfare against almost all shipping in European waters, determined as they were to put an end to Allied purchases of munitions in the United States. The renewal led the United States to break relations with Germany, and ultimately to enter the war in April of 1917. Many of the traditional reasons to account for the American intervention have since been discarded. President Wilson himself contributed to obscuring the issues at the time by seeing the conflict as a defense of international law and freedom of the seas. The fact was that Britain was in desperate straits. By April of 1917, a quarter of her ships leaving home ports never returned. For all the traditional American suspicion of the British, it was nothing compared to this country's abhorrence of the possible victory of the German system with its avowed policy of European domination.

Despite American intervention, 1917 was a year of serious reverses for the Allies. French attempts to break the German lines with shock assaults resulted in nothing but shocking casualties. An Italian drive against the Austrians, timed to coincide with the French offensive, inched forward all summer, only to be hurled back by Austro-German units at Caporetto. After this the British and French had to keep troops in Italy to prevent a separate peace. But the most disastrous collapse of all came in Russia, where her immense efforts had come to nothing. Her economy could not sustain the demands of modern war, and British hopes to establish a supply line either through the Dardanelles or the Baltic had been frustrated. The imperial regime, which had survived the Crimean and Japanese disasters, cracked in March of 1917, with the abdication of Nicholas II being the admission of failure.

A liberal provisional government tried to rebuild the armies in the face of the advancing Germans, while the country plunged deeper into revolution. Communist agents infiltrated the army, further weakening its ability to fight; and when the Communists, pledged to peace at any price, seized control of the provisional government in November, the Russian war effort came to an end. In the general collapse, the Empire had already begun to dissolve. The Poles declared their independence in March of 1917; and in November, the Ukrainians, Estonians, Finns,

Bessarabians, and Latvians followed suit. The climax of the catastrophe came in the treaty of Brest-Litovsk, which the provisional government signed with the Central Powers in the spring of 1918. The Russians formally acknowledged the loss of territories to the former minorities, as well as the independence of Lithuania and Transcaucasia. Following which, the Germans occupied Finland and the Ukraine, hoping the latter would provide the food to offset the effects of the British blockade.

Despite these Allied setbacks, the Germans knew the seriousness of their own situation by the end of 1917. The British were beginning to build merchant ships faster than the Germans were destroying them; and British tanks scored a spectacular, if temporary, breakthrough near Cambrai, which seemed ominous to the Germans who had been minimizing the effectiveness of tanks. Worse, fresh troops from America would soon be crossing the Atlantic to offset the loss of Russia to the Allies. Thus, the Germans gathered their forces in the west for a last great blow, substantially outnumbering the Anglo-French forces. In the crisis, the latter achieved a combined command for the first time in the war in the person of General Foch.

The German push began in March of 1918, and though it reached the Marne east of Paris by May, American troops were then ready to enter the lines. Moreover, French artillery became increasingly effective in breaking up German efforts. By early August, it was clear that the back of the German offensive had been broken and that German casualties had been notably higher than those of the Allies. The initiative passed to the Allies, and the Germans expected a major drive by Foch, which indeed began in September. In the meantime, the Germans opened negotiations to seek a peace before their forces were seriously routed. The Austrians, having tried to coordinate their drive in 1918 against the Italians with the final German push, were so handicapped by wholesale desertions that no success was possible. They agreed to an armistice on November 4.

The methods and the motives of Germany in seeking peace have remained controversial, for they set the stage for further international conflict. Naturally she sought the softest peace possible, and she saw that possibility in an appeal to the well-known idealism of the American president. In a belated enthusiasm for democracy, William II reconstituted his government on October 4 to establish true parliamentary government; and on the same day the German and Austrian governments appealed to Wilson for an armistice based upon his Fourteen Points. These had been set down at the beginning of 1918 as an outline of American foreign policy and amounted to a settlement based upon the rights of *all* nationalities to self-determination. The Fourteen Points, however, had been composed before the Germans had revealed their territorial designs in the treaty of Brest-Litovsk; and they now found that Wilson demanded not simply the acceptance of the Fourteen Points, but cessation of submarine warfare and evacuation of all occupied territory as precedents of an armistice. Indeed, since Wilson had come to believe that the Germans did not truly adhere to his principles, he now agreed with the other Allied leaders that the German surrender must be unconditional.

Consequently, aside from the actual armistice terms, none of the Central Powers knew what the final peace terms would be. Also, William II abdicated on November 9 to make way for a republic, meaning that the defeated regime escaped the responsibility for signing the unconditional surrender. Finally, the German armistice commission was entirely civilian, though the top German generals had been the first to recommend a quick armistice. Thus, did they seek to place the blame for defeat on others and to create the impression that the army had not been defeated—but betrayed. The armistice terms were harsh. Foch required the evacuation of Alsace-Lorraine, the Rhineland, and all occupied territories (the treaty of Brest-Litovsk became a dead letter). Not only arms, but many trucks, locomotives, and freight cars were surrendered to aid the immediate recovery of Belgium and France, whose industrial areas had been systematically razed by the retreating Germans in 1918. The terms were signed on November 11, 1918.

2.   The Russian Revolution

As in the coming of the French Revolution, we must distinguish between the revolutionary *spirit* and the revolutionary *situation* as the prelude to 1917. For one finds in nineteenth-century Russia both an intellectual protest against the premises upon which the autocracy was based, as well as a set of circumstances which the autocracy seemed increasingly unable to manage. In contrast to the French example, however, where the *spirit* and the *situation* long remained so distinct and separate as to preclude describing them as a revolutionary movement, the coming of the Russian Revolution was a more conscious affair. Those imbued with the revolutionary spirit were also close students of actual conditions in Russia; they meant to overthrow the established order long before 1917; and the historical example of the French Revolution made it possible for them to be conscious of what they were setting out to accomplish.

One of the notable consequences in 1917 was an acceleration of the revolutionary cycle. In 1789, most of the revolutionaries expected to reform the monarchy, to bring to an end a constitutional crisis so that financial and economic problems could be tackled. In 1917, monarchical reformers were swept aside in a few days, leaving the stage for a showdown between the Russian "Girondists" and "Jacobins." The hopelessness of reforming the monarchy had earlier been pointed up after 1905 when military disasters fed criticism of the regime. Public disorder and assassination became so serious that the government not only made an untimely peace with the Japanese, but promised the election of a national assembly—the Duma—on a broad franchise. To the despair of liberals, however, the monarchy quickly recovered from its panic of 1905, and the Dumas between 1906 and 1916 turned out to be consultive bodies rather than truly legislative. For all practical purposes, Russia remained an autocracy.

The revolutionary movement had first developed among army officers who saw service in France between 1814 and 1818, and who were shocked to discover the superiority of western conditions of life. From this there arose a spate of secret societies dedicated to political, social, and economic reform in Russia. Their leadership came from the gentry. Some favored the establishment of a French-style democratic republic, others an English-style constitutional monarchy. They engineered uprisings upon the death of Alexander I late in 1825 (the Decembrist Revolt), which were swiftly smashed. Vigorous reprisals by the new czar, Nicholas I, put new teeth in czarist absolutism and alienated the monarchy even more from the liberal gentry.

On the other hand, even well-meaning attempts by the imperial government to reform produced an inordinate amount of dissatisfaction. The emancipation of the serfs by Alexander II after the Crimean War, and the subsequent redistribution of land, angered former landowners, who felt they had been despoiled, and peasants, who believed that they ought not have to pay for lands received. (Not to speak of peasants dissatisfied with what they had received.) Peasant rioting was widespread in the 1860's, often encouraged by the new (1862) Land and Liberty Society organized by liberals and radicals. Peasants generally, however, did not trust intellectuals, many of whom concluded that there was no hope of a revolution based on the rural population. Radical opinion, therefore, increasingly favored terrorism, the traditional weapon of a tiny minority; and in 1879 the Will of the People Society was formed, openly advocating the assassination of the Czar and indifferent to his reformist tendencies—for reforms could preserve the established order and the principles upon which it was based.

Furthermore, rural poverty was hardly abolished with the emancipation decree and the subsequent reforms. A small group of gentry still controlled nearly half the agricultural land, and perhaps a third of the peasantry remained landless right down to 1914. More to the point, the technical level of Russian agriculture remained so primitive that a peasant's productivity was about one-third the yield harvested by a German farmer. The gentry who rented land to peasants for sharecropping often received fifty percent of the crop or other manorial forms of rent, so that serfdom existed despite emancipation.

The reign of Alexander III (1881-1894) coincided with the beginning of industrialization and its usual abuses, creating a new dimension of grievances to which a repressive government was indifferent. By 1914, Russian production of coal and iron per capita was tiny compared to the western countries, and she had no machine-tool industry or chemical plants at all. Yet, what industry Russia had was modern in its high degree of concentration, which inadvertently contributed to the organization and political strength of her industrial workers. The enormous demands made by the war in 1914 upon this infant industry was the final exposure of the backwardness and underproductivity of the entire Russian economy. Leading straight to military incapacity, the situation brought the autocracy to the brink of its third debacle in a half century. As in 1789, the leadership of this old regime was inadequate in the crisis. The bankruptcy was financial as well as moral, government income being a bare ten percent of military expenditures. At a moment when the regime desperately needed to rally the nation, its vision narrowed in a jealous desire to maintain absolute authority.

With industrialization, meanwhile, had come new western-style socialist movements to compete with the native anarchist and terrorist organizations for command of the revolutionary movement. The first Russian

Marxist party was formed by Plekhanov (in Swiss exile) in 1883. In 1898, Martov and Lenin dared to reorganize the party on Russian soil—the Social Democratic party or SD's—with a direct appeal to industrial workers; but they were soon forced to promote their party from exile. True to their Marxist philosophy, the SD's believed that class warfare knew no national distinctions; thus they saw themselves as part of an international movement and favored international organization. Whereas a second socialist party, founded in 1901 by Chernov as the Socialist Revolutionaries or SR's, was more narrowly Russian, saw its cause in national terms, and worked for the improvement of the peasants' lot as had traditional Russian radicalism.

A division of opinion within the Russian SD's appeared in 1903 at their party congress in London. Lenin wanted to restrict party membership to an elite: to a few, highly disciplined professional revolutionaries who could direct the masses. Martov and Trotsky preferred a party open to all supporters as in the case of the German Social Democratic party. The difference reflected a more serious division: Lenin was uncompromising and meant to accomplish his revolutionary goals through violence; the Martov-Trotsky faction preferred to promote the eventual socialist society with parliamentary, evolutionary means. As the Lenin faction gained control of the party in 1903, it was henceforth known as the Bolsheviks (majority); the Martov-Trotsky group was known as the Mensheviks (minority). The party maintained its outer unity, but the split was never healed.

Liberals organized, too, with the Union of Liberation in 1903. Primarily seeking representative government, the liberals were often men who had taken part in local and provincial government after the reforms of 1864 and who wanted those reforms crowned with the creation of a national parliament. The Czar's hasty promise to summon such a parliament in 1905 seemed for a moment to mean victory for the liberals, just then reorganized as the Constitutional Democratic party or KD's. But the regime quickly alienated liberal support by devising a series of checks upon parliamentary power and by rejecting liberal legislation designed to rally the peasantry to the government.

The war, which finally revealed the complete incompetence of the autocracy, at first rallied the public to the regime. Though the reactionary ministers in power succeeded for a time in keeping the true state of affairs at the front from members of the Duma, the specter of disaster loomed large in St. Petersburg by mid-1915. When anxious members of the Duma found themselves powerless to urge abler or more reputable officials upon the regime, the suspicion developed that the autocracy actually connived at a German victory out of sympathy for the German form of government. The outbreak of revolution, however, in March of 1917, was not led by the liberal or the radical parties, but seems to have been a spontaneous outburst of public outrage at a government whose efforts had produced nothing but defeat, food shortages, and serious inflation. A wave of strikes in the capital brought great mobs into the streets, and the government found that it could not rely upon its demoralized troops to keep order. Only after the government lost control of the major cities did radicals organize a workers' council (Soviet) in St. Petersburg, by which time the liberals in the Duma had already notified Nicholas II that his abdication had become necessary. He gave way without a struggle.

The Duma, anxious to prevent the more radical Soviet from assuming power, then created a provisional government under the prime ministry of Prince Lvov, a KD. This new regime, however, was handicapped from the start by the presence of the Soviet, which acted as a rival government, issuing its own orders and establishing soldiers' councils (also soviets) in all army units. It soon became clear that the Provisional Government would have to depend upon the Soviet for military support. That was no problem for the moment, as the Soviet was dominated by Mensheviks and SR's, who favored promotion of the war just as the Provisional Government did. But when that regime announced, as war aims, that Russia would expect to obtain the Straits and Constantinople, the socialists in the Soviet balked. They took the line that wars are imperialistic, and that all peoples should demand that their governments conduct only defensive war and renounce annexationist policies. In any case, it seems likely that the rival regimes would have fallen out sooner or later, especially over SR plans to redistribute land.

This jockeying for control of the revolution between liberals and moderate socialists was soon complicated by the appearance of Lenin in mid-April of 1917. Totally opposed to any further Russian participation in the war (on the grounds that wars are manufactured for the benefit of capitalists), he worked for Bolshevik seizure of the Soviet, after which he planned to end the war and establish a dictatorship of the proletariat. Lenin had been permitted by the Germans to cross their territory to reach Russia in the hope that he would succeed in removing Russia from the war. It was not hard for him to convince the war-weary, land-hungry masses that the time for peace and land redistribution had come, and a government dedicated to pursuing the national interest in the war faced a collapse of the home front. When the general commanding the troops in St. Petersburg tried to halt demonstrations for peace, the Soviet ordered his troops to their barracks. This set the stage for re-constitution of the provisional government in July, with the SR Kerensky assuming the prime ministry.

LENIN [VLADIMIR ULIANOV] (Photo World).

The revolution, therefore, had moved a step to the left. Yet, Kerensky appointed a well-known conservative, Kornilov, to command the armed forces in an attempt to restore discipline. The appointment put the regime in an equivocal position: While seeking harmony and unity with the Soviet, Kerensky also put his military forces in the charge of a man who regarded the Soviet as composed of pro-German traitors. Kerensky never escaped the dilemma of his dual loyalty—his responsibility to maintain the government he headed, and his attachment to fellow socialists in the Soviet who were a continual threat to his government. In the crunch, he could provide no effective leadership; and the crisis came in September when Kornilov informed Kerensky of his plan to crush the Soviet. Kerensky first wavered, then warned the Soviet of its danger. Those who wanted to save the revolution, doubting Kerensky's integrity, felt they had no alternative but to submit to Bolshevik leadership, while railway workers, under Soviet direction, managed to confuse troop movements so thoroughly that Kornilov's coup collapsed without any fighting.

Still, many of the Bolsheviks shrank from the prospect of seizing the Provisional Government, and Lenin had a difficult time convincing his party that their time had come. Kerensky took no effective means to meet the challenge he knew was coming, and in November he fled in disguise to France. In taking power, Lenin at once announced that the war would be immediately ended, and that the property rights of the nobility would be destroyed—hoping to insure his support by the mass of the population, the peasantry. He also gave notice that the revolution in Russia would be a mere prelude to the world socialist revolution. To carry out his promises, the Soviet government ordered an end to private landholding, with no compensation to former landowners. The nationalized lands were to be worked through rural soviets elected by the peasants; these soviets were to be responsible for the distribution of land for individual farming.

As for peace, an immediate armistice was followed in early 1918 by the Treaty of Brest-Litovsk. Lenin might argue that Russia had no power to resist the harsh settlement dictated by the Central Powers, but in fact he was for international socialism and relatively indifferent to the claims of Russian nationalism. In any case, a treaty which cost Russia 1,300,000 square miles of territory and over sixty million people was bound to shock patriotic opinion. Her former allies were caught in a serious bind by Russia's separate peace, which gave the Germans real opportunity for victory in the West. And Lenin compounded the agony by repudiating all debts contracted by the imperial regime, which hit the French especially hard as they had been the primary lenders to Russia.

Lenin postponed an immediate nationalization of industry in the hope of keeping it functioning. Yet, he allowed workers to form soviets for the purpose of supervising managerial personnel, which contributed to considerable confusion and hostility. Having always believed in the dictatorship of an elite, Lenin knew that terror would be necessary to control opposition. "Not a single question pertaining to the class struggle," he said, "has ever been settled except by violence. Violence when it is committed by the toiling and exploited masses is the kind of violence of which we approve." The All-Russian Extraordinary Commission (Cheka) was appointed to shut off opposition and illegal activities, and its chief weapon was terror. The fallen Provisional Government had promised national elections to form a constituent assembly, which Lenin recognized could become a stronghold of opposition, especially since the SR's—the traditional peasant party—might well win the elections. Lenin went ahead with the elections in 1918 only because he had control of the army by then and knew he had the power to dissolve the assembly. When the SR's indeed gained the majority in the assembly and gave signs of seizing control, Lenin disallowed further sessions. The Bolshevik dictatorship had been established.

3.   The Postwar Settlements

The general Peace Conference opened in Paris in 1919 under the chairmanship of Clemenceau, the French Premier, whose main objective was the permanent weakening of Germany for the future security of France. In all, thirty-two states were represented, many having become belligerents late in the war simply to obtain a seat at the conference; and many national groups wishing to become states, aware of Woodrow Wilson's hope that the settlement would be based upon the rights of *all* nationalities to self-determination, also sent representatives. Soviet Russia, having made a separate peace and by then engaged in civil war, was unrepresented, and the defeated powers were not invited. This omission, while avoiding the possibility of the defeated sowing discord in the ranks of the victorious as Talleyrand had managed it a hundred years before, later lent weight to the German claim that Germany had been unjustly treated—indeed, betrayed. On the other hand, the Germans had been defeated in the field. Having offered to surrender on the basis of Wilsonian principles, it became easy to convince themselves that they had so surrendered. When in fact, even Wilson, after Brest-Litovsk, had insisted upon unconditional surrender. Aside from the armistice terms, none of the defeated powers knew what the eventual peace terms would be.

"The Big Four": ORLANDO, LLOYD-GEORGE, CLEMENCEAU, WILSON
(Radio Times Hulton Picture Library).

The harsh settlement that emerged from the conference was by no means easily achieved, and not only because it was difficult to draw neat boundary lines to separate nationalities aspiring to self-government. In 1815, the peacemakers had been assisted by the fact that the principle of *legitimacy,* the basis for political and territorial settlement, was consistent with the Allied method of uprooting French militancy (that is, destroying the vestiges of the French Revolution by restoring the legitimate House of Bourbon). In 1919, because of the overlapping of national claims, the principle of nationality was much harder to apply fairly or to general satisfaction, not to speak of the national claims of the defeated powers. Moreover, the principle was soon found to be inconsistent with the attempt to guarantee that Germany would not revive as a military state. The morselization of Europe, in sum, left an immense residue of bitterness on the part of those nationalities which thought they had been despoiled or which were certain they had not received what was properly theirs; just as it created new states that had no particular geographic or economic viability. The stage was set for the ambitious and the revengeful.

Still, something can be said for Wilson's concern for the rights of nationalities. He had observed the nationalists' passion in the later nineteenth century and knew it to be a major source of conflict and violence. He also knew that nationalism itself had had many constructive features. One might regret that its claims, so long unrequited in the nineteenth century, had turned nationalism into a hate-filled monster. What a difference for Europe, for instance, if the Austrians had discovered early a way to make their cosmopolitan empire congenial to the component nationalities! Like Napoleon III before him, Wilson hoped in 1919 that the ambitions of the various nations could be satisfied all while preserving cosmopolitan Europe through international organizations: his League of Nations.

The Treaty of Versailles (1919) forced Germany to return Alsace-Lorraine to France, to cede two frontier areas around Eupen and Malmédy to Belgium, to give up Posen and West Prussia to the new Poland, and to consent to plebiscites (under the auspices of the League of Nations) that would regulate what part of Schleswig must go to Denmark, what part of Upper Silesia must be given to the new Czechoslovakia, and what the future of the Saar Basin would be. German armed forces were sharply limited to numbers felt to be adequate for policing the coast and maintaining internal order. The creation of Poland (see the map) had the effect of isolating East Prussia from the rest of Germany; and within the "Polish Corridor" separating the two, the German city of Danzig was made a free city under the supervision of the League of Nations. One can see at once how the integrity of the new League of Nations was shackled at its birth to the maintenance of the peace settlement. The Covenant of the League of Nations, in fact, became the first section in the Treaty of Versailles, so that any German violation of the treaty would put her at odds with all members of the League.

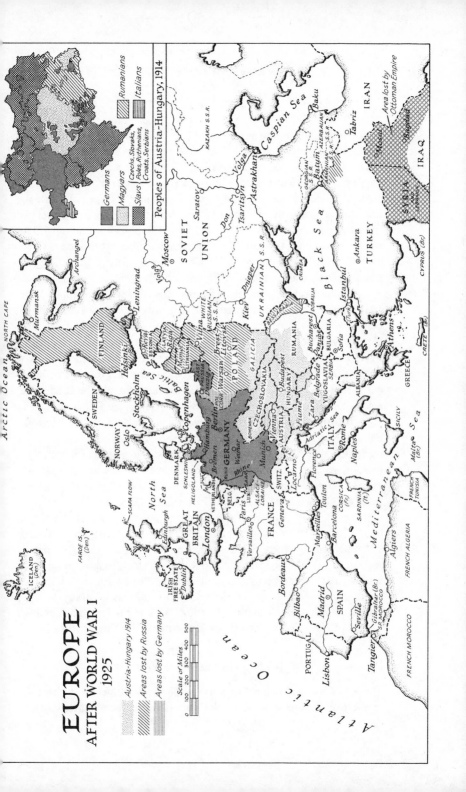

EUROPE
AFTER WORLD WAR I
1925

Scale of Miles
100 200 300 400 500

Austria-Hungary 1914

Areas lost by Russia

Areas lost by Germany

Peoples of Austria-Hungary, 1914

Germans

Magyars

Slavs (Czechs, Slovaks, Poles, Ruthenians, Croats, Serbians)

Rumanians

Italians

Area lost by Ottoman Empire

The "war-guilt" clause in the treaty condemned the Germans to pay reparations for damage done to civilian property and population. The treaty required a token payment of five billion dollars, with an Allied Reparation Committee to set the final figure by May of 1921. Thus, Germany pledged to pay an unknown amount at a moment when her territorial losses reduced her ability to pay. Aside from the loss of her colonial empire (given to the League of Nations for disposal), Germany lost only one-eighth of her territory; but the eighth lost contained sixty-five percent of her iron ore and forty-five percent of her coal. This Allied indifference to some of the economic realities of the peace settlement was repeated in the treaties that broke up the Austro-Hungarian Empire along national lines, destroying an economic unity in central Europe.

Separate treaties were signed with Austria (St. Germain-en-Laye, 1919) and with Hungary (Trianon, 1920). Austria suffered particularly, being reduced to twenty-five percent of her former share of the Dual Monarchy in both population and territory. Two new states comprising western and southern Slavs, respectively, Czechoslovakia and Yugoslavia, were carved out of the old Empire; despite the fact that the component groups, like the Czechs and Slovaks or the Serbs and the Croats, had never been notably congenial. Other Slavic-, Italian-, or Romanian-speaking territories were ceded to the new Poland, to Italy, and to Romania; but the German-speaking South Tyrol was given to Italy upon Italian insistence that the Brenner Pass region was necessary for defensive reasons. Austria was specifically forbidden to seek a union with Germany as a solution to her territorial losses, and a restoration of the Hapsburgs was denied to both Austria and Hungary. The latter retained only about forty percent of her former population. Defeated Bulgaria had to sign the Treaty of Neuilly (1919), ceding territory to Greece and Yugoslavia, which had the effect of cutting Bulgaria off from the Aegean Sea. But the treaty agreed to by the Turkish Empire so outraged Turkish nationalist opinion that it led to the overthrow of the old monarchy and disavowal of the treaty. In any case, Turkey lost her claims upon her vast empire in North Africa and the Near East, and the League of Nations inherited the task of partitioning the territory.

4.   The Climate After Versailles

The Great War had seemed to confirm the nineteenth-century democratization of European society. Not only had the liberal states emerged victorious—with the four major autocracies crumbling—but an international agency to settle international disputes had at last been founded, which would reflect international opinion. Perhaps, then, Europe now had the means to shut off the currents of corrosive nationalism and to approach her problems as a cosmopolitan community. In fact, general war would again break out twenty years later, broader in scope than in 1914. Many factors contributed to the instability of the European order after 1919 and, thus, to the failure of the peace settlement.

The war had left all manner of wounds which drastically affected the social fabric in the belligerent countries. The casualties alone were on an unprecedented scale, the major participants counting over eight million dead and more than double that figure in wounded. France suffered the greatest casualties in proportion to total population; but the Russians, who would soon add millions of dead through civil war, suffered the most in sheer numbers. All the belligerent European countries found themselves with a serious deficit of men after 1918, the discrepancy in Britain approaching the figure of 1100 women for every 1000 men. The European birth rate, already declining by 1914, dropped sharply during the war to forecast a manpower shortage for years to come. During the war, women were mobilized as never before for work on farms and in factories, leading to their greater emancipation. Britain, for instance, rewarded women over thirty with the right to vote in 1918.

Similarly, the total mobilization of national resources, necessary for all the belligerents as the war lengthened, had a lasting effect upon European economic and social thinking. Before 1914, Europe had been part of a world economy—largely an unplanned economy. Despite the rising tariff barriers that reflected the hostile nationalism of the late nineteenth century, international business relations expanded, characterized by increasing economic specialization and trade. Europe increasingly exported capital as well as manufactured goods, London being the most important source of cheap capital for worldwide investment. The wartime economic planning led to postwar demands for peacetime mobilization of the national resources, so that the benefits of industrialization could be more quickly and generally realized. Despite such demands, businessmen naturally tried to resume the prewar patterns of trade; but the impact of the Great Depression after 1929 forced European governments back to planning. Thus, it is fair to claim that 1914 was a watershed between unplanned and planned economies. The nineteenth-century liberal had dwelt upon those things which governments ought not do; postwar liberalism defined new realms for government controls.

Economic planning had been foreshadowed in the late nineteenth century in both government and private business by Bismarck's "state socialism," for instance, and by the social insurance systems available in most western countries by 1914. After 1890, European businessmen showed a new tendency to plan for the future on a grand scale to increase their efficiency and competitiveness, a movement that led to the formation of giant cartels and trusts. Because of this experience, such men were called into government service during the war for economic planning in the emergency, the German Walther Rathenau being a notable example. That the impetus for peacetime planning emerged from the war years can be seen in the military metaphors used in the peacetime planning: agrarian and industrial *fronts,* production *battles, shock* workers, and *brigade* leaders.

The political and economic recovery of Europe after such terrible devastation called for international cooperation and planning, especially through the agency of the League of Nations. Even the victorious Allies, however, soon allowed national interests and prejudices to prevail over international requirements, a condition that gave opportunity to all those who hoped to unsettle the peace rather than maintain it. The first sign of Allied disaffection was the failure of the United States Senate to ratify the Treaty of Versailles. Since ratification of a treaty requires a two-thirds majority, the rejection was the work of a minority. On the other hand, in the face of considerable popular enthusiasm for the League of Nations, this country returned a Republican congress in 1918 and elected a Republican president in 1920, clearly enhancing the probability that the treaty would fail. The public showed itself more eager for rapid demobilization and "normalcy" than for any other cause in the world. Sometimes seen as a sign of American immaturity in international politics, the reaction more likely reflected popular suspicion that American idealism had been trampled under foot by cynical European statesmen in the forging of the peace settlement. Had the war been more realistically approached in 1917, or even before, Americans might have been spared much of the subsequent disenchantment. As it was, those who had approached the war in 1917 as a crusade for international law and freedom of the seas ended in 1920 by refusing to participate in the League of Nations, the most idealistic aspect of the peace settlement.

The prospects for achieving Wilson's goal of "perpetual peace" were immediately dimmed. Marshal Foch had already remarked the previous year that "This is not Peace. It is an Armistice for twenty years." In fact, not only was there no real peace after 1919, but even the "armistice" was too consistently violated to be called a true armistice. Conflicts were limited in scope, some of them taking the nonmilitary form we have come to call "cold war;" but the European climate through the next twenty years was militant.

THE UNEASY PEACE

1. The League of Nations

The League was an association of sovereign states, initially designed to include the thirty-two nations who had broken relations with Germany during the war, plus thirteen neutral nations to be invited to join. Thereafter, additional nations could be elected to membership by a two-thirds vote of the member nations. The League's work was done through a Secretariat, a Council, and an Assembly, located at Geneva in neutral Switzerland. Each member nation was on an equal footing in the Assembly, having three delegates there but only one vote. Five of the nine seats in the Council, however, were given permanently to the great powers—Britain, France, the United States, Italy, and Japan; the remaining seats were to be filled by election from the Assembly to represent the smaller states. Most decisions in both the Council and the Assembly required a unanimous vote, and a nation could resign from the League by giving two years' notice of its intention.

The postwar treaties gave the League responsibility for guiding the development of territories in the former German and Turkish empires. Such territories were mandated to more "advanced nations" by the League for the express purpose of preparing them for self-government, their progress to be reviewed annually by the League. Beyond this specific responsibility, the League was charged with reducing worldwide armaments, the mediation of disputes, and the promotion of humanitarian projects. Armed with no police power to enforce its decisions, the League depended upon the willingness of member nations to honor their obligations to the international community; but the Covenant did contain a clause that obliged all members to break trade and financial relations with any nation which went to war.

Obviously, the League had been designed with an assumption of American participation, and our failure to join raised the immediate prospect that economic sanctions by League members against an aggressive power might not succeed, but would hurt in particular a trading nation like Britain if she supposed such League action. American withdrawal shocked the French for a further reason: Their negotiators at Versailles had demanded, for reasons of security, the Rhine as the northeastern frontier. Opposing this annexation of German-speaking people, the Americans and British persuaded the French to abandon the claim in exchange for treaties guaranteeing French security. Yet, the American Senate refused to ratify a treaty of alliance with Britain and France in 1919 some months before our rejection of the Versailles settlement became known. The French felt betrayed by this collapse of wartime unity, which led them to assume a tougher attitude on the matter of German recovery.

2.   The First Alterations of the Peace Settlements

Turkish nationalists had long suspected the European powers of conspiring to partition the declining Ottoman Empire. When the Sultan agreed to terms in 1920 with the Allies which amounted to his abandoning of all the non-Turkish territories of the old Empire, the nationalists—led by Mustapha Kemal—were prepared to overthrow the monarchy and to disavow the agreement. Consequently, it became necessary for the Allies to occupy Constantinople to save the peace treaty. The Greeks were allowed to occupy Smyrna in Turkey itself, where the population was largely Greek-speaking; and the Italians were confirmed in their possession of Rhodes and the Dodecanese Islands.

Seizing the old city of Angora (later Ankara), the nationalists announced they would establish a liberal republic and destroy the peace settlement, which led the Greeks to march on Angora. While the Greeks had British encouragement, most of the other European powers saw that the nationalists had widespread popular backing in Turkey and concluded that a new understanding with Kemal ought to be reached. In 1922, he drove the Greeks into the sea and proclaimed the overthrow of the Sultanate, following which a new peace settlement was reached at Lausanne in 1923.

Kemal had to accept the loss of the non-Turkish territories, including the Dodecanese and most of the Aègean islands; but he saved Smyrna for Turkey and recovered Adrianople and a portion of eastern Thrace at the expense of Greece. In exchange for this he agreed to the neutralization of the Straits. He also negotiated a compulsory exchange of populations with Greece in order to expel Greek residents from Turkey, where they had lived since ancient times. The League of Nations had to supervise the transfer, which uprooted nearly one million Greeks, while the Turks retrieved about 100,000 of their nationals from Greece. Tiny Greece could hardly absorb such a sudden influx of people, so that the dislocation had grievous political and economic results for Greece. Since the British and French had been on opposite sides at the beginning of the crisis, the squabble marked the beginning of their postwar antagonism which further shattered Allied unity.

Italian nationalists were another group that was dissatisfied with the peace settlement of 1919, though Italy had received the Trentino, South Tyrol, Trieste, Istria, and a few islands off Dalmatia. Given the limited value of Italian military efforts during the war, her Allies had thought these gains to be generous; but Italy had anticipated annexing the city of Fiume and the Dalmatian coast as well. Slavic Dalmatia had been awarded to the new Yugoslavia, and Italian diplomats walked out of the Paris conference when they saw their claim to Fiume rejected. Late in 1919, a small force of Italian war veterans, led by the poet D'Annunzio and wearing capes and daggers, seized Fiume for Italy. Yugoslavia refused, however, to abandon her claim to the city, and the two powers reached a negotiated settlement at Rapallo in 1920 which made Fiume an independent city-state. The compromise outraged nationalist opinion in Italy, giving Mussolini, after his rise to power, the opportunity to curry popular favor by demanding a revision of Fiume's status. The Yugoslavs gave in in 1924 and allowed Italy to annex much of the city, leaving several outlying areas of the port for Yugoslav use.

Meanwhile, Russian nationalists of variout political hues were drawn together in opposition to Lenin and the Bolsheviks. The harsh terms he accepted at Brest-Litovsk (1918) were followed by an agreement to pay Germany six billion marks in reparations, leading many Russians, like their former Western Allies, to believe that Lenin was turning Russia into a German puppet state to permit Germany to turn her full military power into her last offensives of 1918. If Britain and France should fall, Germany would be in a position to annex the entire Soviet Union. Lenin found support from those in Russia who were ready for peace at any price, which gave him time to build the Red (Bolshevik) army. The threatened civil strife was no mere ideological opposition to Bolshevism, but a patriotic outburst in particular. The Bolsheviks moved the capital from St. Petersburg to Moscow as a more secure base to face the storm.

The Great Civil War (1918-1920) was really a series of struggles between the Bolsheviks and many opposition groups, together called the Whites. This White movement, however, including the whole spectrum from monarchists to Mensheviks, was never unified or coordinated, and their patriotic stance was compromised by the appearance of foreign troops—especially British, French, and American—on Russian soil, sent to prevent Russian arms from falling into German hands. Since this intervention inevitably favored the parties opposing peace with Germany, and because the West furnished supplies to the Whites, the Bolsheviks could portray the intervention as an improper interference into Russian politics. As Russian nationalists, the Whites were less than enthusiastic about the new states (Poland, Finland, Lithuania, Latvia, and Estonia) carved out of the old Russian Empire, nor were they sympathetic to demands for autonomy by the Cossacks and the Ukrainians.

This chaos of interests is best illustrated in the Ukraine, where an independence movement had been encouraged by the Central Powers early in 1918. When newly in power, the Bolsheviks overthrew a Ukrainian regime which established itself in Kiev, but they were in turn forced to abandon the province at Brest-Litovsk. With the Germans then collapsing in the West in the summer of 1918, the province was invaded by White forces, backed by a French mission that landed at Odessa. Poland, meanwhile, dissatisfied by her new boundaries, saw in this Ukrainian disorder the opportunity to rectify her dissatisfaction.

The question of a proper frontier between Russia and Poland has been one of the traditional border conflicts in European history. The peacemakers in Paris gave the Poles the Curzon Line, named after Lord Curzon, a British negotiator, as their eastern frontier, thus denying Poland her historical claim to the Ukraine, to a slice of Belorussia, and to the city of Vilna (which was given to the new state of Lithuania). In 1919, when the Bolsheviks were preparing to drive the White forces out of the Ukraine, the Whites tried to draw the Poles into an alliance against the

Red regime; but being unwilling to cede to Poland territory the Whites regarded as properly Russian, no arrangement was achieved. Thus, the Poles stood aside while the Bolsheviks swept the White forces out of the Ukraine, and then opened negotiations with the Bolsheviks for a revision of the frontier, demanding the borders of 1772—those of pre-partition Poland.

These negotiations failing, the Poles overran the Ukraine in 1920 and grabbed the city of Vilna. A Red counteroffensive, however, not only drove the Poles out of the Ukraine, but thrust straight at Warsaw, which the Poles managed to hold with the aid of a French military mission. After this the Reds were forced back across the frontier. A negotiated settlement in 1921 gave the Poles bits of territory beyond the Curzon Line; but the status of Vilna was only settled by a plebiscite held there in 1922—the city voted to join Poland. Lithuanian nationalist opinion was enraged by the outcome. Diplomatic relations with Poland were broken, not to be restored until 1938.

The Bolsheviks, meanwhile, tackled the isolated centers of White resistance in the Ukraine, in the Caucasus, and in Siberia. Japan had taken advantage of the Russian Revolution to land troops at Vladivostok late in 1917, leading the Western Allies also to send troops to Siberia, but principally to contain Japan. As elsewhere, the Allies were hostile to the Bolsheviks for making a separate peace, and an evacuation did not take place until it was clear that the Reds were winning the Civil War. The Japanese were the last to evacuate—in 1922. This foreign presence left a bitter memory in the Soviet Union.

3. War Debts and Reparations

The political bitterness after Versailles was soon reinforced with financial and economic conflict that greatly impeded postwar recovery in Europe. Nationalist rivalry and hostility was easily expressed in high protective tariffs, which inhibited trade. This climate hardly favored a rational resolution of the enormous tangle that the question of war debts and reparations offered Europe after Versailles. The fantastic costs of the war had driven all the belligerents into heavy taxation and borrowing. During the war years, France had doubled her tax income, and Britain had tripled hers; and both governments had been obliged to force the liquidation of overseas investments in payment for badly needed sup-

RUSSIAN TERRITORIAL LOSSES 1917-1921

—— Brest-Litovsk treaty line 1918

▨ Russian territorial losses

NORWAY

SWEDEN

Murmansk

Archangel

Dvina

FINLAND

Helsinki

Leningrad

Reval
ESTONIA

LATVIA
Riga

LITHUANIA

Kovno

Vilna

Moscow

WHITE
RUSSIA

S O V I E T

U N I O N

GERMANY

Warsaw
POLAND

Brest-Litovsk

Baltic Sea

Kiev

Dnieper

UKRAINE

Don

Volga

AUSTRIA-HUNGARY

Dniester
BESSARABIA
Pruth

RUMANIA

SERBIA

MONTE-
NEGRO

BULGARIA

Black Sea

ALBANIA

(Ott.)

GREECE

KARS-
ARDAHAN

OTTOMAN EMPIRE

Scale of Miles

0   100   200   300   400

plies. Inter-Allied borrowing had provided for the assistance of the weaker nations.

At the war's end, therefore, the three wealthiest of the victorious powers emerged as creditor nations—the United States and Britain for roughly seven billion dollars each, and France for two and a quarter billion dollars. Since the repayment of debts first required national economic recovery, most governments again had to borrow to stimulate the adjustment to peacetime production. Thus, by 1922, the United States had risen to be a creditor for ten billion dollars, France for three and a half billion dollars, while Britain had slipped to being a creditor for four and a half billion dollars. As there was no hope of collecting the money lent to Imperial Russia, Britain and France proposed that all wartime debts be written off to the war effort and began granting concessions to their debtors, with only the postwar debts to be binding. But once again, the need for postwar Allied cooperation was shattered in Washington, where the Harding administration insisted on collection of the entire debt. Our attitude forced the European Allies to press for German payment of reparations at the very moment when the British, in particular, had begun to doubt the wisdom and the justice of assessing reparations at all.

The Reparations Commission, in the meantime, presented Germany in 1921 with a reparations bill of thirty-three billion dollars, to be paid in installments over thirty years: a high sum for a country which had just lost substantial resources for the production of goods, and which then had an unfavorable balance of trade. Moreover, Germany emerged from the war with notable inflation resulting from her failure to develop adequate wartime taxation to finance the war. Many Germans immediately began reinvesting their capital abroad to escape the high taxation obviously in the cards at home, a practice that crippled the effort to convert to a productive peacetime economy. The government itself contributed to the inflationary spiral by printing money to meet its expenses and through the necessary purchase of foreign currencies to meet the initial reparations payment. The German mark consequently began to sink on the international market, so that before the end of 1921 the Germans had to notify the Reparations Commission that they would be unable to make the payment due in 1922 and asked for a moratorium of two and a half years.

In the face of American intransigence on the inter-Allied debt and needing immediate economic relief in the devastated areas, the Belgians and the French were opposed to a moratorium, while the British were inclined to leniency. The French, moreover, knew that the sums demanded of Germany were proportionately no heavier than what had been charged them in 1871: that even having lost the resources of Alsace-Lorraine, the French had resolutely set about paying off their indemnity and had done so ahead of schedule. Not merely had the French government faced the unpleasantness squarely, but French capital had not fled from the national responsibility. Consequently, the French in 1921 had no doubt that the Germans could pay the reparations if they had the will to do so, just as the French were indifferent to the charge that the peace terms were unjust. The example of Brest-Litovsk, moreover, left little doubt that peace terms dictated by Germany would have been even harsher than the terms of Versailles. In French opinion, the German financial maneuver in 1921 was merely the second act in the devious drama staged by the Germans in 1918 in attempting to cloud the circumstances of their military defeat.

Early in 1923, the Germans having been declared to be in default by the Reparations Commission, Franco-Belgian forces occupied the industrial Ruhr valley. The evident Allied disagreements about financial matters, however, encouraged the German government to sponsor passive resistence to the military occupation; and the immediate decline in productivity spurred the inflationary spiral to ruinous heights. Allied occupation costs were greater than the reparations purchased by force, and it became clear that new reparations arrangements would have to be made.

The task fell to a new committee chaired by Charles Dawes, which granted a moratorium on payments until 1926. Annual installments were reduced to a point thought to be consistent with Germany's ability to pay—the matter of her unwillingness to pay having not yet been perceived—and the Dawes Committee recommended that foreign loans should be granted to Germany to stimulate economic recovery. In 1929, a second committee, chaired by Owen Young, again reduced the annuities by extending the period of the debt to 1988 and arranged for further foreign financial aid. These remedies soon vanished in the world economic crisis that began in 1929, and it remains unclear today how much Germany had actually paid in reparations before the payments ceased. The suspicion is that she paid less than she received in loans, that the Allies had been led into financing German recovery and at the cost of inter-Allied confidence and cooperation.

In fact, German determination to destroy the peace settlement can also be found in her foreign policy. She signed a treaty of friendship with the Soviet Union at Rapallo in 1922, whose secret clauses provided for the illegal training of German troops in Russia; and she expected that Russo-German friendship would lead to the extinction of the new Poland and the recovery of the prewar eastern frontier. In 1923, her people experienced a psychological and moral collapse at the height of the economic chaos, adding fuel to their sense of outrage that had been cultivated since 1918. From this posture of innocents betrayed would spring the most dreadful barbarity yet experienced by modern Europe, a regime that would ridicule or pervert every great tradition of European civilization to the applause of the German people. This was the peace that never was.

4. The Succession States

This name was given to the new nations that were carved out of the fallen autocratic empires. Satisfying the historical demands for self-determination, these new nations soon demonstrated that the problems generated by nationalism had not withered away with the coming of national independence. All of them suffered economically, for example, from the plethora of new frontiers—which meant barriers to trade, for ancient antagonisms were easily expressed in discriminatory tariffs. Most of them suffered internally from minority problems. Czechs and Slovaks, or Serbs and Croats, might all speak Slavic languages and be able to understand each other; but all had unique ethnic and historical traditions that were soon manifested in mutual hostility when two or more groups were lumped together as a nation-state. Finally, these states all suffered from a schism that was common in most European states after 1919. Those who strove to make European society more democratic were fought by those whose only wish was to destroy the postwar settlement or to recover lost territory and power.

The new Republic of Austria found itself reduced to a state where virtually half the population lived in Vienna and its suburbs. Aside from the economic significance of such an imbalance, the absence of the traditional hinterland threatened to bring to an end the traditional links between the Church and Austrian government. The rural areas, remaining strongly Roman Catholic, became the stronghold of the Christian Socialist party; while the Social Democrats, an anti-clerical party, drew its strength from Vienna (and included the large Jewish community). Thus, regional and religious antagonisms exacerbated the normal tension between a conservative and a liberal party. A small Nationalist party, determined to revise the 1919 settlement, followed a pan-German line and urged *Anschluss* (union) with Germany.

Such political divisions were inimical to the very notion of loyal opposition that democratic government requires. After a dozen years of party strife that frustrated the attempts of the majority Social Democrats to build a more democratic society, and after an attempt in 1931 to integrate Austria into the German economy through a customs union was blocked by the western powers as a covert attempt to seek the *Anschluss* forbidden by the 1919 peace settlement, the desperate Social Democrats felt forced to bring parliamentary government to an end. Without a dictatorship in the name of moderate government, which Chancellor Dollfus inaugurated in 1933, it had seemed only a matter of time before the conservatives, backed by a private army (the Heimwehr), would seize power. As it was, Dollfus was assassinated in 1934 during an unsuccessful attempt by the Nationalists to deliver Austria to Germany. Thus, the democratic forces maintained power, but only at the cost of democracy.

Hungarian political life after 1918 was almost entirely conditioned by the frustration of nationalist ambitions. During the final weeks of the war, the Hungarians had sought to escape from the likely penalties for defeat by dissolving their union with Austria and bringing to power an aristocrat, Count Károlyi, known for his liberal views and his opposition to the war. When it became clear that his projected reforms and his expressions of concern for the subject nationalities would not save Hungary from being treated as a defeated power, he lost popularity and resigned office early in 1919. For the next five months, Hungary was a communist republic headed by Béla Kun, who proclaimed the beginning of a dictatorship of the proletariat. Though representing only a fraction of the Hungarians, he was widely tolerated in anticipation of help from Bolshevik Russia in preventing the loss of territory to Romania and the new Czechoslovakia.

Toward that end, Kun reorganized the Hungarian forces into a Red army and began an invasion of Slovakia and Transylvania. With French encouragement, the Romanians fought back, scattered the Red army, and even occupied Budapest for a time. Kun fled to Russia, abandoned by upper- and middle-class people who had favored his nationalist campaign, and power fell to the conservative aristocrats who had traditionally governed Hungary. Known communists, radicals in general, and Jews in particular were subject to a brief reign of terror; and the right to vote in the future was severely limited. In early 1920, Hungary's short experience with a republic came to an end with the reestablishment of monarchy, really a regency under Admiral Horthy, since Hungary's new neighbors threatened war in the event of a Hapsburg restoration. During the next two decades, Horthy's regime catered to the great landowners, crushing demands for social reforms, yet enjoyed considerable popularity deriving from widespread belief that he would ultimately succeed in revising the peace settlement in Hungary's favor and make possible a Hapsburg restoration. Revenge was the paramount issue.

No doubt the Hungarians were hostile to democracy as a principle espoused by the victorious powers, but democracy fared poorly elsewhere in central and eastern Europe despite initial intentions to promote democracy. In the new Yugoslavia, for example, the royal house was the former house of Serbia; and since nearly fifty percent of the population was Serbian, most Serbs thought of the new state as simply a greater Serbia and favored a highly centralized state that would inevitably be dominated by them. The minority Croats and Slovenes, regarding themselves culturally and economically superior to the Serbs, preferred decentralization to preserve ethnic uniqueness. When the Constitution of 1921 proved to be the embodiment of Serbian principles, the minorities opened a campaign in Parliament for autonomy that soon made a chaos of political life and which culminated in 1928 with the murder of the Croatian leader on the floor of Parliament. To preserve the nation, King Alexander I then dissolved Parliament and embarked upon a royal dictatorship, which had the effect of driving the opposition underground. In Yugoslavia's three Balkan neighbors—Greece, Romania, and Bulgaria—experiments with parliamentary government were equally unsuccessful; but perhaps better should not have been expected. None of them had any parliamentary tradition nor any understanding of orderly party government, and all ended with royal dictatorships in the 1930's.

The restored Poland, too, became a disappointment for the democra-
tizers; but here the critical factionalism that proved to be disruptive of
parliamentary government was the traditional cleavage in Poland between
the conservative gentry and the liberal bourgeoisie. Marshal Pilsudski, a
national hero for his part in establishing an independent Poland and for
his subsequent defense of Warsaw against the Red army in 1920, presided as Chief of State until the democratic constitution of 1922 was
ready. Modeled on that of the French Republic, the constitution provided for a weak executive and a dominant parliament—a structure fatal
in a country so deeply divided. As in Hungary, the Polish gentry was
able to obstruct needed agrarian reforms, and in 1926 Pilsudski put an
end to parliamentary wrangling by overthrowing the constitution and
becoming a dictator. Though he had flirted with socialism in his earlier
years, Pilsudski disappointed both rural and urban workers who looked
to him for social reform. Thereafter, Poland remained a military dictatorship, the government primarily devoted to preserving Polish independence from both Germany and Soviet Russia, who were rightly suspected of a collaboration detrimental to Poland.

Czechoslovakia proved to be the succession state where democracy
functioned most successfully during the interwar period. She had various
nationalities within her frontiers—Czechs, Slovaks, Germans, Hungarians, and Ruthenians (Ukrainians)—and frictions there certainly were,
some of them of ancient origin. The Germans, who were really Austrians
inhabiting the area of the Sudeten Mountains in particular, found it
awkward to have to abandon the preferred status they had enjoyed under the Hapsburgs. The Czechs, Slovaks, and Ruthenians, if linguistically
close, all had different ethnic backgrounds. Somewhat more culturally
and industrially advanced, the Czechs were also inclined to anti-cleri-
calism, which did not sit well with the more agrarian, Roman Catholic
Slovaks and Ruthenians.

On the other hand, Czechoslovakia had assets that overcame these
liabilities. Her natural resources, her industry and agriculture, gave her a
more balanced economy than her neighbors possessed; and in Thomas
Masaryk, she was blessed with political leadership of the highest order.
Massaryk, originally Slovak, had become an internationally famous scholar at the University of Prague, thus himself bridging the gap between
Czechs and Slovaks. The new state was planned from the start on the
assumption that cooperation between national groups would be funda-

mental to statehood, and Masaryk, as the first President, provided an inspiring example of democratic leadership in his fairness toward all groups. Not until external interests began to exploit the national divisions within Czechoslovakia did her experiment begin to crack. Meanwhile, she had demonstrated that—with good will and good leadership —a cosmopolitan state could be viable.

THE GREAT DICTATORSHIPS

1. Fascist Italy

One should not fail to note that the Czechoslovakian leadership after 1918 was enormously assisted in its attempt to plant vigorous democratic institutions by the existence of a balanced economy that gave the promise of a progressive prosperity. In much of Europe, however, parliamentary government was undermined by economic dislocation, uncertainty, and fear, themselves the offspring of war, war debts, reparations, and discriminatory tariffs. Economic recovery generally was so slow, in no small part due to the collapse of Allied cooperation, that it soon became apparent that it had made little difference whether a country had come out on the winning or the losing side in the war. That perception itself was the cause of great bitterness. The longer the propertied classes felt the pinch, the more their faith in the democratic processes flagged. In the background was the success of the Bolsheviks in Russia, whose propaganda appealed to working people everywhere, especially in those years of hardship and dismay. As a consequence, many middle-class people came to believe that a Rightist dictatorship would be at once a guarantee of economic recovery and a barrier to communism. Much of Europe, therefore, drifted toward totalitarian regimes. Individual rights vanished; the rights of the State becoming paramount; and intellectual freedom gave way to thought-control programs administered by ministers of propaganda. Except in a few liberal bastions in western and northern Europe, the long progress of European civilization toward freedom and justice seemed stifled by totalitarian states of the Left and Right whose methods and standards were remarkably similar.

Italian bitterness was rooted, in the first place, in the frustration of national ambition. No other Allied power had entered the war with such naked territorial motives, and though Italy came out on the winning side, her contributions to the victory were a good deal less spectacular than the prizes she claimed. On the other hand, her military and economic costs had been high, making the mediocre military results a matter of national humiliation. Though the Italian negotiators gained much territory for Italy in the peace settlement, their failure to obtain every last claim led them to walk out on the conference, personifying the national hypersensitivity.

In the second place, grievous economic problems proclaimed the emptiness of the Italian victory. Agricultural productivity had declined during the war, leading to an unfavorable balance of trade; the government had borrowed heavily to prosecute the war, also printing paper money toward that end. The upshot was serious inflation, especially distressing to people who lived on fixed incomes or who had bought government bonds during the war. For purposes of wartime morale, the government had promised—once peace should come—a redistribution of land to help a peasantry whose plots were notoriously small. By 1920, with economic conditions actually deteriorating, both rural and industrial workers began seizing properties, no doubt stimulated by exaggerated rumors from Soviet Russia about the immediate benefits that would follow proletarian direct action. The police gradually restored order, and the danger of a revolution faded in 1921. Even so, the propertied classes had been frightened, and, fearing the spread of Bolshevism, fell upon the Fascist movement as their salvation.

Founded in 1919 by Mussolini, who had broken with the Italian Marxists, the Fascist party was not only vehemently nationalistic, but originally embodied the socialist, republican, and anti-clerical views of its founder. Only when Mussolini saw that the road to power lay not in trying to gain leadership of the Marxist movement, but in appealing to the propertied classes, did he revise his principles to appeal to them, to the Church, and to the monarchy. Retaining his nationalism, he emerged as an anti-communist and a champion of order. Yet, as an ex-Marxist, he knew the need for social reforms and was a master of the egalitarian rhetoric that enthralled the working classes and won their adherence. Some of the moderate politicians in Italy thought that Mussolini, therefore, could be a useful ally in promoting Italian recovery, yet were uneasy about the street gangs he was developing into paramilitary units. Their equivocation, plus Mussolini's threat to use violence, led the King to name him Prime Minister in 1922.

BENITO MUSSOLINI (Photo World).

Everything in Mussolini's rise to power indicated that he would follow a militant foreign policy, attack Italian economic problems, and meet political opposition with terror. Upon reaching the prime ministry, he ordered that an official Fascist philosophy be constructed to provide the ideological justification for such policies. The quickly cooked result, a mixture of Sorel, the usual misinterpretations of Nietzsche, and nineteenth-century racial theories, seems to have been influenced by the work of one of Sorel's disciples, Vilfredo Pareto, especially his *Treatise of General Sociology* (1916). He accepted Marx's fundamental idea of class struggle, but rejected the idea that a victory for socialism and the proletariat would produce a classless society—merely a new governing elite. By elite he meant people of notable intelligence, character, skill, or capacity. And because he believed that mankind in general—the inferior people—is irrational, it must be governed by superior people, either by force or by cunning. He seems to have favored force as the better outward sign of strength; and he argued that an elite lost its mandate to govern only when it lost the willingness to use force to obtain what was rightly its own. A new elite, constantly generating among the inferiors, would then seize power. As Mussolini would recast the idea, "The Fascist State is a will to power and to government."

There followed several decades of bullying and blustering at home and abroad out of which a revived Roman Empire was presumably to emerge. Mussolini's heroics, however, always smacked of thuggee, and the suspicion remains that he always picked on the weak. In 1923, for example, the Italian member of an international commission investigating a Greco-Albanian border dispute was murdered. Mussolini assumed that the assassin had been Greek and ordered the bombardment and occupation of Corfu, demanding a large indemnity as the price for withdrawal. Greece appealed the matter to the League of Nations, where it was thought that the dispute ought to be referred to the World Court in the Hague. Whereupon the western powers, fearful of destroying Italian loyalty to the League, advised the Greeks to pay the indemnity. It was a black day for the integrity of the League. We have already noted Mussolini's quarrel with Yugoslavia over Fiume, settled in favor of Italy in 1924 because of Yugoslav weakness.

On the home front, Mussolini sought to stimulate economic productivity, first by reducing taxation made possible by rigorous government economies—though he did raise the income tax rates. Public works were launched to provide work for the unemployed, and both strikes and lockouts were made illegal, which became a permanent feature of what Mussolini called the "corporate state." He originally took office with a coalition government, but as his paramilitary groups had become a militia paid by the State, he could more easily intimidate and purge the opposition. His old associates, the socialists and communists, were the first to feel his venom, and in 1923 he pressured Parliament into passing an electoral law giving the political party with a plurality of votes two-thirds of the seats in Parliament. With twenty opposition parties to split the vote, the elections of 1924 gave the Fascists their two-thirds majority. Thereafter, the terror and censorship were more blatant, and parliamentary life was a farce. By 1928, all candidates for public office had to be approved by the Fascist party. Since all party officials were appointed rather than elected, all vestiges of democracy had been destroyed, and an "elite" held power.

Mussolini's dictatorship clearly represented the interests of the Right, yet the basic ideas for his "corporate state" came from the extreme Left—as he had—and more particularly from that part of the nineteenth-century labor movement called syndicalism. The phenomenon is hardly trivial since it contributed to the similarity of Leftist and Rightist dictatorships after 1918, led by men who accepted violence as the solution to social and international problems, and who generally began political life on the extreme Left imbued with ideas that we may loosely call "Sorelian." In the case of Fascist Italy, where independent labor and management associations were illegal, syndicates were organized within each industry to which both employers and employees belonged. All disputes had to be settled within the syndicate, and no strikes were allowed—hardly a Leftist ideal. Syndicates were also created for the professions and the trades, and the officials who directed the syndicates had to be Fascist party members. The system subjected the entire economic life of the country to the State. It eliminated much strife, and economic recovery and material progress did result. All it cost was political and personal liberty.

2. The Third Reich

While Germany seemed to follow Italy into fascism, the German situation after 1918, because it was more complex than the Italian, has been the subject of greater controversy. The debate has focused first upon the sincerity of German support for a parliamentary republic (the Weimar Republic) and ultimately upon the reasons for abandoning that republic. As late as 1928, the moderate political parties committed to making parliamentary government work heavily out-polled the extremist parties that were not devoted to the constitution. Moreover, the Weimar Republic weathered several armed attacks, crushing the Left-wing Spartacists in 1919 who favored close ties with the Russian Bolsheviks, and breaking the back of the Kapp Putsch in 1920, a Right-wing attempt to restore the monarchy. On the other hand, no single moderate party ever achieved a majority that might have given parliamentary government vigorous direction, so that parliamentary government never seemed to function satisfactorily. The inherent weakness of coalition government was ominously revealed when the moderates needed Right-wing support to control the Spartacists in 1919 and Left-wing support to contain the monarchists in 1920.

Several myths were abroad in the 1920's that clearly compromised popular loyalty to the republic. The first was that Germany had surrendered in 1918 on the basis of Wilson's Fourteen Points and had then been betrayed by the victors; and the second was that the republic had betrayed Germany by accepting the terms presented at Versailles. In fact, the surrender had been unconditional beyond the actual armistice terms, and the real military collapse meant that *any* German government would have had no choice but to accept whatever terms were offered. When we see the popular drift toward Hitler's National Socialists (or Nazis) after 1928, a party whose platform rested upon those myths, we must wonder whether the initial popular loyalty to the republic was genuine or an expedient.

In the matter of reparations, no German political party was convinced that Germany could pay the sum demanded, an attitude that weakened the national resolve to pay. Most Right-wingers were openly obstructionist on the issue, arguing that Germany should resist the "unjust" demands for payment. Many moderates, however, favored paying what was possible while working for a reduction in the amount due. When the western countries found themselves unable to relax their demands, the Weimar Republic sought political and economic ties with the Soviet Union in 1922 as a way of exerting pressure upon the Allies. Their agreement at Rapallo not only threatened the integrity of the new Poland, but was the first signal that Germany meant to evade the responsibilities agreed to at Versailles.

Out of the subsequent Allied occupation of the Ruhr region in 1923 came passive resistence encouraged by the government, and the loss of productivity—the final contributions to runaway inflation. Even though all the nations concerned then came to recognize that new reparations arrangements would have to be made which would provide opportunity for German economic recovery, the shock of those dreadful days of economic chaos left an immense residue of bitterness to feed the popular notion that the Germans had been repeatedly betrayed. Moderate, parliamentary government did not survive the next crisis to afflict the Germans, and the drift to extremism came after the stock market crash of 1929 in the United States, which triggered a general economic crisis.

The primary cause of that crash—if not the only cause—was an overexpansion of credit. Public interest in the stock market greatly increased during the 1920's, and many of the purchases by both large and small buyers were on margin. That is, the investor put up only a fraction of the purchase price for stocks, the broker advancing the rest by borrowing from banks. Perhaps as much as ninety percent of the transactions were speculatory rather than permanent investments. This speculation forced prices (and profits) to a point in 1929 where they had no real relation to wages. When the inevitable break in the market came, investors rushed to sell their holdings, merely fueling the collapse. Because the world economy was still highly integrated, the American disaster soon had international repercussions, especially critical because of the unresolved war debts and reparations.

The economic chaos that ensued not only drove European governments to permanent economic planning, as we have noted earlier, but proved to be fatal to the idea of a single world economy. London's traditional financial monopoly gave way to rival financial centers like New York, just as the world economy was replaced by many national economies. The high protectionist duties of our Hawley-Smoot Act of 1930, consistent in spirit with our policy of debt repayment though hardly conducive to making payment possible, provoked retaliatory trade measures elsewhere. Many countries found high tariffs alone insufficient to promote their economic nationalism and imposed rigid import-export quotas. Still, unemployment figures continued to rise, reaching about three million in Great Britain by 1932 and between six and seven million in Germany.

The hardships endured by German business and labor were at once reflected in the rising strength of extremist political parties on both Right and Left. In 1930, Chancellor Brüning, a member of the moderate Centrist (Catholic) party whose personal conservatism and economic orthodoxy made him fear the Left more than the Right, took office. He called for new parliamentary elections, hoping to appeal to the nation to rally to the parties known to support the republic. As earlier in Italy, the moderate parties failed to join forces to face the challenge of extremism; and when the elections enabled the Communists to increase their seats from 54 to 77, and the Nazis from 12 to 107, Brüning declared the state of emergency that entitled him to suspend constitutional rights and to govern by decree.

This drift toward authoritarianism that culminated in the appointment of Hitler as chancellor in January of 1933 featured intense jockeying for power among ultra-conservative factions and personalities. The military and the old aristocrats believed that they could regain control of national affairs in coalition with Hitler's Nazis, as social distinction divided them more than political principle; whereas the Nazis saw such a coalition as a mere step to power. By 1932 the Nazis had become the largest of the Right-wing parties, and they had recruited a party police, the storm troopers, to bully the opposition. Even so, the decision to allow Hitler to become chancellor was a strategem of the Papen faction to outmaneuver the Schleicher faction. The cabinet contained only two other Nazis; the rest were true conservatives who could guard against the Rightist radicalism the Nazis represented; and Papen himself was vice-chancellor.

Since the Nazis were not a majority party when Hitler assumed office, he called new parliamentary elections, preparing for them with a frenzied campaign against Communists. His strength only rose to forty-four percent of the vote, but with the aid of the monarchical Nationalist party, he had the votes in parliament to have himself given dictatorial powers; and after he expelled the Communist members, his majority was absolute. The symbols of the Weimar Republic were at once replaced with the symbols of the Nazi party, including the national flag, and the state was renamed the Third Reich. Since no one could mistake what Hitler stood for, his rise to power depended upon widespread popular enthusiasm for his views (witness forty-four percent of the vote) and not simply upon the intrigues of Right-wing politicians whose plans went awry. Such politicians, it is true, particularly agreed with Hitler on the goals for German foreign policy. But much of the Nazi vote had come from middle-class people whose judgment had been warped by economic distress, not to speak of university students who saw in Hitler the opportunity to attack the entire social order and to bring about a future in which they would presumably have a greater part. Hitler's radicalism, however, had failed to attract industrial workers, who adhered to the traditional Left-wing parties.

In moving quickly to consolidate his position, Hitler recognized that his most imminent danger lay in those conservatives whom he had outmaneuvered in achieving dictatorial powers. In June of 1933, his storm troopers carried out a brutal purge of nearly a thousand Rightists to prevent a new coalition against him. Meanwhile, he established a Ministry of Propaganda and Enlightenment, acting on his belief that the masses are moved not by intelligence but by inflaming their irrational prejudices. Official propaganda not only hammered away on the old themes of betrayal at Versailles and the subsequent republican duplicity, but

ADOLF HITLER (Radio Times Hulton Picture Library).

introduced a new party line arguing for the superiority of the German race and nation and warning against the national danger which the presence of Jews presumably constituted.

In the campaign to purify Germany, the police were given orders to shoot Communists on sight; but in introducing the official harassment of Jews, Hitler was implementing the Nazi race theory which came close to being the only "intellectual" justification the regime found. Like the racists of the late nineteenth century, the Nazis believed that race is the prime determinant in society. The party line held that pure Aryans (which meant Nordic people) are inherently superior and are biologically destined to rule over Slavs, Latins, Negroes, and Jews; and that Jews in particular contaminate a society. Hitler began by dismissing "non-Aryans" from official, military, and professional posts in 1933, a non-Aryan being defined legally to include anyone with one Jewish grandparent or Aryans who married non-Aryans. The government incited mobs to attack Jews and their property; in 1935 they were deprived of citizenship, and many of them were put in concentration camps. Other Germans who objected to this inhumanity or who objected to the intellectual absurdities upon which the racial policies rested were themselves liable to confinement. The sad fact was that German culture fell into the hands of the government censors and propagandists, so that the purpose of all learning and the arts came to be the support and the glorification of the State. The educational system, too, was soon geared to prepare the young for nothing but service to the State and to wish for nothing but total subservience to the State. And that State was in the hands of Hitler and his party cohorts, who called themselves an elite, but whose social or intellectual credentials for such a claim were entirely invisible—men who were not so much indifferent to, as ignorant of, the morality and law that make society possible.

This totality of State control was extended to the national economy. In that era when most European governments experimented with economic planning and with limited economic controls, Nazi Germany devised extensive economic planning. The goal was to provide the means for war. Private enterprise still existed, but the State attempted to regulate production and distribution, banking, investment, and trade, not to speak of manpower. The high degree of coordination within German business and industry that had been developing for several decades before 1933 facilitated the Nazi economic policy, as the great cartels could be used as agencies to promote government designs, a fact which rallied many industrialists to the Nazi cause. Hitler also sponsored a public works program to eliminate the grievous unemployment, though by 1938 his rearmament program had created a virtual war economy that itself guaranteed full employment.

Control of foreign trade had initially been introduced in 1931 to stop the flight of capital, but in 1934 the Nazi's introduced their New Plan which was designed to reduce imports and to force the use of substitute products that could be made in Germany. Toward that end, importers had to hold balances in special marks rather than in freely convertible currency, and the government limited export commodities to items of nonstrategic value. This New Plan aimed at once at autarky—economic self-sufficiency—and at blatant trade discrimination; and it could only have succeeded in that day of international business recession. In any case, what the Germans attempted in the 1930's amounted to a reversal of the tendency toward economic specialization that had characterized the world economy in the nineteenth century. The practice of autarky was both a preparation for war and a deliberate looting of struggling foreign economies.

3.   The Soviet Union

Whereas Italy and Germany were governed democratically for brief periods after 1918, democracy in the Soviet Union was a sham from the outset. Lenin's constitution of 1918 did provide for a national parliament, the All-Union Congress, but it met only once every two years, mainly to ratify the work of the cabinet—known as the Council of People's Commissars. Moreover, the voting system was highly complex, indirect, and discriminated against the rural population. Entire groups of people believed to be sympathetic to pre-Bolshevik regimes were simply disenfranchised. The Communist party was the only legal party, and it comprised a bare one percent of the population, an elite which in theory submitted absolutely to party discipline. At first the party had its own tribunal, the *Cheka,* which tried political opponents before executing them. But in 1922, the Cheka was abolished and its function was assumed by the OGPU, a division of the national police; the transfer illustrated the fact that the party and the State were identical.

Because Lenin's leadership of the Russian Revolution was cut short when he suffered a stroke in 1922, a struggle for power began at once even though Lenin survived into 1924. His favored successor was his long-time associate, Trotsky, an intellectual and the man credited with building the Red Army which had triumphed in the Civil War. His chief rival, Stalin, was regarded by Lenin as a man so utterly ruthless that his leadership could jeopardize the integrity of the revolution. Yet, Stalin, then secretary-general of the party, ultimately gained the ascendancy, partly because his control of the party machinery proved to be the most powerful position in Russia, and partly because a majority of the Bolshevik leaders feared his intellectual mediocrity less than they did Trotsky's brilliance.

As their rivalry intensified during the 1920's, Stalin and Trotsky became identified with different revolutionary programs. Trotsky, sticking closely to the Leninist line, continued to see Russia as the generator of international revolution. Stalin, seeing the failure of Marxist parties elsewhere by 1923, argued for Russian isolationism, and for building Russia into a strong socialist state capable of resisting attack from the capitalist nations if that should come. Though most of the Bolsheviks rallied to Stalin's party line, he knew that many of them had been reluctant to abandon the dream of world revolution, leading him to declare the Trotskyite position as anti-revolutionary and subversive. Trotsky and his friends were expelled from the party in 1927, and he from Russia two years later.

With the question of leadership settled, Stalin could turn to the economic reorganization of the country—to the construction of a totally planned economy. The first Five Year Plan (1928) was designed to transform an underdeveloped country into an industrial state without depending upon either foreign or domestic private investors. Toward that end, the government decided upon the collectivization of Russian agriculture as the quickest way to modernize it and to produce the agricultural surpluses necessary to free manpower for industrial labor. What is more, collectivization struck at the heart of a serious source of opposition to the regime—the wealthier peasants (or *kulaks*) who had resented the food rationing and price-fixing that had made agriculture relatively unremunerative. During the 1920's, the resentful kulaks had often limited their production to their own needs, refusing to deliver food to the cities.

The kulaks resisted collectivization even more vigorously, destroying farm animals and equipment, until Stalin virtually declared war upon them as a class. Some two million of them, who survived a campaign of terror, ended in forced labor camps in remote areas of the Soviet Union. Not until collectivization was completed in 1931 could the State claim that private enterprise had been destroyed, with the State capturing the entire economic system. No doubt the very vastness of Russia and her economy enhanced the possibility of economic isolation, which was the counterpart of Stalin's political isolation. The government limited imports to materials vital for the developing industry, and the volume of foreign trade remained low. The standard of living also remained low as the government concentrated on heavy industry, upon mechanizing agriculture, and upon military preparations. Emphasis on consumer goods would have to wait. A second Five Year Plan was inaugurated in 1933, a period which saw Russia emerge as an industrial nation.

Stalin granted a new constitution in 1936 which was heralded at home and abroad as a great advance in democracy and personal liberty.

It provided for a bicameral parliament, one house to represent the many nationalities in the Soviet Union, the other house to be elected directly by the people. Not only did the continuation of one-party government reveal the reform to be mere window-dressing, but it came at a moment when Stalin was engaged in a vast paroxysm of terror designed to consolidate his absolute authority. Beginning in 1935, he carried out a systematic purge of the party hierarchy, including many of the "old Bolsheviks" suspected of enjoying prestige or popularity. Some of the most prominent were induced to confess their betrayal of the revolution in trials whose evident aim was to influence world opinion. No doubt there had been criticism of Stalin's abandonment of world revolution, of his harsh treatment of the kulaks, and of his unwillingness to provide more consumer goods; just as he no doubt believed that the rearmament of Germany under the Nazis was a serious military threat to Russia and required greater unity to meet the danger. But the very savagery of Stalin's purges, which only ended in 1938, revealed a pathological distrust of those around him. It is hardly a matter of idle curiosity that the two men—Hitler and Stalin—whose personal regimes required the death of countless millions, were both evidently victims of paranoia. We shall probably never know how many innocent millions Stalin sent to death or to labor camps, for the purges reached far beyond the party hierarchy in almost total disregard for human life.

4.   Fascist Spain

Democracy also failed in Spain in the 1930's, but the particular brand of fascism that emerged was really a variant of ancient political traditions in Spain. Spanish national unity had been born of a late-medieval crusade led by the Christian monarchy against the Moslem Moors, the memory of which kept many Spaniards traditionally loyal to the monarchy, the army, and the Church. Yet, the brilliant successes enjoyed by these foundational institutions well into the sixteenth century were much rarer thereafter, for Spain lacked the economic resources to compete successfully with the other Atlantic states. Her response was to turn inward in defense of her traditional institutions—to reject innovations bred north of the Pyrennees. The loss of her Latin American empire not only contributed to her isolation, but dealt a serious blow to the prestige of the traditional triumvirate governing Spain. In the nineteenth century, therefore, the monarchy faced increasing demands to decentralize the nation, particularly from the Basques and the Catalans; the army could no longer justify its claim on a major slice of the national budget; the Church was so conservative that it was occasionally chided by Rome; and those Spaniards wanting to stem the national decline by bringing Spain into the ranks of the progressive countries began to toy with liberal and radical ideas coming from outside, notably anarchism. Military defeat by the United States in 1898 was a humiliating blow, and when the army could not even contain an uprising in Morocco in 1931, the anti-monarchical forces were finally able to win the national elections and force the abdication of the monarch, Alphonso XIII.

Unfortunately for the new Spanish Republic, its supporters were divided into nine political parties, ranging from liberal to anarchist, making coalition government necessary. In the short history of the republic, no cabinet ever enjoyed the backing of a parliamentary majority in the hands of one party. This inherent instability was all the more threatening as only fourteen of the 470 delegates elected to the Constituent Convention had had previous parliamentary experience. Grasping for the few issues upon which all republicans could agree, they fell upon anti-clerical and anti-military legislation. The army was substantially reduced in size, many superfluous officers being retired on full pay; clerical control of education was sharply reduced, and the State confiscated all ecclesiastical property.

Such extreme measures served to rally the traditional factions to attempt a comeback, but in the 1930's they saw in fascism the ingredients for a Right-wing dictatorship likely to be more effective than a restored monarchy. Thus the Spanish fascist movement, calling itself the Falange, took the anti-communist line common to fascist parties elsewhere and declared itself opposed to the republic on the grounds that the republic was communist-ridden. While there can be no doubt that the communists, as one of the republican parties, did make trouble for the more moderate republicans, the poverty of the Falangist charge was revealed in the elections of 1936, when the communists won only two and one-half percent of the parliamentary seats.

The actual attempt to overthrow the republic began as a military coup in Morocco, and rebel officers quickly seized control in portions of south, west, and northwest Spain; but the coup failed as much of the southwest, the north, and the heart of Spain remained loyal. Thus, the country plunged into civil war, with the rebel government establishing itself at Burgos, and General Franco emerging as the rebel chief. Both sides appealed for foreign aid—the rebels to Germany and Italy, the republic to France and the Soviet Union. Hitler responded with transport planes (especially needed to bring troops from Morocco, since the Spanish Navy remained loyal to the government) and later with new military aircraft. Mussolini sent troops, ultimately 40,000 supported by tanks, though their performance was unimpressive.

Russian aid to the republic, through the Mediterranean, was limited by the presence of German and Italian submarines. But Soviet aid compromised the noncommunist majority in the Spanish government, who were continually hampered by radical uprisings in the rear. To have refused the nominal cooperation of the radical parties would have been to write off Soviet aid. Therefore, the government would have greatly preferred its military assistance to come from the western democracies for both logistical and political reasons. Léon Blum, the socialist prime minister of France in 1936, favored giving such assistance—so great was his horror of European fascism—but that critical aid never came. The wonder is that the Spanish army, with substantial foreign aid, took three years to destroy the republic. Madrid, bitterly defended by its citizens, fell only in 1939, at a moment when the communists were making a last bid to seize control of the republic.

Many in the civil war died anonymously. Casualties from both battles and purges probably cost over a million lives. The Franco regime, posing as a regency to prepare for a Bourbon restoration, was in fact a corporate state modeled on Mussolini's Italy. The international aspects of Franco's victory, however, revealed the true decay of western nerve when faced with the responsibility to maintain the settlement of 1919. The western policies of nonintervention in Spain were ostensibly based on a pathetic hope that they would induce the fascist powers to cut off support to Franco and upon the fear that general intervention could lead to general war. On the other hand, the evil that the totalitarian states represented by the 1930's, whether Rightist or Leftist, was so transparent and so menacing to the remaining bastions of human liberty and decency, that western failure to save a moderate republic in fact reflected a moral crisis in western society.

It is no doubt true that western resolve was handicapped by the very fact that the danger appeared simultaneously from the extreme Left and

Right. To some, neutrality seemed to be the moral alternative to an alignment with any totalitarian regime. Yet, a great body of western opinion had been so antagonized by the foreign and domestic policies of the Bolsheviks after 1917 that there remained a genuine reluctance to aid any regime that accepted communist support as the Spanish Republic had, which became a tendency to tolerate any regime that was avowedly anti-communist. But the failure of the western democracies to act in their own interest in Spain primarily revealed the disenchantment which they, the victors in 1918, felt about the peace that had crowned a victory won at such terrible cost.

From the outset there had been no Allied agreement as to the proper treatment of defeated Germany. The British and Americans, in particular, tending to suffer from bad consciences about the harsh settlement, were susceptible to German complaints and inclined to overlook treaty violations—to the intense distress of the French. The meager fruits of victory taught an entire generation the virtues of pacifism, a public attitude that enfeebled every western government when forced to face the teeth of militant totalitarianism. This weakness, when coupled with the collapse of democratic governments on all sides, made many in the West question the vitality and future of democracy—in the very countries that in the nineteenth century had been the hope of all peoples seeking freedom. The disillusionment reached its apex in France, where the sense of betrayal by her wartime allies was a contributing factor.

THE CRISIS OF THE 1930's

1.   French Disunity

French economic recovery in the 1920's had been remarkable and had been accompanied by administrative and tax reforms which ought to have produced a sense of confidence and security. French uneasiness, however, was not solely rooted in the decay of the wartime alliances, but in an awareness of a declining population and in the dislocation of many people as France experienced a new thrust of industrialization. The demographic crisis reached its peak in 1935, when the number of deaths exceeded the number of births. If the loss of young men in the war was the direct cause, France had long experienced a declining birthrate, sharpening the sense of a loss in vitality.

The postwar industrialization gave France a more balanced economy than she had had in the nineteenth century, and her resulting stability made her the last major European country to be affected seriously by the stock market crash of 1929. As in the case of Germany, however, that collapse ultimately brought economic depression and unemployment, causing the industrial workers in particular to demand social legislation. The Rightist parties regarded such Left-wing demands as the probable beginning of a Bolshevik revolution, so that by 1932 a national crisis was brewing. Coalitions of Leftist parties controlled the governments at that point, but the cabinets were never stable given party differences as to the degree of nationalization of business and industry necessary to meet the economic crisis. And the multi-party system contributed to the difficulty of getting tax increases and other anti-inflationary measures through parliament.

The result was near paralysis, a rapid succession of "caretaker" cabinets, which not only undermined public confidence in democratic procedures, but encouraged the revival of all those elements in French society that had been hostile to the republican form of government after 1870. This internal disunity contributed to a weak foreign policy when it came to facing the menace of Hitler and Mussolini, further convincing some Rightists that only a fascist-style regime in France could cope with both internal and external pressures. The so-called Popular Front, a new coalition of Leftist parties formed in 1936 under Blum, did save the democratic republic from that Rightist solution; but by then the national weakness had been revealed to those who wished the destruction of the Versailles settlement.

Meanwhile, uncertain of British and American support, the French had been trying to bolster that settlement through alliances in 1934 with Czechoslovakia, Yugoslavia, and Romania, a system known as the Little Entente, and ultimately with the Soviet Union in 1935. The military value of such alliances for French security, however, was doubtful, while the tie with the Soviet Union served to heighten Rightist suspicions. As Blum discovered in 1936, no firm commitment to the cause of republican Spain was politically possible, however necessary it may have been for French integrity and security.

2. Economic Depression in Britain

Disenchantment with victory overcame the British even earlier than the French, principally because Britain did not enjoy the economic recovery experienced by the French in the 1920's. At the root of the problem was Britain's traditional preeminence in industry. Whereas the French had to rebuild much of their industry after the war, the British resumed competition in the world market with an established industry that was outmoded and relatively inefficient compared to that of Germany, the United States, and Japan, late-comers to industrialization. During the dark years of sacrifice that culminated in victory, the public had come to anticipate a postwar Eden: prosperity and social reform. Instead, British export trade proved to be shockingly low in volume, and as production necessarily fell off, unemployment soared. Membership in the Labor party rose rapidly as a consequence, mainly at the expense of the old Liberals; and Labor formed its first government in 1923 under Ramsay MacDonald.

The Labor party, which had housed some pacifists during the war, also profitted from a postwar wave of pacifism, as many of the disillusioned came to believe that no victory could be worth its cost. Rapid postwar disarmament reflected both this pacifism and the need for government economy. Continued depression led to a strike in the coal industry in 1926, and thanks to the ineptitude of the leaders in government, labor, and industry, the coal strike expanded into a general strike that inflamed class tensions. The middle class tended to see the general strike as Bolshevik-type direct action, and thus as revolutionary and a rejection of traditional parliamentary procedures, often losing sight of the workers' genuine grievances. After the failure of the strike, the Labor party sought to educate, and recruit from, the middle class to reduce hostility and enhance understanding.

Therefore, faced with the global economic crisis after 1929, the British parties tended to close ranks and to cooperate in defense of the British system and way of life. Unemployment remained high right down to the outbreak of World War II, but only a few extremists suggested in the 1930's that the parliamentary democracy be scrapped in favor of an authoritarian regime. Though preserving internal unity better than did the French, the British domestic scene precluded rearmament even when the designs of the facist states became transparent, providing the foundation for a foreign policy even weaker than that of France.

3. The Years of Appeasement

The failure of the western powers to counter the fascist intervention in Spain was only one of several instances in the 1930's when the western powers showed themselves ready to pay any price necessary to avoid another war. Because general war eventually came despite their good intentions to avoid it and despite their willingness to appease those determined to revise the status quo, world opinion ultimately condemned western statesmen for not putting the brakes to the likes of Hitler and Mussolini before they became so arrogant in their power and so much more difficult to defeat. The criticism misses several key points: that it was proper to seek peace; that it was not wrong to employ diplomacy to settle issues; that democratic governments cannot long act in defiance of public opinion; that when public opinion leads to disarmament (as in Britain) or to support for a military establishment essentially defensive in character (as in France) or to feigned neutrality (as in Belgium), a statesman's latitude is constrained, and he has no convincing response to those who respect only force.

One can understand the roots of popular pacifism after World War I and sympathize with its motives, while lamenting the rising barbarism which cared not for people, much less for their peace. So the day came, as it must to all civilized men, when the menace had to be destroyed if civility were to endure. The fault of the statesmen of the 1930's was their failure, as cultivated men, to recognize the essential barbarism of the movements they faced and to treat them simply as national or territorial claims and interests, more or less justified, as is proper in normal foreign relations. To have perceived exactly what Hitler represented, which was hardly the national German interest, would have been to cry out in alarm for the immediate mobilization of the national resources in defense of both decency and the national interest.

The first act of aggression to be challenged weakly by the western powers in the 1930's was in fact committed by Japan in 1931. Using a minor incident in Manchuria as a pretext, the Japanese overran that Chinese province and established a puppet state called Manchukuo, accomplishing what they had failed to do at the turn of the century. China appealed to the League of Nations for assistance, but Japan ignored a League request for a negotiated settlement; and when the League formally condemned the Japanese aggression, the Japanese gave notice of intention to withdraw from the League. By 1935 Japan had pursued her invasion of North China, occupying three more provinces without any punitive response from either the League or the United States.

In 1935, Hitler made his initial challenge to the Versailles settlement by denouncing its disarmament clauses, an action that led directly to the Franco-Russian alliance, but which failed to provoke the military reaction Hitler feared. The British, in fact, seeing the Franco-Russian pact as a further example of unfairness to Germany's legitimate rights, actually encouraged German rearmament by concluding a naval agreement with Hitler that year. Though Hitler agreed to limit his navy to thirty-five percent of the tonnage of the British Commonwealth fleets, he clearly gained an enormous political victory.

Mussolini made his move in 1935, too, following an incident on the frontier between Ethiopia and Italian Somaliland. The Italians had had an eye on Ethiopia since the 1890's, and Mussolini boasted that he would accomplish its seizure. The League moved quickly to halt his aggression by voting to impose economic sanctions against Italy. But Britain and France, hoping to draw Mussolini into a common front against German military revival, connived to have coal and oil excluded from the commodities to be denied to Italy. No doubt Italy could have bought the oil from American producers in any case, but the western connivance in Mussolini's aggression only increased his contempt for democracy and his preference for Germany. The League's sanctions went unenforced while Ethiopia fell to Italian arms. When the League lifted the useless sanctions in 1937, Mussolini expressed his contempt by taking Italy out of the League. The collective security, presumably to be promoted by the League of Nations, was obviously nonexistent. By then, the Spanish Civil War was compounding the humiliation of the democratic states.

From then on the initiative belonged to Hitler. In 1936 he ordered the military reoccupation of the Rhineland—forbidden by the Versailles settlement—to which the western powers made no military response. To have acted to preserve the demilitarization of the Rhineland would no doubt have brought war with Germany, as Hitler's political future would have given him no choice but to fight. The crisis revealed especially the political and military vulnerability of France: A caretaker government was still in office; and the military establishment, designed solely for national defense and not for quick counterthrust, was poorly equipped for offensive warfare. The army, in fact, confessed its weakness. Many Rightists, angered by the recent alliance with the Soviet Union, openly favored strengthening Hitler as a bulwark against communism. Moreover, world opinion had gradually bought the German line that the Versailles settlement had been unjust and that Hitler was only rectifying a wrong. What the French revealed to Hitler, by not taking firm measures to safeguard their own frontiers in 1936, was the unlikelihood of their going to war on behalf of an ally.

The Versailles settlement had also forbidden the union *(Anschluss)* of Germany and Austria. In his own book, *Mein Kampf* (1923), Hitler revived pan-Germanism, claiming that Germans everywhere should be united into a greater Germany. He particularly desired the annexation of his native Austria. However many Austrians had been eager for *Anschluss* after 1918 as the solution to Austrian economic problems, the idea appealed considerably less after 1933. The Christian Socialist leadership in Austria sought closer association with Mussolini, expecting that Italy would not want a strong Germany on her northern frontier. But Mussolini's ultimate collaboration with Hitler not only isolated Austria, but commenced the slow erosion of Italy into a German satellite.

In 1938, after an unsuccessful attempt by the Austrian National Socialists (Nazis) to seize power, Hitler brought overwhelming pressure to bear on the Austrian government. Seeing no effective support from either Italy or the western powers, the Austrian government let itself be bullied out of office in favor of the local Nazis. *Anschluss* followed at once. Hitler then held a plebiscite to ask the Austrians if they approved union with Germany, and ninety-nine percent of the population dutifully accepted the accomplished fact. Germany thus acquired over six million new citizens.

Hitler next turned upon Czechoslovakia, where he had been encouraging the three million German minority, known as *Sudetens,* to enlarge upon alleged discrimination by the Czechs and to demand *Anschluss* with Germany. To have tried a bald annexation as in the case of Austria would have been risky, for unlike Austria the Czechs had strong defenses and alliances with France and Russia. The Germans knew they had the military power to reduce Czechoslovakia in 1938, but not the strength to resist simultaneously an Anglo-French invasion from the west. Poland, on the other hand, with an eye on Czech territory in case of partition and eager to appease Hitler, let it be known that she would not allow Russian troops to cross Polish territory to aid Czechoslovakia.

Even so, Hitler thought it best to try to gain his ends by negotiation, especially after Prime Minister Chamberlain of Britain claimed that one must work out crises with Hitler in good faith to prevent war. Daladier, then prime minister of France, saw the danger Germany posed more clearly than Chamberlain, but was constrained by the French army's lack of readiness for offensive warfare and felt that France could not risk a campaign without direct British support. Given Chamberlain's insistence on a negotiated settlement, the Sudetens stepped up their demands for *Anschluss*. The agony of the Czechs was complete when both Poland and Hungary also made territorial demands, and when the Slovaks were induced to demand autonomy.

On September 29, 1938, Hitler entertained Chamberlain, Daladier, and Mussolini at a conference in Munich, deliberately omitting the Russian who might have supported the western powers. Chamberlain, determined to save the peace, and having publicly said that "If we have to fight, it must be on larger issues than . . . a quarrel in a faraway country between people of whom we know nothing," did not even insist that the Czechs be allowed to send representatives. They were given no alternative but to surrender twenty-five percent of their territory and to grant Slovakian autonomy.

Chamberlain claimed that he had "won peace in our time," but when Hitler occupied the remainder of Czechoslovakia without resistance six months later, Chamberlain's faith in the integrity of the likes of Hitler was shattered. Daladier already knew that the British and French had abdicated as great powers by their refusal, or inability, to exercise their responsibilities at Munich. Russia subsequently made great political capital from her exclusion from Munich, claiming that she would have honored the collective responsibility to block Hitler. In fact, the Russians made no military preparations to aid Czechoslovakia and privately notified the Germans that the Sudeten issue did not concern the Soviet Union. But at least the Russians had no illusions about Hitler's ultimate intentions and were deliberately buying time.

Since 1933, the Soviets and Nazis had religiously denounced each other's ideologies and declared themselves to be mortal enemies. Moreover, Hitler had made no secret of his determination, once Germany had the military strength, to acquire what he called *Lebensraum* (living space) in Eastern Europe. Even so, Stalin had long recognized the actual community of Russo-German interests: Both powers were antagonistic to the post-World War I territorial settlements, and both knew that secret German rearmament in the Weimar period had been abetted by Russian connivance. In particular, both had in the partition of Poland the grounds for eventual agreement in Eastern Europe. By 1939, Russia had the choice of either working out closer ties with the Anglo-French to check German expansion in Eastern Europe or of approaching Hitler to work out an agreement for the division of Eastern Europe between them.

The military weakness of the West hardly recommended the first option, especially after Munich; the Russians knew only too well the long term western hostility to the Soviet system and doubted effective cooperation; and Stalin's proposal to occupy all of Eastern Europe from Finland to Turkey as the key to blocking Germany could hardly be conceded by the West when informed of the probable Russian terms. Thus, when Hitler turned his attention to Poland after the occupation of Czechoslovakia in 1938, Stalin took steps to implement his second alternative.

The Versailles settlement had given Poland territories in the west that included German-speaking people, and she had expanded to the east at the expense of the Soviet Union in the troubled years following the Russian Civil War. The treaty had also created the Free City of Danzig as an enclave, a city too German to be given to Poland. Polish nationalists nevertheless assumed that the city must eventually become theirs. Indeed, the architects of Polish foreign policy, banking on eternal Nazi-Soviet hostility, favored reaching a friendly understanding with Hitler as the basis for a greater Polish role in Eastern Europe. Consequently, they were considerably unsettled, at the end of 1938, when Hitler informed them that Danzig must become German; and in the ensuing months, they seemed slow to realize that Hitler's intentions included no room for Polish ambitions.

Meanwhile, the clear threat to Poland led the British and French governments to warn Hitler in the spring of 1939 that they would act to resist any attempt upon Polish independence. To this Hitler responded by acknowledging the repeated overtures from the Soviet Union. On August 23, 1939, a German-Soviet Pact was signed. Even though most of its terms remained secret, its implications came as a bombshell, for the Pact publicly announced that in case one of its signatories were to go to war, the other would remain neutral.

While the German-Soviet Pact enabled Hitler to launch an attack upon Poland, which he did in great confidence one week later, the Pact was an enormous diplomatic victory for Russia. It led to embroiling Hitler with Britain and France, who honored their pledge to Poland by declaring war on Germany, and bought the Soviet Union valuable months to prepare for the eventual collision with Hitler in Eastern Europe. It bought territory, too: The secret clauses provided for the partition of Poland, for Lithuania to become a German "sphere of influence," but for Finland, Latvia, and Estonia to come within the Russian sphere.

Evidently, Hitler presumed that his conquest of Poland, launched with no declaration of war, would be so swift that the western powers would reluctantly accept it as they had his prior annexations. By then, however, even Chamberlain had recognized that the world faced something quite different from the alleged German claims to rectify the "wrongs" of the Versailles settlement. As he put it, "We have a clear conscience, we have done all that any country could do to establish peace, but a situation in which no word given by Germany's ruler could be trusted, and no people or country could feel themselves safe, had become intolerable. . . . For it is evil things we shall be fighting against, brute force, bad faith, injustice, oppression, and persecution. But against them I am certain that right will prevail. And so the war, which the men of peace had said was intolerable, came in September of 1939.

WORLD WAR II

1. The Italy-German Offensives

For all its militant bluster, the Italian government had watched the approach of war in 1939 with considerable misgiving, rightly doubtful of Italy's ability to sustain a major conflict. Yet, Mussolini's feeble appraisal over the years of where true Italian interests lay had culminated in a formal alliance with Germany early in 1939 (the "Pact of Steel") and left Italy at the mercy of German foreign policy. Even so, Italy did not immediately honor her alliance after the Anglo-French declaration of war upon Germany, but adopted the "wait-and-see" tactics she followed in 1914. What she saw was encouraging. While the western allies found themselves unequipped to give Poland any direct help, the Germans turned upon the Poles the new tactics of *blitzkrieg* (lightning war). Aircraft, especially dive bombers, were used as artillery to break up enemy formations and to destroy communications; after which swiftly moving armored divisions took advantage of enemy confusion to range far behind enemy lines and to develop encircling movements that cut the enemy into isolated pockets. Air attacks were used simultaneously against the civilian population to increase confusion and demoralization.

The Poles, outnumbered, outgunned, and unprepared to cope with such methods, capitulated after twenty-seven days, and the campaign would have been even shorter had Warsaw not held out heroically when all else was lost. Russia, meanwhile, occupied the Polish and Baltic territories specified in the deal with Hitler, and approached the Finnish government with a proposal for an exchange of territory ostensibly to improve the defenses of Leningrad. Determined to do everything possible against the anticipated day of Russo-German conflict, the Russians attacked the Finns late in 1939 upon Finnish rejection of the proposal. Though the Russians made a poor military showing against the valiant Finnish defense, the Finns ultimately were obliged to make the territorial concessions in 1940. Inactive on the western front, the Anglo-French had been struggling to put together an expedition to aid the Finns. Hitler used the knowledge of these futile preparations as pretext to occupy both Denmark and Norway in early 1940, claiming that the Allies planned to use a Scandinavian route to attack his ally, Russia. This series of calamities forced Chamberlain from office, and his long-time critic, Winston Churchill, took the prime ministry.

Now powerfully based on the continent, Hitler suddenly broke the calm on the western front with an invasion of the Netherlands and Belgium on May 10, 1940. The tactics of blitzkrieg were again employed to produce paralysis and demoralization, now augmented by parachutists and subversives who seized vital centers of communication. A Dutch surrender came after five days. For years, the French had spent millions on their Maginot Line, a defensive work of undeniable strength extending along the northeastern frontier from Switzerland to Belgium; but it had never been extended to the sea for fear of weakening Belgium's resolve to resist a German attack. Consequently, the Anglo-French rushed troops into Belgium to help stem the German drive, only to be confronted by the unexpected capitulation of Leopold III on May 28. His surrender had the effect of isolating the Allied forces in Belgium, and their necessary retreat was blocked by a German breakthrough at Sedan that had completely bypassed—or outflanked—the Maginot Line.

Though the French fought a successful rearguard action that enabled the bulk of the British forces, nearly 340,000 men, to escape by sea through the port of Dunkirk, the magnitude of the defeat and the outflanking of the Maginot Line convinced the French military that the defense of France had become impossible and that an armistice must be sought. At that juncture, Mussolini deemed it prudent to begin an assault against the French southeastern frontier. After an agony of indecision, the French signed an armistice on June 22 which gave Germany all of northern France and the Atlantic coastal zone. General de Gaulle, who had opposed the armistice, flew to London to organize a Free French movement, and some of the units of the French navy joined his cause. Much of the navy remained loyal, however to the new French regime which established itself at Vichy in southern France under the leadership of Marshal Pétain. This regime, openly collaborationist with the victorious Germans, was no doubt supported by some who felt that defeated France had no alternative; but the regime brought to power men and factions who had long been antagonistic to the democratic Third Republic and whos aw in its defeat the opportunity to construct an authoritarian (and antisemitic) state.

The fall of France left Britain alone against the continent, almost as she had been in 1807. She had sacrificed much of her military equipment at Dunkirk in favor of rescuing her men, but she did have naval control of the Channel as a barrier to German invasion. But the Germans saw that if they destroyed the Royal Air Force, the British fleet would not dare to operate in the narrow confines of the Channel. German air attacks upon Britain began in July of 1940; but the British aircraft, though outnumbered, proved to be substantially superior to the German and were assisted in seeking their targets by a new device called radar. The German air losses over Britain became so costly that plans for an invasion had to be postponed. German bombing did, of course, hamper British industrial production, and submarines inflicted heavy losses on merchant shipping. At that point in 1940, President Roosevelt, convinced that a British defeat would be catastrophic for the United States, took the lead in getting help to the British despite his country's substantial isolationism. Roosevelt traded fifty overage destroyers for convoy duty to Britain for long leases on British bases in the Caribbean and Atlantic. Early in 1941, Roosevelt secured the Lend-Lease Act, which gave him authority to provide American help to any nation whose defense was vital to American security.

The Italians endeavored to contribute to knocking Britain out of the war in 1940 by taking aim at British positions in Egypt and the Near East, to be accomplished by an offensive eastward from the Italian colony of Libya and by the conquest of Greece. These campaigns were not

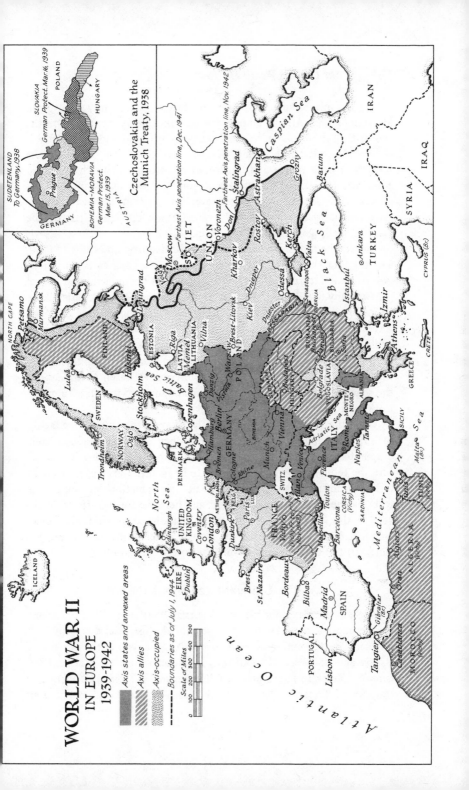

WORLD WAR II
IN EUROPE
1939-1942

Axis states and annexed areas
Axis allies
Axis-occupied
Boundaries as of July 1, 1944

Scale of Miles
0   100 200 300 400 500

Farthest Axis penetration line, Nov. 1942
Farthest Axis penetration line, Dec. 1941

Czechoslovakia and the Munich Treaty, 1938

SUDETENLAND
To Germany,1938

SLOVAKIA
German Protect. Mar.16, 1939

POLAND

HUNGARY

BOHEMIA-MORAVIA
German Protect.
Mar. 15,1939

Prague

GERMANY

AUSTRIA

ICELAND

NORTH CAPE
Petsamo
Murmansk

NORWAY
Trondheim
Oslo
Luleå
SWEDEN
Stockholm

FINLAND
Helsinki

Leningrad
Moscow

SOVIET UNION

Voronezh
Don
Rostov
Stalingrad
Astrakhan
Grozny
Batum

ESTONIA
Riga
LATVIA
Memel
LITHUANIA
Vilna

Baltic Sea

Kharkov
Dnieper
Kiev
Dniester
Odessa
BESSARABIA

Copenhagen
DENMARK
Danzig
Warsaw
Brest-Litovsk
Vistula

North Sea

UNITED KINGDOM
Edinburgh
Coventry
London
Dunkirk

EIRE
Dublin

NETHER.
BELG.
LUX.
Paris
Hamburg
Bremen
Cologne
Berlin
Rhine
GERMANY
BOHEMIA
Munich
Vienna
SWITZ.

POLAND
SLOVAKIA
HUNGARY
Budapest
RUMANIA
Bucharest
Danube
BULGARIA
Sofia
YUGOSLAVIA
Belgrade
ALBANIA

Black Sea
Sevastopol
Kerch
Yalta
Istanbul

TURKEY
Ankara
Izmir

IRAN

IRAQ

SYRIA

CYPRUS (Br.)

CRETE

GREECE
Athens

Brest
St.Nazaire
Bordeaux
FRANCE
Vichy (to Nov.1942)
Marseilles
Toulon

Milano
Venice
Florence
Rome
Naples
Taranto
ITALY
Adriatic Sea
Tyrrhenian Sea

MONTE-
NEGRO

SICILY

Malta (Br.)

Mediterranean Sea

CORSICA
(Vichy)
SARDINIA

Barcelona
Madrid
Bilbao
SPAIN
PORTUGAL
Lisbon

Gibraltar (Br.)
Tangier
Oran
Algiers
ALGERIA
(Vichy)
MOROCCO
(Vichy)
Casablanca
Tunis
TUNIS

Atlantic Ocean

only miserable failures, but gave the British opportunity to overrun Mussolini's East African empire and to inflict heavy damage upon the Italian fleet in the Mediterranean. On the other hand, though Hitler was furious at the Italian bungling, German troops were sent to bail out the Italians in both Africa and Greece, in the process of which he forced Romania, Hungary, and Slovakia to join the war against Britain and Greece; and German troops were even sent to Italy to bolster Mussolini's regime against popular criticism. Despite the Italian fiascos, the war was really going badly for Britain.

Indeed, the threat of increasing aid to Britain from the United States, and the fact that Britain began to have the resources to begin serious bombing of Germany in 1941 did suggest that the moment had arrived for Germany to risk an all-out assault upon Britain. Instead, Hitler chose to create a two-front war by invading the Soviet Union on June 22, 1941. Expecting no invasion from the Atlantic side, Hitler calculated that he could conquer Russia during the summer. Once he should have the great food-growing regions of the Soviet Union in hand, he could then easily finish off the British in the Afro-Mediterranean theater. Confidence in the scheme was so great that the Germans launched it with no preparations for a winter campaign in Russia.

When the Russians retreated swiftly to avoid the outflanking tactics of blitzkrieg and scorched the earth as they retired, Hitler's schedule evaporated; and the fundamental unsoundness of attacking Russia before the reduction of Britain proved to be fatal to Germany. She might inflict dreadful casualties upon the Russian population, but was unable to bring the Russian armies to bay, and her own forces suffered miserably in the Russian winter. Worse, supplies began reaching the Soviet Union from Britain and from the United States (under the Lend-Lease Act), most of them by way of the laborious Iranian route.

2.   The United States Enters the War

Japanese territorial ambitions on the Asian continent had been evident for decades, and in 1936 Japan promoted close relations with Nazi Germany in recognition of common goals to be won at the expense of Russia and the West. Consequently, the Russo-German Pact of 1939 came as a shock to Japan, but the following year she joined Germany and Italy in the Tripartite Pact, evidence that Japan had been assured of an ultimate German invasion of the Soviet Union. Since the Japanese had long seen their own plans in global terms, they logically came to see the increasing American commitment to Britain and Russia as aimed also at Japan in the long run, not simply at Germany and Italy. Moreover, American aid to the embattled European powers meant that American industries were being retooled for military production, and the signing of the Tripartite Pact in 1940 led the Roosevelt government to request funds for a "two-ocean" navy and to adopt for the first time universal military training in peacetime. The Japanese decided to strike before American mobilization could be completed.

Six months before the Japanese surprise attack upon our fleet based at Pearl Harbor (December 7, 1941), Japan extorted military control of Indo-China from the powerless Vichy French, thus obtaining an advanced base for an assault upon the Philippines, Hong Kong, and Malaya, which were struck the same day as the Japanese attack upon our Pacific islands. While the United States was recuperating from the initial blows, the Japanese achieved the surrender of Hong Kong, Singapore, the Dutch East Indies, and the Philippines; forced an alliance upon Thailand; and occupied Burma to cut off the chief western supply route to Nationalist China. The consequent loss of prestige by the old European colonial powers contributed to the early independence of the southeast Asian colonies in the postwar period.

The American declaration of war against Japan after the surprise attack brought Germany and Italy into the war against us under the terms of the Tripartite Pact, forcing the Roosevelt administration to meet the crisis with a global strategy. Given the strength of the Japanese position by 1942, Roosevelt's decision was to contain further Japanese expansion, while concentrating American energies to winning first in Europe where the enemy was overextended and already in some difficulty. The defeat of Japan would be the secondary goal. This European orientation, however logical, was controversial in this country, where many citizens had been resolutely turning their backs on Europe since 1919 and where resentment over the Japanese "sneak" attack was keen.

The strategy in the long run, of course, worked; yet, 1942 was a desperate year in Europe with Hitler dangerously close to accomplishing in Russia and the Mediterranean what he had failed to accomplish in 1941. Much of the continent was being mobilized for Nazi military requirements and forced to accept Nazi ideology as well, thus participating in what Hitler called the "final solution" to the Jewish question. From all parts of Europe Jews were shipped in cattle cars to concentration camps, where ultimately about six million of them met death after unspeakable suffering. Those who had early recognized the essential barbarism of the Nazi movement now had their proof; and whatever the dictates of military strategy, it was proper—and overdue—that we recognized what was our primary enemy. Soviet Russia's own record in the systematic liquidation of political opponents perhaps gave her no moral claim to be a champion of humanity, but there could no longer be any doubt that Britain must be saved and France and the Low Countries liberated if civilization were to endure. Toward that end, the Soviet Union was embraced as a valiant ally, and the long western antagonism to the Bolsheviks and their dictatorship was overlooked. This necessary but uncomfortable alliance was the price we paid for our withdrawal from postwar European affairs, and the immense Russian contribution to the final defeat of Hitler gave Russia an undeniable role in the peacemaking.

German failure to win in either Russia or North Africa in 1942 passed the initiative for the first time to the Allies. Anglo-French landings in Morocco and Algeria caught the Italo-German armies from the rear, ending the stalemate in Egypt. By May of 1943, the entire North African coast was in Allied hands, Italy lay open to invasion, and the Russians were regaining much territory in the Ukraine. In Asia, meanwhile, an Allied fleet had successfully defended Australia from Japanese invasion by repulsing the invasion fleet in the Coral Sea (May 7, 1942), and a month later a Japanese fleet approaching Midway Island was driven off with heavy losses. Such victories would have been impossible had the United States waited until Pearl Harbor to increase its naval strength.

Early in 1943, Roosevelt and Churchill met at Casablanca to plan the invasion of Europe, naming General Eisenhower as the supreme commander and announcing, as their war aims, an unconditional surrender by the enemy. They wanted no room for German equivocation as after 1918. Their decision to invade Italy rather than western Europe in the summer of 1943 has remained controversial, because the Italian campaign turned out to be more costly than was anticipated and was subsequently criticized as ill-advised. The western leaders were eager to mount an offensive against the continent at the earliest possible date to divert German pressure from the Russians, as the Germans had launched a new campaign in Russia that spring. The thoroughness of German defenses along the Atlantic coast would have required greater Allied preparation than the Italian invasion seemed to require, so that the decision to strike northward from Africa provided relief for the Soviet Union months before an invasion of the Channel coast could have.

An Allied invasion of Sicily began July 10, 1943, and its success within two weeks was so obvious that the Fascist Grand Council overthrew Mussolini in favor of Marshal Badoglio, who opened secret negotiations for peace. At the beginning of September, Allied troops crossed the Straits of Messina into southern Italy, and Badoglio was granted an armistice on the basis of unconditional surrender. The Germans, however, meant to make a fight of it, taking advantage of the rugged Italian terrain. They poured reinforcements into Italy, which were badly needed on the Russian front, but managed to delay the capture of Rome until the following summer. And they rescued Mussolini and established him as a Nazi puppet in northern Italy—the role he had unwittingly chosen even before the war by rejecting Anglo-French and Austrian overtures.

The assault upon the heavily defended Channel coast was finally launched on June 6, 1944. It required an overwhelming air cover, a massive fleet to provide fire against shore batteries, and enormous stockpiles of supplies in Britain in anticipation of serious initial losses. The most novel feature of the Normandy invasion was the creation of artificial ports for landing troops and supplies, done by sinking rows of ships and concrete caisons. Enemy communication lines were pounded from the air to impede strong counterattacks; but only when American armor broke through southward into Brittany, and then eastward toward the valley of the Seine, were the Allies firmly established on the continent.

In August, an American-Free French expedition from Italy and North Africa was landed on the Mediterranean coast between Nice and Marseilles to drive northward up the Rhone valley. Both Paris and Brussels were liberated before the summer's end, whereupon the Allies had to face the stubbornly held defenses of Germany itself. The German position became hopeless before the end of 1944. Russian troops had been moving westward into Estonia and Poland, and after the Ukraine was

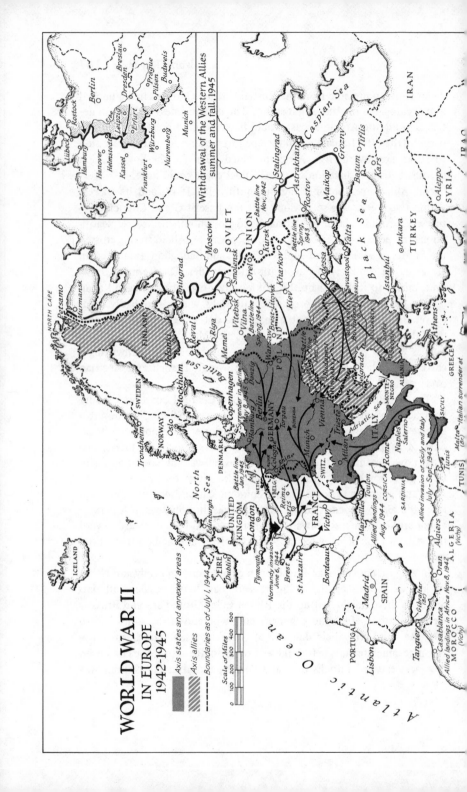

WORLD WAR II
IN EUROPE
1942-1945

Axis states and annexed areas

Axis allies

Boundaries as of July 1, 1944

Scale of Miles
0 100 200 300 400 500

Withdrawal of the Western Allies summer and fall, 1945

ICELAND

NORTH CAPE

Petsamo
Murmansk

Trondheim

NORWAY
Oslo

SWEDEN
Stockholm

FINLAND
Helsinki

Leningrad

Moscow

SOVIET UNION

Smolensk
Orel
Kursk
Battle line
Spring, 1943
Kharkov

Battle line
Nov. 1942

Stalingrad

Astrakhan

Rostov
Maikop

Grozny
Batum
Tiflis

Kars

Black Sea

TURKEY
Ankara

Istanbul

Yalta
Sevastopol
Odessa
Kiev

SYRIA
Aleppo

IRAQ

IRAN

Caspian Sea

Vitebsk
Vilna
Battle line
Spring, 1944
Warsaw
Brest-Litovsk
POLAND
Danzig
Battle line
Jan. 1945

Reval
Riga
Memel

Baltic Sea

Copenhagen
DENMARK

North Sea

UNITED KINGDOM
Edinburgh
London
Plymouth

EIRE
Dublin

Surrender in Berlin
May 8, 1945
Hamburg
Berlin
Torgau
GERMANY
Cologne
Rhine

NETH.
BELG.
Reims
Paris
FRANCE
Vichy

Brest
St Nazaire
Bordeaux

Normandy invasion
June 6, 1944

Munich
Vienna
BOHEMIA

SWITZ.
Milan
Trieste

Adriatic Sea

MONTE-NEGRO
Belgrade

GREECE
Athens

ITALY
Rome
Naples
Salerno

SARDINIA
CORSICA

SICILY

Allied invasion of Sicily and Italy
July – Sept. 1943

Marseilles
Toulon
Allied landings
Aug. 1944

SPAIN
Madrid

PORTUGAL
Lisbon

Tangier
Gibraltar
(Br.)
Casablanca

MOROCCO
(Vichy)
Oran
Algiers
ALGERIA
(Vichy)

TUNIS
TUNISIA

Malta
(Br.)

Italian surrender at

Allied landings in Africa Nov 8, 1942

Atlantic Ocean

Lübeck
Rostock
Berlin
Breslau
Hamburg
Hanover
Helmstedt
Leipzig
Dresden
Prague
Pilsen
Budweis
Kassel
Erfurt
Frankfurt
Würzburg
Nuremberg
Munich

recovered, the Russians swept into the Balkans and from there north-ward into Hungary. Only Nazi determination to continue fighting pre-vented an end to the war.

Nazi fanaticism in part rested upon a sure knowledge that the regime could not survive defeat, and the government had long since perfected the instruments of terror necessary to keep the population in the war. Moreover, Nazi propaganda had convinced many Germans that a Russian victory and occupation would be worse than the most appalling costs from continued fighting. But the Nazis also hoped that the presence of the Russians advancing through eastern Europe would awaken the historical western antagonism to the Soviet regime; and German propa-ganda pleaded for the western powers to join Germany in an anti-Bolshevik crusade. The Nazi line was especially clever, because it sought to exploit wartime troubles between Russia and her western allies. As early as 1938, the Russians had revealed their desire to dominate eastern Europe, and during the war they had pointedly refused to recognize governments-in-exile (notably the Polish) and had cooperated exclusively with resistance movements led by communists. To Allied complaints, the Russians sometimes hinted that the West connived at a Soviet defeat by failing to apply sufficient pressure upon Germany. The charge was unwarranted, but was widely believed in Left-wing circles in Europe af-ter the war. Through it all and despite the susceptibility of some Right-wing elements in the West to the German propaganda line, the alliance held firm on the common assumption that Hitler and his regime must be destroyed.

With the end in sight, Churchill, Roosevelt, and Stalin met at Yalta in the Crimea in February of 1945 to discuss plans for defeated Germany. They included an arrangement to divide Germany into four occupa-tional zones (British, French, Russian, and American) with a joint con-trol commission to be seated in Berlin, and an agreement to convene an international conference in San Francisco in April to draft a charter for a permanent international organization: the United Nations. The nego-tiators at Yalta also recognized the Russian right to reorganize eastern Europe, to which Churchill and Roosevelt really had no alternative unless they were prepared to drive the Russians from eastern Europe by force. And that would have been unthinkable given the popularity the Russians had gained during their desperate defense against invasion, not to speak of a war with Japan yet to be won. The historical reasons which had required the West to need, and to accept, Russia as an ally led to a peace settlement which could not ignore her interests, however little the West liked the price that had to be paid.

2.   1945: The End of World War II

By February of 1945, Anglo-American troops had crossed into Germany and quickly destroyed the formidable defenses on the left bank of the Rhine. Simultaneously, the Russians approached Berlin from the east and invaded Austria from Hungary, cutting off the German forces in northern Italy from the mother country; while Anglo-American forces inflicted heavy defeat on the enemy in the Po valley. Mussolini, fleeing to Switzerland, was caught by anti-Fascist guerillas, shot, and left hanging head-down in a Milanese square. The news of his death seems to have convinced Hitler that suicide was the preferable end. Russian and Western troops met at the Elbe river on April 26. Three days later the German forces in Italy capitulated, followed on April 30 by Hitler's suicide in besieged Berlin. But not before dictating his final diatribe against "international Jewry." "It is untrue," he stated, "that I or anybody else in Germany wanted war in 1939. It was wanted and provoked exclusively by those international statesmen who either were of Jewish origin or worked for Jewish interests. . . . Above all," his testament concluded, "I enjoin the government and the people to uphold the racial laws to the limit and to resist mercilessly the poisoner of all nations, international Jewry." Such was the quality of thought that led a great nation into chaos.

Hitler's death ended German resistance. The German military surrendered unconditionally to Eisenhower on May 7 at Rheims, and to Marshal Zhukov in Berlin the next day; and the four victorious powers assumed their respective occupational zones as delineated at Yalta. No doubt the end would have come more quickly had the United States not had the simultaneous task of containing Japanese expansion, something Russian critics of American efforts persistently ignored.

In fact, as American strength in the Pacific theater increased, the Japanese were forced to the defensive as early as 1943. American strategy produced an island-hopping campaign: isolated, small-scale, but murderous assaults upon Japanese-held garrisons designed to provide the Allies with bases for the ultimate invasion of the Philippines and

CHURCHILL, ROOSEVELT, and STALIN at Yalta, 1945 (Photo World).

Japan itself. A British-led Allied force began to drive the Japanese from Burma in 1943, eventually reopening the ground route to Nationalist China and likely saving India from Japanese invasion; but the Pacific remained the principal theater of the campaign against Japan.

General MacArthur's campaign to retake the Philippines opened late in 1944, while plans went forward to attack the island of Iwo Jima and Okinawa, so close to Japan that they would provide bases for intensive bombing of the home islands. Consequently, the Japanese defended the two islands with great tenacity, but the former fell in mid-March of 1945, Okinawa in June. The very bitterness with which the Japanese had defended their shrinking empire led to the inescapable conclusion that the home islands would be defended with fanaticism, and that the invasion of Japan could be successful only after terrible cost to both attackers and defenders. At Yalta, Stalin had promised to join his Western allies against Japan after a German surrender; but after May 8 he had made no move to do so, and the betting was that he would maintain a benevolent neutrality as long as possible to allow Russia to recover in Europe. The American decision to use atomic bombs to demonstrate to the Japanese the futility of resistance and to bring the war to an end as cheaply and quickly as possible became the last major, and most controversial, decision of the war.

At the time, some scientists participating in the development of the atomic bomb argued against its actual use on the grounds of its terrible destructiveness. The mere threat to use it should suffice to compel a hasty Japanese surrender. American political leaders, however, had little confidence that a mere threat would intimidate the Japanese military, especially when the details of the new weapon would be seemingly out of science fiction. Why not, then, stage an announced demonstration of the bomb's awesome power by exploding one near Japan but at an altitude that would spare the Japanese population? Here the flaw lay in American uncertainty as to whether the bomb would actually explode as advertised; a technical failure could convince the Japanese that we had been bluffing. An unannounced demonstration would have avoided that risk. But even a successful demonstration, unannounced or otherwise, might not have convinced the Japanese that we meant to use such a weapon, since the mere demonstration would have suggested our reluctance. Hence the painful decision to drop the bomb without warning on a Japanese target.

The initial bomb was dropped over Hiroshima on August 6, but it failed to provoke the expected offer to surrender—though it brought the Russians into the war against Japan out of fear of being denied a part in the East Asian peace settlement. On August 9, the second bomb was dropped on the naval base at Nagasaki; but even then the Japanese cabinet took six days to reach a decision to surrender unconditionally, perhaps the most astounding of the many evidences the Japanese gave during the war of their willingness to fight against great odds. The bombs cost approximately 130,000 fatalities and many thousands of wounded. From the immediate military point of view, therefore, since it had been feared that no Japanese surrender could be expected until an invading army had killed many times that number of Japanese, the decision to drop the bomb seemed wise.

The controversy, on the other hand, did not end with the Japanese surrender in August of 1945, but assumed new dimensions as the world awoke to the horrendous realization that mankind now possessed a weapon that could end life as we know it on this planet, either from direct bombing or from radiation poisoning that can alter genetic structure and produce incalculable mutations in future generations. In a world where colored peoples were everywhere rising to independence, the use of such a weapon against Japan, when it had not been used in Europe, was taken as proof of western disdain for the lives of non-Whites. The actual fact that the bomb was not available in time for use against Germany carried little weight in impassioned racial debate. The colored found it inconceivable that we would have used the bomb against Germans, an opinion that must be questioned in view of Allied saturation bombing of German cities and the fire-bombing of Dresden in particular.

The Japanese surrender left the United States in control of Japan and her island possessions. But the Russians, who had been at war with Japan only seven days, recovered the southern half of Sakhalin and won recognition of Outer Mongolia as their sphere of influence. It is surmised that had the western leaders at the time of Yalta known that they would soon possess an atomic weapon they would not have felt so great a need for Russian assistance and would have been able to stand firmer against Russian territorial ambitions in eastern Europe and Outer Mongolia. That probability led to later speculation that was less well-grounded—to the charge that the atomic bomb had been dropped primarily to impress and to warn the Soviet Union, not Japan. This ingenious line came to be cited in discussion about the origins of the "cold war" after 1945, but no evidence has ever been uncovered to suggest that the United States had by then formulated a policy to take advantage of our nuclear monopoly and to provoke a showdown with Russia. On the other hand, neither did the United States foresee how alarming that monopoly would appear to the Soviets. Awakening their historical distrust of the capitalist West, the Russians were the more determined to retain a protective screen of satellite states. The groundwork had been laid for another uneasy peace.

But the effects of Hiroshima far transcended international politics. Beginning after mid-nineteenth century, many Europeans within the literary culture had come to suspect that the technology born of science would lead to materialism and decadence, that the day would come when God would call a halt to man's insatiable quest for knowledge and new powers and close us down. The exhibition in 1945 of what science and technology could do seemed to such people evidence that scientific knowledge leads only to evil; or more pointedly, that evil is in knowledge and not in man. Should that notion become increasingly popular, as it steadily has since 1945, it could some day be reckoned as the most important product of the atomic bombardment of Japan. For it would be hard to generate an idea more inimical to civilization.

SUGGESTED READINGS

Birdsall, P. *Versailles Twenty Years After.* New York: Reynal, 1941.*

Cairns, John C. *France.* Englewood Cliffs, N.J.: Prentice-Hall, 1965.

Craig, Gordon A. *From Bismarck to Adenauer: Aspects of German Statecraft.* Johns Hopkins Press, 1958.

Curtiss, John S. *The Russian Revolutions of 1917.* Princeton, N.J.: Princeton University Press, 1957.

Eubank, Keith. *The Origins of World War II.* New York: Thomas Y. Crowell, 1969.

Feis, Herbert. *The Road to Pearl Harbor: The Coming of the War between the United States and Japan.* Princeton, N.J.: Princeton University Press, 1950.

Feis, Herbert. *Churchill, Roosevelt, Stalin: The War They Waged and the Peace They Sought.* Princeton, N.J.: Princeton University Press, 1957.

Finer, Herman. *Mussolini's Italy.* New York: Grosset & Dunlap, 1965.

Fischer, Fritz. *Germany's Aims in the First World War.* New York: Norton, 1967.

Fowlie, Wallace. *A Guide to Contemporary French Literature from Valéry to Sartre.* New York: Meridian Books, 1957.*

Gilbert, Felix. *The End of the European Era, 1890 to the Present.* New York: Norton, 1970.*

Greene, Nathanael. *From Versailles to Vichy, The Third French Republic 1919-1940.* New York: Thomas Y. Crowell, 1970.*

Holborn, Hajo. *The Political Collapse of Europe.* New York: Knopf, 1957.

Hughes, H. Stuart. *Consciousness and Society: The Reorientation of European Social Thought, 1890-1930.* New York: Knopf, 1958.

Jordan, W.M. *Great Britain, France, and the German Problem, 1918-1939.* Oxford: Oxford University Press, 1943.

Kennan, George F. *Soviet-American Relations, 1917-1920.* 2 vols. Princeton, N.J.: Princeton University Press, 1956-1958.

Mayer, Milton. *They Thought They Were Free.* Chicago: University of Chicago Press, 1955.*

Mosse, George L. *The Culture of Western Europe: The Nineteenth and Twentieth Centuries.* Chicago: Rand McNally, 1961.

Nolte, Ernst. *Three Faces of Fascism: Action Francaise, Italian Fascism, National Socialism.* New York: Holt, Rinehart & Winston, 1966.

*An asterisk indicates that a paperback edition is available.

Pipes, Richard. *The Formation of the Soviet Union: Communism and Nationalism, 1917-1923*. Cambridge, Mass.: Harvard University Press, 1954.

Remak, Joachim. *The Nazi Years, A Documentary History*. Englewood Cliffs, N.J.: Prentice Hall, 1969.*

Snell, John L. and others. *The Meaning of Yalta, Big Three Diplomacy and the New Balance of Power*. Baton Rouge: Louisiana State University Press, 1956.

Thomas, Hugh. *The Spanish Civil War*. New York: Harper, 1960.*

Thorne, Christopher. *The Approach of War 1938-39*. New York: St. Martin's, 1967.

Tillman, S.P. *Anglo-American Relations at the Paris Peace Conference of 1919*. Princeton, N.J.: Princeton University Press, 1961.

Treadgold, Donald W. *Twentieth Century Russia*. Chicago: University of Chicago Press, 1959.

Tucker, Robert C., and Cohen, Stephen F., eds. *The Great Purge Trial*. New York: Grosset & Dunlap, 1965.*

Walters, F.P. *A History of the League of Nations*. Oxford: Oxford University Press, 1960.

Weber, Eugen J. *The Action Francaise*. Stanford, Ca.: Stanford University Press, 1962.

Weinberg, Gerhard L. *Germany and the Soviet Union, 1939-1941*. Leyden: E.J. Brill, 1954.

PART IV

Epilogue:
Europe Since 1945

FROM HOT TO COLD WAR

1. The Idea of One World

Because the Second World War completed the devastation of Europe that was begun in 1914, the pivotal position of Europe in the world was gone by 1945. Gone, too, was the notion that the rest of the world was simply an extension of European ideas and power. At the same time that independence and uniqueness were being championed throughout the world, the global dimensions of the recent war had convinced many statesmen that most international problems could no longer be geographically confined, and that an international organization that was truly global in composition must emerge to guarantee the maintenance of peace. After 1918, the League of Nations had claimed to be a global association. In fact, it was Europe-centered and dominated. The two great powers who came to dominate the United Nations after 1945 were never members of the League. In contrast, the United Nations, with its capital in New York, with a Burmese secretary-general after 1962, has clearly been far more global and egalitarian than its predecessor.

On the other hand, the overwhelming military resources of the United States and the Soviet Union after 1945, especially after Russia acquired her own nuclear capability in 1949, had the effect of dividing the members of the United Nations into two partisan camps, jeopardizing the organizational effectiveness in maintaining the peace. Just as there had been localized wars between 1919 and 1939, so have there been numerous localized wars since 1945. Yet, the world has so far escaped a general conflict for a period longer than the interwar years, and if anything the prospects for such a conflict are fading rather than increasing. The final irony may be that the terrible weapons produced by science and technology have created a balance of terror more effective in producing restraint than the political institutions created for that purpose have been. Other reasons than terror have also made coexistence practical, for neither of the super-powers is nearly as dissatisfied with the status quo as major powers were on the eve of the two World Wars.

2. Political Reorganization of Europe

The uneasiness of the wartime alliance with Russia lived on to haunt the Western powers as they faced the reconstruction of Europe. On some issues there was general agreement: that Germany must be demilitarized, for example, and that her industrial production ought to be curbed in favor of agriculture to reduce her military capacity and give her a more balanced economy with a standard of living commensurate with that of her neighbors. All of the Allies agreed to be responsible for the denazification of Germany and to participate in an international court (at Nuremberg) to try the Nazi leaders, ten of whom were executed. Moreover, the fruits of the narrow economic nationalism after 1918 had convinced a whole generation that the problem of recovery was European in scope and that it must be approached realistically rather than with prejudice and hatred. And no doubt the economic plight of victor and vanquished was so similar in 1945 that it encouraged a spirit of cooperation.

Yet, for all the resolve to construct a happier world, the historical and ideological antagonisms that had divided Russia from the West since 1917 were exposed anew as soon as the common enemy was prostrate. Areas liberated by Anglo-American troops were generally reorganized politically to conform to the western ideals of political democracy. In eastern Europe, where Russia had been the liberator, single-party Communist dictatorships ostensibly representing "the people" were organized with Russian blessing. Resistance to this particular brand of democracy was particularly strong in Czechoslovakia, where Western-style democracy had prospered before the war, until it became necessary in 1948 to stage a Communist coup to establish the regime Russia demanded. The plight of the Czechs, who had been on the Western conscience since 1938, forced many westerners to the distasteful conclusion that the exigencies of politics had made them collaborators in the establishment of a Russian colonial empire in eastern Europe. Denazification meant different things to the wartime Allies. Whereas the Russians understood denazification as a mandate to eradicate "bourgeois capitalism" from their occupational zone in Germany, the three Western powers proceeded against individuals in their zones in a manner consistent with Western canons of justice. The inevitable slowness of such judicial procedures convinced the Russians that the West was insincere in its pledge to uproot Nazism, while the West saw the socialization of the Soviet zone as more Russian colonialism.

No one, however, expected that Europe ought simply to be returned to her prewar political or economic order. The weakness of parliamentary democracy in the 1930's when confronted with its mortal enemies precluded a return to that "normalcy," while the war years sharpened popular demand to democratize Western society further by reducing the power of the greatest of the capitalists through the nationalization of key industries and utilities. And those Europeans who had contributed to the horror of the war years by collaborating with the Nazis now felt the full wrath of those who had preferred resistance. In France, where the grievance settling reached its peak, 40,000 collaborators were tried and sentenced within the first year of liberation. Members of the Vichy regime all stood trial as collaborationists, old Marshal Pétain suffering imprisonment until his death.

Once the Allies had a chance to survey the German scene, they became aware that their initial design for the German economy would have to be modified; and the United States in particular soon recognized that the problem of European economic recovery would require an approach quite different from our posture of the 1920's. Warfare had traditionally devastated those rural areas where armies fought, but the novel nature of the total war in Europe between 1939 and 1945 means that she emerged with wholesale destruction of urban areas in particular; and large populations had been displaced by the Nazi practice of using conquered peoples as forced labor. The problem of resettling these displaced people was made even more difficult by the flight or expulsion of German minorities from eastern Europe at the end of the war—in all a gigantic refugee problem. (Restored Poland, having been forced to give up Polish territory to Russia in the east, was given a western frontier along the Oder and Neisse rivers at the expense of Germany.)

Just as the West was beginning to recognize that the enormous devastation and the large numbers of refugees in Germany would require an adjustment of Allied plans for German recovery, it became apparent that the Soviet Union had no intention of permitting the eventual reunification of Germany for fear that reunification would mean the collapse of the Communist regime being established in the Russian zone, not to speak of a united Germany again becoming a military threat. Consequently, when the Western occupational authorities concluded that they could only cope with the magnitude of the collapse in Germany by increasing their reliance upon German administrators and by encouraging a degree of industrialization not previously anticipated, the Russians interpreted the modification as a conspiracy to revive Germany as an anti-Soviet ally. The unwitting employment of men later revealed to be ex-Nazis seemed to give credence to the Russian charge. Relations between Russia and the West soon deteriorated to a point where there were really two Germanies, an East and a West, subject to two different political and economic policies.

The term "cold war" came to be applied to the postwar tension between Russia and the West. Each suspected the other of imperial ambitions, and each side took what it considered to be proper defensive measures that generally appeared to be offensive in nature to the other side. The American decision to halt Lend-Lease aid to Russia at the end of the war was perhaps logical, but it really reflected American disapproval of Russian plans for eastern Europe and our embarrassment at having had no option but to give the Russians a free hand. Thus, American action was seemingly unfriendly, especially in view of obvious

Russian need for economic assistance and her eagerness to accept it. When, in 1947, the United States announced the Marshall Plan to provide financial aid to implement European reconstruction plans, intending to provide aid to victors and vanquished alike, American generosity was rebuffed by the Russians, who also prevented their satellites in eastern Europe from accepting American aid.

Consequently, American aid went to the non-Communist countries alone, deepening the rift between East and West, a division that Churchill called the iron curtain. In 1948, the Russians showed their teeth by cutting off all land and water communications to Berlin, an enclave of Allied control within the Russian zone, evidently hoping to force the Western powers out of the city so that it could be integrated into the Russian zone. The West responded to the blockade by supplying the city by air for nearly a year until the Russians abandoned their campaign. In 1958, the Russians renewed the pressure by announcing that they meant to turn over their Berlin obligations to the puppet East German regime in the Soviet zone, a regime unrecognized by the West; and the iron curtain became a physical fact in 1961 when the Russians and East Germans built a wall of barbed wire and concrete to prevent the flight of East Berliners into the freer society of the West.

This tension between the Communist and non-Communist worlds in both Europe and Asia led to the formation of vast systems of alliance in which Russia and the United States were inevitably the senior partners. In Europe, these alliances were gradually consolidated into two major blocs, the Noth Atlantic Treaty Organization, or NATO (1949-1952), bringing northern, western, and southern Europe into alliance with the United States; and the Warsaw Pact (1955), which defined the relationship of Communist eastern Europe to the Soviet Union.

Meanwhile, Soviet Russia had turned her European bloc into something more far reaching than a military alliance. She meant not simply to aid recovery in eastern Europe, but to supervise and coordinate the economic efforts of the various Communist regimes: to promote the collectivization of agriculture, to stimulate industrialization, and to restrict trade as much as possible to countries within the eastern bloc. Toward that end, she stationed troops in eastern Europe to encourage cooperation—not to speak of secret police. While there can be little doubt that economic improvement did take place, this Russification of eastern Europe was particularly profitable for the Russians and grated upon nationalist sentiments in the satellites. It led, in 1948, to a break between Communist Yugoslavia and Moscow.

Fearing to foment a general war in the crisis, the Russians refrained from a military intervention, well aware that the Yugoslav regime enjoyed widespread support and would make a fight of it. After this President Tito of Yugoslavia charted an independent course, turning his country into a halfway house between East and West, where private and collective ownership coexisted. "Titoism" was such a tempting example in eastern Europe that Stalin determined to purge from Communist party leadership any eastern European politician thought to be enticed by the Yugoslav example. From the crisis, therefore, strong leaders emerged to dominate the various communist parties, all of them presumably loyal to Stalin. By the time Stalin died in 1953, he seemed to have achieved personal control, not only in the Soviet Union, but of a vast, integrated empire.

The West achieved in the postwar years a measure of integration, too, but never at the expense of national sovereignty or independence. Here the critical problem was West Germany. Having believed in 1945 that the demilitarization and deemphasis on industrialization was necessary, the Western Allies had been forced by the chaos in Germany to encourage more industrialization than planned—all while profoundly distrusting the former enemy. In addition, faced with the unpleasant reality of the cold war and a Soviet empire in the east, the West came to believe that it could not afford to sacrifice a German contribution to Western industrial and military strength. Indeed, the memory of Russo-German cooperation in the past was still sufficiently bitter to suggest the inadvisability of perpetuating German weakness to a point of driving the Germans to seek an accommodation with Russia. The West, therefore, and not without misgivings, accepted West Germany as an ally, but with provisions to prevent her from again seeking hegemony on the continent. Thus, the degree of economic integration ultimately achieved was partly political in motivation.

To begin with, the West German Federal Republic was given the responsibility for administering what had been the Western occupational zones in 1949, with the proviso that the West Germans must accept Allied control of German industrial development. This was guaranteed by the creation of the European Coal and Steel Community in 1951, an outgrowth of the French Schuman Plan to provide a transactional body to regulate the prices and the production of coal and steel. France, Belgium, the Netherlands, West Germany, Italy, and Luxembourg joined the community.

The second regulatory device was NATO itself, which created a joint military organization for its member nations. Any German rearmament in the future would be subject to NATO control. The treaty required the United States to maintain troops in Europe as a member state and committed us to maintaining Western security; and Eisenhower became the first supreme commander of NATO forces in 1950. The final step to integrate West Germany into the Western camp was taken in 1954 when the sovereignty of the Federal Republic was formally acknowledged, and West Germany joined NATO. France became reconciled to the concomitant German rearmament only because of a renewed British pledge to keep troops stationed on the continent.

Meanwhile, the European Coal and Steel Community began to function to such mutual satisfaction that its members envisioned new dimensions of unity. At Rome in 1957 they founded the European Atomic Energy Community to make the uses of atomic energy available to all members; and they established the Common Market, an ambitious program of total economic integration aimed at the gradual elimination (over a period of fifteen years) of trade barriers between members and bringing about uniform working and social conditions. Inefficient sectors of the members' economies soon felt the pinch after the Common Market, administered from Brussels, began to function in 1959, but the long term effect on economic growth in every member nation has been spectacular.

British application for membership was blocked in 1963 by President De Gaulle of France. He saw Britain as an outpost of American interest and influence, not to speak of tied to the British Commonwealth outside Europe. Believing that American power and investment in postwar Europe was entirely too great for the good of European integrity and morale, De Gaulle advanced himself as Mr. Europe. While maintaining formal friendship with the United States, he continually worked to reduce the American presence in Europe. The relative high cost of British industrial productivity, plus the liquidation of much British capital overseas to finance the late war, meanwhile left the British on the brink of economic disaster, for which eventual entry into the Common Market seemed to be the only solution.

But even as a good European, De Gaulle became a symbol of national sovereignty, hostile to the idea that Europe ought to evolve into a united state. He was, in fact, a Romantic, cosmopolitan nationalist of early nineteenth-century vintage, believing that each nationality's unique qualities must be preserved through liberty and self-government for the enrichment of European civilization as a whole, and supremely confident in the French ability to provide European leadership. He was, moreover, an elitist with a passion for greatness and a hatred for the conventional and the commonplace. Until his death in 1970, he was held to be an anachronistic obstructionist by those who labored to bring Europe more squarely into the era of social democracy and international integration— a new cosmopolitanism. But he took to his grave something of Europe's past greatness.

3.   From Laissez-faire to Welfare

Thanks to two World Wars and the great depression in between, Europe not only ceased to be the pivot of global politics, she ceased to be the pivot of the world economy. Beginning in 1914, European capital available for export began to decline, and by 1945 much capital invested abroad had been liquidated to pay for wartime imports. The Second World War, in particular, had been extremely destructive of capital equipment, and Europe experienced a sharp decline in her agricultural and industrial production, crippling her export trade. Consequently, she could not expect to import commodities essential to recovery, nor could she, by 1945, expect even to recover the standard of living of 1939 without outside help. That outside help could only come from the United States, which had gradually become the center of global economic power in the twentieth century, was confirmed by the Second World War.

While the second war was more truly global than the first war, the first was far more destructive of the European population. If one is to understand the catastrophic effect of the casualties upon the morale and vitality of Europeans ever since, one must include in the calculation of the losses not simply battle casualties, but the rise in the civilian death rate and the reduction in the birth rate for which the war was responsible.

In other words, several generations have to pass before population losses can be reasonably reckoned, and we can as yet have no figures for the second war that are comparable to those of the first war. The latter cost Europe, excluding Russia, between twenty and twenty-two million people, approximately seven percent of the population. Russian losses, to which have to be added those lost in the revolution and the civil war, are estimated to have been twenty-eight million, or about eighteen percent of the population. In the 1930's it was already noticeable that the western European populations were aging, a factor in both economic vitality and social welfare. By 1945, a continent that in the nineteenth century had experienced a population explosion and peopled all parts of the world with emigrants had reached a point of near stabilization of population growth with little emigration.

As we have seen, liberals had traditionally opposed government regulation as champions of individual liberty. But the very magnitude of the disaster between 1914 and 1918 shocked liberals into a reversal of position. Led by Lord Keynes in Britain and Gunnar Myrdal of Sweden, they came to see that economic life in the highly complex modern society is not self-regulating. If economic recovery and social welfare were to be attained, governments would have to engage in economic planning and management. Keynes recommended such devices as the regulation of interest rates, of production ceilings, of subsidies, the raising or lowering of taxes to encourage or restrict investment, and programs of public works to provide employment. Beginning in 1932, the Social Democratic Party in Sweden used such devices to eliminate unemployment at a moment when it was widespread elsewhere. Keynes meant to revolutionize "the way the world thinks about economic problems," and since the alternative to the Keynesian revolution in the twentieth century became total economic planning by the State, as in Nazi Germany or in the Communist states of eastern Europe, it is fair to support Keynes' own contention that he meant to preserve liberal capitalism by the use of limited controls to prevent the ruinous "boom and bust" cycles of laissez-faire capitalism. The international economic planning in the years after 1945 simply confirmed and extended the Keynesian principles.

European recovery after 1945 also depended upon new technologies and new efficiency, as well as upon American financial aid. Industrialization and urbanization, long a fact of European economic life, continued to intensify, dependent in part on new forms of power and upon the techniques of mass production—really a new degree of the specialization of production processes and labor—as well as upon new technologies born in the laboratory. The older industrial pioneers (Britain, France, and Belgium, in particular) had a more difficult time adjusting to the new techniques than those countries who came later to industrialization: Germany, Russia, Japan, and the United States. As diesel and internal combustion engines began replacing those powered by steam, the new demand for petroleum matched the decline in the demand for coal. Though it is true that by 1950 European productivity surpassed the capacity of 1929, one gets a better perspective by also noting that the productivity of 1928 had barely exceeded that of 1913. Two wars and a depression had clearly left their mark. Yet, by 1970, European productivity amazed all who knew the earlier devastation.

While the political division of Europe between East and West after 1945 was particularly the offspring of antagonisms born during World War I, we should not overlook the historical administrative and doctrinal differences that have divided the continent along the iron curtain since Roman times. Subsequently, there were really two Europes, albeit similar in their common Roman and Christian foundations. Moreover, only eastern Europe endured lengthy occupation by Asian conquerors, Mongols and Turks, whose exactions of tribute left the occupied regions impoverished. And the East never enjoyed the river and ocean communications of the West. The economic underdevelopment of eastern Europe, in other words, when compared to that of the West, is both a contemporary and an historical phenomenon. In our own time, eastern Europe has been relatively unproductive: The rates of disease have been higher, and there have been more infant mortality, more malnutrition, and more bad housing than in the West. In Europe, at any rate, such conditions have not fostered political democracy, democratic governments proving to be vulnerable to extremist movements that fed on popular desperation. When one charts the interwar political record, one notes that democracy survived in only the few countries with the highest per capita income. By that standard, eastern Europe had little chance, either before or after 1945, to make a success of Western-style democracy.

Economic productivity, if an important key to the standard of living, is not the only key. In the twentieth century we have come to add as important measures of standard of living a sense of economic stability and security, the social services that are available, the shortening of work hours, physical health, and life expectancy. Creation of a mass market for nonessential consumer goods has perhaps been the most recent measure of the affluent society. In all such categories western Europe has the superior standard of living, but eastern Europe has been the scene of notable economic development since 1945; though some insist that Eastern development could have been greater than it has been if the region had not been so rigidly tied to Russian economic and political requirements.

The recent progress, on the other hand, shoud not obscure the enormous damage to the European economy and psyche that the twentieth century brought, for Europe has lived almost continually with either war, revolution, or economic crisis since 1914: a period of relative insecurity of life and property, a period of many and great purges and confiscations, of refugees and displaced peoples, an era of concentration camps and genocide unexampled in modern Europe. Such insecurities and imperfections, in view of the democratization of society and the general awareness that European civilization held the promise of a better life for all, produced increasing demands for social justice.

We must note in passing that universal manhood suffrage was a commonplace in Europe after 1918. What was new after that date was a growing tendency to give the vote to women, a movement more precisely egalitarian than democratic. Norway was the first European nation to extend the vote to women (1907); and except for Switzerland, the practice was general by 1950. Democracy and industrialization had always implied the need to provide increased public instruction for an expanding electorate and the technical requirements of a complex economy. Especially after World War II, European opportunities for secondary, technical, and higher education were multiplied; but with an uneasy awareness, thanks to interwar memories, that a rising literacy rate in itself did not necessarily guarantee a more enlightened electorate.

Mass literacy had at once opened the door to greater learning and made the population more reachable by propaganda and advertising. The dilemma harkened back to the cultural despair of many intellectuals in the later nineteenth century, who had equated democratization with vulgarization. A resolution of that dilemma has since become clearer: a more sophisticated public education dedicated to making each citizen aware of the complexity of causality and aware of the "two cultures" whose rift remains to be bridged. The historical alternative to a democratic society is just as clear: an authoritarian society governed by an elite of some kind, the preference of some European university students in the 1960's who declared their abandonment of liberal democracy, unwittingly following the example of their German counterparts of the 1930's.

Meanwhile, the most systematic response to the clamor for social justice, especially intense after the economic collapse of the 1930's, came from an economist named William Beveridge in his *Report on Social Insurance and Allied Services* (1942). His formula to provide social security "from the cradle to the grave" and to eliminate extremes of wealth and poverty became a creed for postwar social reformers. It meant state responsibility for full employment as well as for education, insurance, and health. It often meant public ownership of resources or industries to force social progress.

Some nationalization of property had already begun, it is true, in the 1930's as a response to economic disaster. For example, the coalition of Leftist parties in France known as the Popular Front in 1936-1937, established the French National Railways Company, a mixed corporation with the state holding fifty-one percent of the stock. The most striking example of the welfare state in action, however, came after the British Labor Party took office in 1945: a National Insurance Act, a National Health Act, the Coal Industry Nationalization Act, the nationalization of the Bank of England, and the Transport Act to supervise all public transport, all enacted in 1946 and 1947. Similar developments took place under the new Fourth Republic in France. It would be wrong, consequently, to think of postwar Europe as divided into two communities: one of total free enterprise, one of total collectivization. Everywhere in Europe national economies functioned under greater regulation than ever before—and for the general good. In the East, the economies were controlled by single-party dictatorships; in the West, certain enterprises were nationalized only after popular vote had sanctioned such policies.

THE STATE OF THE TWO CULTURES

1.   Science

In the twentieth century, modern man has had to cope with much more than new knowledge unsettling to traditional belief. No understanding of the new knowledge, in fact, was even possible until he learned to accept new dimensions of vastness and minuteness, dimensions that challenged both the imagination and credulity. In 1900, for instance, the distances of only about twenty stars were known with any assurance; whereas today the distances of several thousand stars have been ascertained using improved telescopes and photography. The notion of galaxies other than our own, perhaps a hundred million of them, and the necessary use of the light-year as a measure (light travels at the rate of 186,000 miles per second), totally defeats our normal assumptions about space and distance. The nearest galaxy is at least 500 million light-years away—and possibly receding.

At the other end of the scale, until the end of the nineteenth century the atom was conceived as a hard, solid object, and as the smallest unit of physical reality. In the 1890's, however, Joseph Thomson found particles within atoms which carried negative charges of electricity, particles he called corpuscles but which came to be called electrons, and which showed that atoms are composite entities. The evidence suggested, furthermore, that electrons were identical in all atoms. Subsequently, protons were discovered: particles charged with positive electricity equal in amount to the negative charge on the electrons. It meant that each atom of a given element possessed an equal number of electrons and protons (making every atom electrically neutral). It followed then that the atoms of different chemical elements must be formed of *differently arranged groups* of electrons and protons.

In 1911, Lord Rutherford further refined atomic theory by proposing that atoms are largely empty. He saw the atom as a central nucleus with a positive electrical charge, surrounded at a distance by an outer shell of negatively charged electricity: a model that suggested nothing so much as a miniature solar system involving much empty space. Matter, in other words, was to be regarded as more empty than "material." A second inference was that if atoms differed chemically because of the different numbers of protons and electrons of which they are composed, then could they not be transmuted? The description of radioactivity had already shown certain elements to be in the process of disintegration. Rutherford achieved the first such transformation in 1919 by bombarding more complex elements with alpha particles to produce a simpler element—hydrogen. Further experiments showed that not only could transmuted elements be produced, but even some synthetic elements be created, such as plutonium, berkelium, and californium.

The apparent simplicity of Rutherford's atom soon underwent modification with the discovery of additional components. In 1932, Chadwick described the neutron, an uncharged particle with a mass equal to that of the proton. Then came Anderson's positron (1933), with a mass equal to that of an electron, but with a positive charge. And finally mesons, particles of short life, being variously charged or neutral. The atom, in other words, was rapidly taking on the aspects of a cosmos, just when the cosmos itself was becoming a complexity almost beyond our ability to imagine, much less comprehend. The minuteness that atomic theory requires us to accept had an analogy in the germ theory of disease. When it had been established in the nineteenth century that bacteria are the agents of disease, it became immediately possible that even more minute agents of disease existed—what we have called viruses since 1935. What viruses are—whether they are living agents or not—is not yet entirely understood.

When physicists learned in our century to measure the rate of disintegration of radioactive substances into lead or helium, it became possible—by measuring the proportion of lead and helium in radioactive materials—to establish the age of the rocks in which such minerals occurred. This has enabled contemporary geology to confirm the great age of rocks —in the millions of years. Consequently, geological time became another measure of vastness leading to incomprehensibility. Postwar generations that were particularly motivated to demand new degrees of security were not being given by science the easy or absolute answers that many people require for security. New discoveries deepened the mysteries about reality which only confident personalities and generations find thrilling.

These new realms of vastness were the more extreme in that they were set within the narrowing of time in all other aspects of modern man's life, namely, the acceleration of the pace of change and the new speed of communications. The European of 1860 would have found the pace of life in the twelfth century more similar to his own than that of 1960. The later he lives in the twentieth century, the more pressure there is upon him to accommodate to change, a factor which hampers the development of an integrated civilization. Since 1945, moreover, he has had to face a new dimension of destructiveness which atomic theory produced. Experiments to transmute atoms by bombarding them with high-voltage devices called cyclotrons or atom smashers led to a successful splitting of the nucleus of a uranium atom into two parts—atomic fission—by Hahn and Strassmann in Germany (1939). After this came a letter from Einstein to President Roosevelt explaining the military possibilities of atomic fission that would require a political decision of the utmost gravity. Einstein not only knew the terrible destructiveness inherent in an atomic weapon, but what it would mean if Hitler's Germany alone developed it.

Atomic explosion was not the only European concern. Already in the nineteenth century some European intellectuals worried about the population explosion in Europe itself, whereas by 1945 the anxiety had become global. The biologist Julian Huxley, a neo-Malthusian, was the man most responsible for making the world conscious of the population problem: he was the great figure at the Conference on World Population held in Rome in 1954. Here the first international survey of the population problem was made; an estimate that the world population of 1920 would double by the early 1980's. Such a projection implied that if food and population growth were not soon brought into balance, the world would face miseries and frustrations more explosive than any other human factor. More pointedly, that they would become the chief motives for future wars.

2. The Literary Culture

The vitality of the sciences in twentieth-century Europe has been in sharp contrast to the spiritual despair revealed in arts and letters. While a reflection of the political and social crisis in which Europe has lived since 1914, European intellectuals had already felt threatened by violence and vulgarity in the later nineteenth century, and were often further benumbed by their inability to see any purpose in the universe. Having by and large rejected metaphysical truths and put their faith in science to provide the ultimate answers, they lived to learn that modern science, almost by definition, could not provide the answers they sought. Their growing alienation from science, therefore, went beyond their earlier objection to the birth of a materialist society founded upon technology. The road to metaphysics lay open to those who came to understand the limits of science, but it has been a road not overburdened with traffic. Instead, the tendency has been to close the shutters and to seek a private truth within the recesses of the self.

The sudden increase in the size of the reading public, by contributing to a mass of writing that reflected popular taste rather than literary merit, exacerbated the literary agony. The cheap press did attract some eminent writers, men like G.K. Chesterton and G.B. Shaw, who may well have influenced people to acquire an interest in better literature, ideas, and politics. On the other hand, radio and television came to share with literature and journalism the task of informing the public; and the educational possibilities inherent in such media have too often been offset by their exceptional effectiveness in spreading partisan propaganda. We are only beginning to suspect, however, that the most critical aspect of the new media is to blunt the mind by encouraging the notion that learning is an easy and passive thing. The necessary contemporaneity of much journalism, radio, and television may also have contributed to popular indifference to traditional values, to anything which may be of permanent value, to history itself.

But if the literary culture has to a certain extent lost its market to the new media, the fault is not entirely due to the attractive slickness of the new media. Twentieth-century poets, for instance, have been passionately concerned about violence and social issues, yet much less effective than their nineteenth-century counterparts in influencing national thought. New poetic techniques, while innovative and subtle, have amounted to a failure to speak to people and only to the poetic elite. Novelists like James Joyce, Virginia Woolf, and Franz Kafka have been much akin to the new poets, developing a highly symbolic, often obscure, narrative to be interpreted by each reader—really an appeal to a limited audience.

Another group of twentieth-century novelists, of whom D.H. Lawrence and Marcel Proust are representative, have been in what we might call the Freudian tradition, emphasizing not our rational selves but the unconscious or the irrational, and imbued with a pessimistic view of man's nature and his fate. Some of the early twentieth-century novelists revealed the optimism of scientific humanism which one found earlier in Flaubert; but the farther this group got into the century, the more they saw science as nothing more than nonmoral, manipulative technology, as in H.G. Wells, *The Shape of Things to Come,* or in Aldous Huxley's *Brave New World.* The ultimate horror—the use of technology to enslave mankind entirely—was predicted in George Orwell's *1984.*

In 1918, Oswald Spengler published his massive work *The Decline of the West,* a curious mishmash of learning and fantasy. He drew a parallel between European civilization in the twentieth century and that of the ancient world in its last stages. Using analogies drawn from the life cycle, he portrayed the rise and fall of civilizations as a matter of inevitability and beyond our control through reason. This prophet of doom was widely quoted by European intellectuals in the interwar period, congenial as his message was to the literati, though in retrospect it seems unlikely that many of the quoters were qualified to judge the validity of his analogies. Part of Spengler's popularity derived from a willingness to pronounce on the state of civilizational health. Arnold Toynbee's twelve-volume *Study of History* also became well-known through the publication of an abridgment after the Second World War. Toynbee used an organic approach to history, though his results were less pessimistic than Spengler's

During the First World War, Karl Barth, a Swiss theologian, began to preach what has been called a "theology of crisis," clearly a response to deep shock. He became a modern prophet defining sin for modern man, condemning the sinfulness of modern civilization, and called for repentance, for men to live in awe, fear, and trembling. Barth represented a revival of Kierkegaard's view (and perhaps Calvin's) that God cannot be intellectually investigated. In this view, only God's love makes possible the otherwise unbridgeable distance between man and God; and His revelation in the Bible is the unique source of His truth for us. Thus, the revelation was a miracle. Barth's fundamentalism has been in sharp contrast to the social gospel of many contemporary churchmen, who have devoted themselves to practical, secular social programs. Whereas he would argue that they mistake temporal goals as the Kingdom of God, they would argue that there can be no salvation for men reduced to a brutish state by social or economic oppression.

The private agony of many in the literary culture was especially revealed in the philosophy of existentialism. With its roots deep in the nineteenth century, notably in the ideas of Kierkegaarde and Nietzsche, existentialism did not really flourish in Europe until after the holocaust of two World Wars. Existentialism has been somewhat difficult to define, because by 1945 it encompassed a variety of creeds, some of them Christian like Paul Tillich's, some of them atheist as in the case of Jean-

Paul Sartre. The most popular writer in the movement was Albert Camus, whose principal existentialist work was *The Myth of Sisyphus*
(1942).

ALBERT CAMUS (Henri Cartier Bresson/Magnum).

Whatever their other differences, all existentialists opposed a systematic philosophy, seeing truth or reality only in subjective, personal
terms. Thus, thought has to do with a particular person in a particular
situation, but always against a background of deep anxiety. For the existentialist, man cannot know reality through the use of detached or
objective reason, almost suggesting an anti-intellectualism. Existence
alone becomes reality, a fearful and agonizing plight. Men are seen as

cast into an alien and hostile world with death as the final absurdity, each man inevitably alone both in his knowledge and his values. This view goes beyond the idea that we are all unique and that some things can be known to us alone. It means to assert that there are no eternal or universal truth, and that human life has no meaning or purpose beyond what we ourselves invent in our search for security. It means that man has no place in the rationale of nature.

When the novelist-physicist C.P. Snow commented in 1961 on the rift between the scientific and the literary cultures, he did so as a man who had bridged them and who knew that the incomprehension and mistrust separating the two cultures is as unnecessary as it is dangerous. The literati, who had had no part in the technical advances of the two previous centuries, hated the Industrial Revolution for its presumed brutalization of the working classes and its emphasis upon material gain. Remaining relatively indifferent to man's social condition, these "humanists" were preoccupied with man's tragic destiny as an individual. They saw scientists as blindly optimistic, since the scientists were confident in the possibility of improving the social condition of man. Snow argued that the two views of man can and must coexist: that they are not incompatible perception of man's lot. In essence the message was not new, however timely. Man requires bread to live, but cannot live by bread alone.

Others who bridged the two cultures also avoided the agony of despair so common after 1914. In his *Science and the Modern World* (1925), the philosopher-mathematician Alfred North Whitehead noted that "successful organisms modify their environment," and that the various species, if often regarded as hostile, are actually mutually dependent. "A forest," he put it, "is the triumph of the organization of mutually dependent species." Similarly in society, different races and nations are necessary if a higher civilization is to be produced. Racial or national uniformity would produce stagnation, not to speak of boredom. Whitehead believed modern science to be the enterprise which challenges us to change, to grow, to enable us to modify our environment for the better; which forces us to see the future as necessary change, which forbids us the "placidity of existence" which may be comfortable, but which is suicidal for civilization.

Change no doubt involves us in dangers and includes the risk of uncertainty, but it avoids the certain disaster that intransigence implies.

SIR CHARLES P. SNOW (Wide World Photos).

Indeed, as the philosopher-mathematician Bertrand Russell claimed, hope for the future is at least as rational as fear. As for those who seek to make their peace with the two cultures and to reconcile themselves to the mysterious, the unknown, or the uncertain, there has been no better guide than history.

SUGGESTED READINGS

Deutch, Karl W. *et al. France, Germany and the Western Alliance— A Study of Elite Attitudes on European Integration and World Politics.* New York: Scribner's, 1967.

Dobzhansky, Theodosius. *Mankind Evolving.* New Haven, Conn.: Yale University Press, 1962.

Fontaine, André. *History of the Cold War.* 3 vols. New York: Pantheon, 1968-1969.

Feis, Herbert. *Between War and Peace: The Potsdam Conference.* Princeton, N.J.: Princeton University Press, 1960.

Feis, Herbert. *Japan Subdued: The Atomic Bomb and the End of the War in the Pacific.* Princeton, N.J.: Princeton University Press, 1961.

Friedrich, Carl J. *Europe: An Emergent Nation?* New York: Harper, 1970.

Herberg, Will, ed. *Four Existentialist Theologians.* New York: Doubleday Anchor, 1958.*

Hughes, H. Stuart. *The Obstructed Path.* New York: Harper, 1968.*

Lukacs, John. *A New History of the Cold War.* New York: Doubleday Anchor, 1968.

Maier, Charles S., and White, Dan S. *The Thirteenth of May: The Advent of de Gaulle's Republic.* Oxford: Oxford University Press, 1968.*

Ortega y Gasset. *The Dehumanization of Art and Other Writings on Art and Culture.* New York: Doubleday Anchor, 1956.*

Pierce, Roy. *Contemporary French Political Thought.* Oxford: Oxford University Press, 1966.*

Rees, David. *The Age of Containment: The Cold War 1945-1965.* New York: St. Martin's, 1967.*

Shamos, Morris H. *Great Experiments in Physics.* New York, London: Holt, Dryden, 1957.

Snow, C.P. *The Two Cultures and a Second Look.* New York: Mentor, 1964.*

Thomson, David. *Democracy in France Since 1870.* Oxford: Oxford University Press, 1969.*

Whitehead, Alfred North. *Science and the Modern World.* New York: Mentor, 1948.*

Willis, F. Roy. *France, Germany and the New Europe 1945-1967.* Oxford: Oxford University Press, 1968.*

*An asterisk indicates that a paperback edition is available.

INDEX